Read Him Again and Again

Read Him Again and Again

Repetitions of Job in Kierkegaard, Vischer, and Barth

ANDREW ZACK LEWIS

◈PICKWICK *Publications* • Eugene, Oregon

READ HIM AGAIN AND AGAIN
Repetitions of Job in Kierkegaard, Vischer, and Barth

Copyright © 2014 Andrew Zack Lewis. All rights reserved. Except for brief quotations in critical publications or reviews, no part of this book may be reproduced in any manner without prior written permission from the publisher. Write: Permissions, Wipf and Stock Publishers, 199 W. 8th Ave., Suite 3, Eugene, OR 97401.

Pickwick Publications
An Imprint of Wipf and Stock Publishers
199 W. 8th Ave., Suite 3
Eugene, OR 97401

www.wipfandstock.com

ISBN 13: 978-1-62032-314-4

Cataloguing-in-Publication data:

Lewis, Andrew Zack.

Read him again and again : repetitions of Job in Kierkegaard, Vischer, and Barth / Andrew Zack Lewis.

xviii + 196 pp. ; 23 cm. Includes bibliographical references and index.

ISBN 13: 978-1-62032-314-4

1. Bible. Job—Criticism, interpretation, etc. 2. Kierkegaard, Søren, 1813–1855. 3. Vischer, Wilhelm, 1895–1988. 4. Barth, Karl, 1886–1968. 5. Bible—Hermeneutics. I. Title.

BS1415.52 L394 2014

Manufactured in the U.S.A.

For Melanie

"For he crushes me with a tempest, and makes my wounds many for nought."
—Job 9:17

"Although I have read the book again and again each word remains new to me. Every time I come to it, it is born anew as something original or becomes new and original in my soul."
—Søren Kierkegaard, *Repetition*

Contents

Preface • ix
Abbreviations • xii
Introduction • xv

1 Job in Great Time • 1
2 Gregory, Aquinas, Luther, Calvin, and Kant on Job as Predecessors to Kierkegaard, Vischer, and Barth • 38
3 Each Time I Come to a Word, It Is Again Made Original: The Repetition of Job in Kierkegaard's Young Man • 67
4 The Goodness of God beyond Good and Evil: Wilhelm Vischer on Job as a Witness to Jesus Christ • 104
5 A Witness to the True Witness: Karl Barth's Unique Contribution to the Interpretation of the Book of Job • 135
6 Evaluation and Conclusion • 163

Bibliography • 179
Index • 197

Preface

MY FIRST ENCOUNTER WITH the Kierkegaardian category of repetition was in the book *The Moviegoer* by Walker Percy. The protagonist, Binx Bolling introduces the category after he watches a western movie in the same theater where he had watched a western movie fourteen years previous. The experiences were so similar that he declared the repetition successful. "What is a repetition?" Binx asks. "A repetition is the re-enactment of past experience toward the end of isolating the time segment which has lapsed in order that it, the lapsed time, can be savored of itself and without the usual adulteration of events that clog time like peanut in brittle."[1]

The year after I read *The Moviegoer* for the first time, I took a class on the book of Job set in Vancouver's Downtown Eastside, known as Canada's poorest postal code. We were encouraged to use Job as a template on which to view the poor and marginalized today. The class served as my first formal study of the book of Job and what I learned there—the people I met and the books that we read[2]—remains the groundwork for all my subsequent study on Job.

A few years later, I stumbled my way into writing a master's thesis on the use of Genesis 1–3 in the Prologue of Job. It was a historical-grammatical reading of the narrative portions of Job, approaching the book from an angle different from the liberationist model in the earlier class, but my first encounter remained in my mind throughout the process. Perhaps Binx Bolling would agree that in a way the second encounter was a repetition of the first.

Years later, pursuing a PhD in Hebrew Bible at the University of St. Andrews, I was persuaded by Professor Chris Seitz to look at Karl Barth as biblical exegete, specifically his essay on the book of Job. In his essay, Barth refers to Kierkegaard's book *Repetition* where he was attracted to Kierkegaard's use of the category of repetition as tool for describing Job's

---

1. Percy, *The Moviegoer*, 79–80.
2. Particularly Gutiérrez, *On Job*.

encounter with God's voice in the tempest. My dissertation would, in part, deal with Barth's reception of repetition, but only as a way of approaching Job again, from yet another angle—that of reception history. Thus, I carried out another repetition . . . in a way.[3]

As will become evident in the following book, the meaning of the philosophical category of repetition is rather elusive. It does not merely refer to "repeating" any old thing. Binx Bolling's experiment in repetition, like Constantin Constantius in *Repetition*, throws the reader off the scent. These unreliable speakers mirror Job's friends' unreliability and require repeated readings to grasp their significance. The category of repetition may have a specific meaning that might require a more accurate English word to help pinpoint, but Kierkegaard clearly wants his readers to play with other meanings of "repetition" in the process, thus I feel comfortable with the subtitle of this book.

The book of Job, after all, requires repeating, no matter the finer points of the meaning of the term. Anyone who claims to know the right interpretation of Job has likely not thought through all of the problems of their interpretation. It therefore seems appropriate that in my second "repetition" of the book of Job, I study three other "repetitions" of the book.

Though behind the category of repetition lies an interest in self-discovery and though I, like many before me, am drawn to Job for self-discovery, I do not reveal much in the way of my own self here. I do, however, want to acknowledge at least some other individuals who made this book possible.

Of those I want to mention by name, I must start with Dr. Mark W. Elliott who took my doctoral supervision under unusual circumstances but who definitely turned out to be the right person to oversee my work. His vast knowledge of what seems to be all subjects, academic and cultural, was my best resource for such a diverse topic. He was also patient with me and prompt with his feedback. I also would like to thank the rest of the St. Mary's faculty and staff for their help and advice, specifically Nathan MacDonald, Gavin Hopps, and Stephen Evans during his brief time in St. Andrews. I should also thank Dave Diewert, Iain Provan, and Chris Seitz for

---

3. In another type of repetition, I would reread Gutiérrez's *On Job* and rediscover his reliance on Barth's interpretation on Job. While Gutiérrez supports much of the exegesis of individual verses or words with popular commentaries by Habel, Westermann, Alonso Shökel, and Dhorme, he chooses to read Job through the Satan's primary question, "Does Job serve God for nought?" It is Barth whom he cites here and on whom he relies through much of his book. Job, according to Gutiérrez, is about the possibility of disinterested religion (5ff.) and the freedom of God (72ff.). In many ways, Gutiérrez applies Barth's Job to his situation among the poor in Peru. In fact, he also supports his exegesis with Kierkegaard, but his Kierkegaard resembles Barth's Kierkegaard. Thus, my first experience of Job anticipated my third—another repetition.

introducing me to and advising me on Job before I dove headfirst into the long and tortuous work on this specific book.

Much of the time I spent on the early drafts of my work was in the Rutherford room of the medieval Roundel in St. Andrews, Scotland. Rutherford is large and I shared it with many people who helped me in several ways, often with much welcomed comic relief. I specifically name Jeremy Gabrielson, Chris Hays, Theng Huat Leow, John Edwards, and Allen Jones. Though I would have been happy merely to have become good friends with all of these men, I was also fortunate to have their projects relate to my own in surprising ways.

I also value the conversations I had with others in the Roundel outside my immediate confines. These include but are not limited to: Seth Tarrer, Stephen Presley, Tim Stone, Jason Goroncy, David Lincicum, and Daniel Driver.

I have also had the privilege to share the unusually large flat at Priorsgate with close friends who were able to aid me in my research and thoughts on my project. Paul Warhurst helped facilitate my understanding of the works of Søren Kierkegaard. Amber Warhurst was a great help in questions about the Hebrew Bible. I also valued discussions with Meg Ramey on the use and influence of the Bible in the modern era.

I would also like to thank Alan Lewis and Shelley Jacobsen for reading over parts of my thesis as I was preparing to finish. They were selfless in their help and gave valuable advice.

The one person who fulfilled all of the offices mentioned above—supervisor, encourager, friend, and editor—is my wife Melanie. She sacrificed much to accompany me to Scotland, has supported me throughout the writing process, and it is hard to imagine doing this without her. Her patience was monumental.

Lastly, I would like to acknowledge the encouragement and love from my parents, Courtland and Rich, and my children, Elaine and Micah. My parents have aided me in countless ways, not the least of which was the generosity with the occasional flight home. Elaine and Micah often made it difficult to concentrate, but instantly refreshed me from a day's work when I arrived home. Love to you all.

Abbreviations

AAR American Academy of Religion
AB Anchor Bible
ACCS Ancient Christian Commentary on Scripture
AnBib Analecta biblica
AThR *Anglican Theological Review*
AUSS *Andrews University Seminary Studies*
BETL Bibliotheca ephemeridum theologicarum lovaniensium
BZAW Beihefte zur Zeitschrift für die alttestamentliche Wissenschaft
CBQ *Catholic Biblical Quarterly*
CD *Church Dogmatics*
Di *Dialog*
EQ *Evangelical Quarterly*
ETR *Etudes théologiques et religieuses*
FAT Forschungen zum Alten Testament
FoiVie *Foi et Vie*
FOTL Forms of Old Testament Literature
HAR *Hebrew Annual Review*
HAT Handbuch zum Alten Testament
HTR *Harvard Theological Review*
IJST *International Journal of Systematic Theology*
Int *Interpretation*

Abbreviations

IVP	Intervarsity Press
JBL	*Journal of Biblical Literature*
JNSL	*Journal of Northwest Semitic Languages*
JQR	*Jewish Quarterly Review*
JR	*Journal of Religion*
JSOT	*Journal for the Study of the Old Testament*
JSOT Press	Journal for the Study of the Old Testament Press
JSOTsup	Journal for the Study of the Old Testament: Supplement Series
LQ	*Lutheran Quarterly*
NIB	*The New Interpreter's Bible*
OBT	Overtures to Biblical Theology
OTL	Old Testament Library
ProEccl	*Pro Ecclesia*
Proof	*Prooftexts: A Journal of Jewish Literary History*
PRSt	*Perspectives in Religious Studies*
RSPT	*Revue des sciences philosophiques et théologiques*
RTP	*Revue de théologie et de philosophie*
SCH	Studies in Church History
SJT	*Scottish Journal of Theology*
SPCK	Society for Promoting Christian Knowledge
StPatr	Studia patristica
ThTo	*Theology Today*
TJ	*Trinity Journal*
VT	*Vetus Testamentum*
WBC	Word Biblical Commentary
WUNT	Wissenschaftliche Untersuchungen zum Neuen Testament
ZAW	*Zeitschrift für die alttestamentliche Wissenschaft*
ZB	Zürcher Bibel

Introduction

THE HISTORY OF THE interpretation of the book of Job bears witness to its difficulty. Though the book tackles many great questions that humanity has been asking for millennia, it does not answer these questions in very straightforward ways. Each successive interpretation of the book of Job seems to raise more questions than it answers, and that inspires later interpreters to enter into the book as well, perhaps hoping for more definitive results. The following book, rather than making another definitive stab at the "meaning" of the book of Job, intends to examine the interpretations themselves—specifically the interpretations of Søren Kierkegaard, Wilhelm Vischer, and Karl Barth.

At its heart, this book is a reflection on biblical hermeneutics. It asks how these scholars come to the conclusions they do in their readings of Job. What preconceptions, prejudices, historical circumstances, and theologies lie behind the hermeneutical moves they attempt? How do they perceive the nature of the biblical canon that inspires some of their interpretive claims? How do they respond to their predecessors in biblical interpretation and the interpretation of the book of Job in particular?

Of course in examining the hermeneutics that undergird the scholars' theses, the book also examines the interpretations themselves. The main reason for examining these three readers in particular is their shared themes of the book of Job that they emphasize. The latest of the three interpreters, Karl Barth, refers explicitly to the earlier interpreters, highlighting Vischer and Kierkegaard as his most important predecessors in his reading of the book of Job. Vischer offers Barth his most important hermeneutical key for reading the book of Job—the question whether Job fears God for nought. Kierkegaard offers Barth his most important philosophical insight in understanding the phenomenon of what Job experiences—the category of repetition. By looking at these three readers, in particular, especially as filtered through Barth's eventual reading, we gain a better understanding of Barth's own hermeneutic, but more importantly, we gain a deeper understanding of the book of Job, itself. Beyond these filters into which Barth, Vischer, and Kierkegaard read Job, the important theme of divine and human freedom as postulated in the book of Job emerges. All three see Job as arguing against his friends for being too tied to human formulations of God. God cannot be bound by these formulations because of God's freedom. The dogma posited by the friends may be sound to an extent, but in the end it limits God's freedom. The book of Job, these three scholars contend, presents the character of Job as free as well, paralleling the freedom of God. Job, through his sufferings, is able to break free of the constricting dogma of his friends and become his own free agent. In his freedom, unrestricted by the dogma presented by his friends, he can recognize God's freedom and learns to rely on God and not the law that God purveys.

As one examines Kierkegaard, Vischer, and Barth and their hermeneutics, one notices that they stand out from the crowd. They tend to buck the common trends of their eras. Historical criticism acts as a tool, perhaps, but the results of historical criticism are not the final goals. They do not discount the validity of biblical scholarship, but recognize that biblical scholarship limits the freedom of the interpreter. The three scholars are critical of systems that place artificial parameters around the text. In this way, their interpretations of Job allegorize the story of Job as they perceive it. Job, like Kierkegaard, Vischer, and Barth, stands away from the crowd and conventional wisdom. Historical criticism takes on a mask of retributive theology, with its system and limited outcomes. By looking only at the roots of the text, historical critics appear like Eliphaz, Bildad, and Zophar, working backward from the results to what must have been the cause, while Job looks beyond the limited scope to God.

One of the tools these scholars use that puts them outside of the mainstream of their times is, in fact, allegory itself. Specifically, they utilize the narrower type of allegory called, alternatively, typological and figural interpretation. In the case of Vischer and Barth, they use typological interpretation to aid their readings of Job. Kierkegaard also incorporates allegory and typology into his interpretation, but his looks very different from the later two scholars' use of it. However, within his interpretation he presents a typological theory that buttresses Vischer and Barth's canonical typology. Thus, Kierkegaard's theory undergirds Barth's hermeneutic and Vischer's exegetical observations undergird Barth's interpretation. Any reader will notice that the allegorical interpretations of these three differ greatly from much of the allegory used in the early Middle Ages to the point that they

Introduction

tend to deny utilizing allegory at all.[4] Nevertheless, as I hope to show, allegory and typology are important aspects of their hermeneutical method of the interpretation of Job.

Included in the reflection on the biblical hermeneutics of these three scholars is an exploration on the role of the reception history of biblical texts in biblical interpretation. Reception history has become more and more prevalent in recent years, but relatively few theories have emerged to help explain its relevance to biblical studies. Chapter 1 attempts to add to this inchoate discussion using the literary theories of the Russian scholar Mikhail Bakhtin as a starting point. Bakhtin argues that great texts exist in great time, a phrase I will unpack below. He also argues that dialogue exists in perpetuity. The forward focused vision of dialogue that Bakhtin presents relates to the temporal aspects of typological interpretation. Chapter 1 continues with an examination of typology and allegory and how they relate to the hermeneutics of Vischer, Barth, and Kierkegaard.

Noting in chapter 1 that texts do not rise up out of nowhere, it is also important to note that *interpretations* of texts do not rise up out of nowhere. Chapter 2 maps the Joban interpretations of major Christian readers from Gregory the Great to Immanuel Kant, setting the stage for Kierkegaard, Vischer, and Barth. Attention will be paid primarily to instances of allegory and freedom in their readings.

Chapter 3 tackles the particularly complex interpretations of Job offered by Søren Kierkegaard. Just as the first two chapters of Job differ generically from the following thirty-nine chapters, Kierkegaard breaks his interpretation of Job into two generically different documents. He explores the words of Job in the prosaic prologue in his autonymous upbuilding discourses, but saves his reading of the poetic dialogues for the pseudonymous novella *Repetition*. The generic differences require attention and explanation by the reader of Kierkegaard before one can make sense of the readings themselves.

Several decades after Kierkegaard, in the interbellum period in Germany, the Old Testament scholar Wilhelm Vischer presented his interpretation of Job in the form of a mini-commentary. Chapter 4 presents a close reading of this commentary, noting its historical context and the theology

---

4. Erich Auerbach, in his important essay "*Figura*," recognizes this semantic problem when he writes, "The strangeness of the medieval view of reality has prevented modern scholars from distinguishing between figuration and allegory and led them for the most part to perceive only the latter" (Auerbach, "Figura," 74). On the other hand, though Auerbach makes important distinctions between figuration and allegory, their differences are perhaps too sharply defined. Below, I argue, along with Henri de Lubac, that figuration and typology do not differ greatly from allegory. Rather, I suggest that typology is a type of allegory—not equivalent, but subsumed under it.

xvii

that Vischer intends to convey in his reading. Of special significance is his thesis that Job cares not for goods or the Good, but only for God's goodness that resides beyond good and evil—a clear reference to Nietzsche's book on morality called *Beyond Good and Evil*. Vischer's Job is a character who comes to realize that his devotion to God means he must look beyond the laws and morality that God puts forward to the God who puts them forward. His is a deeply personal God, not in the sense that God is his property, but that God is a personality and not a purveyor of a system.

Pivoting off of Vischer, and with direct dependence on Kierkegaard, is Karl Barth's reading of Job, which is found in the small print of his *Church Dogmatics*, and is examined in chapter 5. Vischer's essay presents Barth with what Barth would come to see as the key to understanding the book of Job. Vischer's emphasis of the wager between the Satan and God, culminating in the Satan's question over whether Job serves God "for nought" inspires Barth to explore the rest of the book of Job through the wager. He eventually argues that Job is a type of Jesus Christ, "a witness to the true witness," whose devotion to God is free from *quid pro quo*. Both Job and God are free agents who freely choose each other.

While chapters 3 through 5 explore Kierkegaard, Vischer, and Barth independently, the sixth chapter of the book evaluates the three interpretations of Job next to each other. Specifically, it evaluates Barth's interpretation of Vischer and Kierkegaard in his reading of Job, and it continues by looking at the picture of freedom all three interpreters present to their readers.

The book concludes with a brief example of how the observations on Job of these three scholars might benefit the exegesis of specific passages in the book of Job. I apply Kierkegaard, Vischer, and Barth to the first speech of Bildad the Shuhite in chapter 8, a passage the three scholars do not look at very closely. The intention is to show how the conversation on the book of Job, which has been ongoing since before the version we have was even written down, continues into the future. As Bakhtin would say, the dialogue is "unfinalizable."

1

Job in Great Time

IN AN ARTICLE ENTITLED "Reconsidering Job," published in 2007 in *Currents in Biblical Research*, Carol Newsom writes,

> reception historical studies either tend to provide broad overviews or to focus on specific periods or traditions. Moreover, they also tend not to be methodologically self-reflective. As biblical scholars increasingly begin to do reception historical work, this area of study is likely to be reconfigured, since biblical scholars will have to think through what it means for reception history to be considered an integral part of biblical studies.[1]

A few years earlier, in her well received book *The Book of Job: A Contest of Moral Imaginations*, she concludes her study with the advice, "The only conclusion to a study of the dialogic structure of Job can be the advice to go and reread the book in the company of others who will contest your reading."[2]

My intention in this book is to read the book of Job in the company of others in such a way as to self-reflect methodologically on reception historical exegesis. In taking Newsom's advice in her book, I believe that one must integrate reception history into biblical studies. The company of others need not exclude the dead, after all. Moreover, if one takes Newsom's admiration of the literary theory of Mikhail Bakhtin seriously, one must include the interpretations of a book like Job throughout history as utterances in an

---

1. Newsom, "Reconsidering Job," 176–77.
2. Newsom, *Moral Imaginations*, 264.

ongoing dialogue that began before the book of Job existed in any form. This last statement may confuse at first, but should become clear presently.

Because the book of Job has generated so much interest over the centuries, a comprehensive study of the reception of the book would necessarily be a broad overview and would not provide one with much more than a survey of the landscape.[3] This work, by contrast, focuses on a particular strand of thought in Job interpretation. In particular, I look at the readings of Job by Søren Kierkegaard, Wilhelm Vischer, and Karl Barth—a philosopher, a biblical scholar, and a theologian, respectively—who focus much of their attention in their readings of Job to notions of divine and human freedom and incorporate aspects of allegory into their exegetical methods.

In this section I intend to show how Mikhail Bakhtin's discussions on time can help in developing a theory for reception history of the Bible. As Newsom suggests, though biblical scholars are beginning to incorporate the history of interpretation into their research, we lack sufficient arguments for its inclusion in the process of exegesis and perhaps even knowledge of how some seemingly antiquated ideas might fit into our modern readings. Newsom highlights Susan Schreiner's work on Calvin's sermons on Job as very important in current research on Job, but it does remain difficult to know how to incorporate Calvin's panegyrical descriptions of Elihu into modern readings that are even critical of Elihu's inclusion in the book as well as what Elihu says.[4] Even stranger to modern ears are the allegorical interpretations of Job by Gregory the Great.[5]

Bakhtin, however, seems to argue, though not directly, that if one accepts his dialogical theories, one must take into account the reception history of a text, particularly a great work like the book of Job. In order to show this, we must review the confluence of several of Bakhtin's various concepts that lead up to his later works that invoke the idea of great time.

Before doing so, however, it will be useful to present a brief explanation of why Bakhtin proves a useful thinker to utilize over other hermeneutical and literary theorists. Bakhtin does share many similarities to other major hermeneuts both on the Continent and in the Anglo-American tradition. It would go beyond the scope of this book to go into much depth with these

---

3. See Stephen Vicchio's three-volume work on Job throughout history, which impresses with its breadth but lacks much insight into the many works he covers. Vicchio, *Job in the Ancient World*; Vicchio, *Job in the Medieval World*; Vicchio, *Job in the Modern World*.

4. Newsom, "Reconsidering Job," 176. See Schreiner, *Where Shall Wisdom be Found*.

5. Pope Gregory I, *Morals on the Book of Job*.

similarities and differences, but a brief overview will go far in defending Bakhtin's inclusion in this book.[6]

David Paul Parris presents, in an entire monograph, his theoretical justification of reception historical exegesis using the work of Hans-Georg Gadamer and Hans Robert Jauss. There are many similarities between Parris's analysis of Gadamer and Jauss and mine below of Bakhtin. For instance, Bakhtin's discussion of addressivity and genre memory relates well to Gadamer's position that *Vorurteil* is inherited from tradition and contains an anticipatory nature.[7] Gadamer's understanding of the importance of the individual events of history relates to Bakhtin's.[8] *Vorurteil* in Gadamer's thought also coheres well with Bakhtin's favoring one's particularity in history and culture as a starting point in dialogue with an ancient text from another culture. One should also note that Parris holds that Gadamer promotes active dialogue with tradition rather than passive obedience, a sentiment seemingly shared by Bakhtin.[9] Likewise, Bakhtin shares some similarities with Jauss, particularly with Jauss's seven theses in his landmark essay "Literary History as a Challenge to Literary Theory."[10] Of particular interest in his essay is his fourth thesis in which he writes:

> The reconstruction of the horizon of expectations, on the basis of which a work in the past was created and received, enables us to find the questions to which the text originally answered and thereby to discover how the reader of that day viewed and understood the work. . . . [This reconstruction] brings out the hermeneutic difference between past and present ways of understanding a work, points up the history of its reception—providing both approaches—and thereby challenges as platonizing dogma the apparently self-evident dictum of philological metaphysics that literature is timelessly present and that it has objective meaning, determined once and for all and directly open to the interpreter at any time.[11]

---

6. For a more in depth analysis of Bakhtin's similarities and differences with other major scholars of philosophical hermeneutics, I direct the reader to Gardiner, *Dialogics of Critique*. See especially chapter 4, "Bakhtin's Critical Hermeneutics."

7. Parris, *Reception Theory*, 3.

8. Ibid., 4.

9. Ibid., 10.

10. Jauss, "Literary History as a Challenge to Literary Theory," 7–37.

11. Ibid., 18–19.

As will be shown below, Jauss picks up on the gap between the present reader and the original text that draws the reader to the history of the text's reception in a way similar to Bakhtin.

On the other hand, Bakhtin's differences between these two German thinkers help us think about the reception history of the Bible in fresh, and perhaps, more useful ways. Michael Gardiner points out many similarities between Gadamer and Bakhtin, suggesting that dialogue could be a synonym for hermeneutics in the Gadamerian sense. Gadamer's description of dialogue, however, appears much more sanguine than does Bakhtin's. Gardiner's main criticism of Gadamer is that Gadamer's hermeneutics "ignores the crucial dimension of power, and of the specifically *ideological* deformation of language-use."[12] Bakhtin's work on carnival and the carnivalesque as responses to hegemonic power structures, however, displays a keen understanding of power and that understanding lies in the subtext of much of his other work. While dialogue and self-understanding to Gadamer seem to bring about mutual understanding on their own, Bakhtin's recognition of the problem of power makes him more appropriate for the incorporation of dialogue in the interpretation of the Bible. The Bible, after all, is a hegemonic text which has been interpreted by the powerful in its history. In looking at the book of Job, in particular, which is a story of a man in dialogue with the representatives of the more powerful ideas of their time, the recognition of the problem of power is important. Gardiner does fault Bakhtin for not addressing the problem of power in an entirely coherent manner, but commends him for his general awareness of the problem.[13] In the case of reception history of Job, we will be dealing with the powerful interpreters up until the enlightenment, when we will shift to thinkers who are battling the dominant theories of their day. Power, therefore, should be accounted for when looking specifically at the interpretations of Kierkegaard and Vischer in particular and should not be a forgotten entity in the exploration of Barth, either.

As a student of Gadamer, Jauss inherits some of these same problems, which Shepherd discusses at length in two essays cited above. One concern of several of Jauss's critics is the vagueness of his term "horizon of expectations." At times the horizon of expectations seems to be a property of the text's readers while at other times it appears to be a property of the text itself, betraying a "lack of rigour" on Jauss's part.[14] In the end, David Shepherd faults Jauss for betraying his initial confidence in the history of reception by

---

12. Gardiner, *Dialogics of Critique*, 116.
13. Ibid.
14. Shepherd, "Bakhtin and the Reader," 102.

falling back to more traditional notions of inherent meaning within the text itself.[15] The problem with this is that the readers in Jauss's dialogue become less stable and independent and the dialogue ceases to be true dialogue. This is not to say that Bakhtin's dialogue regards all interlocutors as equal in power. Rather, it forces successive interpreters to allow the other voices to speak so that true dialogue can happen, but which recognizes the disparity of power and allows those less historically powerful voices to be heard.

I do not want to overstate the usefulness of Bakhtin over and against Gadamer, Jauss, and others and want to stress that Bakhtin himself suffers from vagueness, based largely on his unsystematic writing style. He does not present an independent theory of reading, after all, but posits several ideas over many articles, monographs, and years that one must piece together. Some of the differences above may also appear as mere hair-splitting, for, in the end, if Bakhtin, Jauss, and Gadamer can all lead us to the importance of including the history of a biblical text's reception, each scholar's views should actually lend credence to its inclusion in the process of interpretation. Bakhtin's theories, however, seem more ready to take into account the complex history of the Bible.

It is Bakhtin's broad scope and attention to history that makes him uniquely useful to biblical scholars. Consider Walter Reed's early book on Bakhtin and the Bible.[16] Bakhtin's theory of language and literature, Reed contends, "positions itself between the fragmenting referentiality of the historical view and the consolidating authority of the theological perspective."[17] Bakhtin, therefore, promotes the reading of the Bible as a powerful utterance in a dialogue rather than "merely a part of a much larger archive of documents and other cultural evidence of human expression"[18] on the one hand and the inerrant or infallible self-contained word from God on the other. In practice, the Bible has maintained a place between these two extremes, for even those who hold the Bible as the inerrant Word of God find themselves in sharp disagreement as to what the message of that Word might actually mean. Bakhtin allows us to recognize the cultural power of the Bible without that power being distorted beyond its practicality and use.

The years following Reed's exploration of the Bible as dialogical utterance have seen the proliferation of many and diverse uses of Bakhtin in biblical studies. Very often, scholars have seen Bakhtin's importance in the development of genre studies as fruitful for furthering our understanding

---

15. Ibid., 103.
16. Reed, *Dialogues of the Word*.
17. Ibid., ix.
18. Ibid., ix.

of the diverse witnesses in the Hebrew Bible, in particular. See especially the anthology *Bakhtin and Genre Theory in Biblical Studies*, edited by Roland Boer.[19] That book shows, among other things, the similarities between genre studies and form criticism and how Bakhtin's theories of genre can "enliven" form criticism and genre studies. What this chapter means to do, then, is to take Bakhtin's theories of dialogue and history even further.

Note, for instance, form criticism's interest in the history of the text. When we look at other historical-critical methods, however (text criticism, in particular), the history of the text is complicated. Text criticism's attempts to recover the original text from the many versions that it has given rise to leads one to question what text we are trying to recover. Bakhtin's language and literary theories allows one to recognize the problems that arise in text critical examinations without having to smooth them over in order to interpret the text.

Barbara Green hints at Bakhtin's usefulness for reception theory, referring her reader back to Shepherd's brief works on Bakhtin and reader oriented criticism.[20] While Shepherd focuses some on Jauss's theories, he tends more to pit Bakhtin against reader oriented theorists like Iser and Fish. I would like to push Bakhtin even further than Shepherd, to gear Bakhtin's ideas specifically to the Bible and history of its reception. The key idea from Bakhtin that leads to a defense of reception historical exegesis is embedded in his somewhat elusive term great time.

The Bible as Unfinalizable Dialogue

Bakhtin's most extended discussion on great time comes from his "Response to a Question from the *Novyi Mir* Editorial Staff" in the book *Speech Genres and other Late Essays*.[21] This rather brief essay raises important concerns about the goal of interpretation of ancient texts. What he says seems to conflict with Paul Ricoeur, among many other hermeneuts, who explains that "to 'make one's own' what was previously 'foreign' remains the ultimate aim of all hermeneutics. Interpretation in its last stage wants to equalize, to render contemporaneous, to assimilate. . . . This goal is achieved insofar

19. Boer, ed. *Bakhtin and Genre Theory in Biblical Studies*.

20. Barbara Green, *Bakhtin and Biblical Scholarship*, 28. Green writes, "Considering that Bakhtin situated the role of the author as simultaneously a reader, and in some ways as almost a peer of authored characters, one is led to ask how can these insights be aligned with reception theories as they have developed in the last couple of decades?" Though Green does not do the aligning herself, she later, in a footnote, refers to Shepherd's works cited above.

21. Bakhtin, "Response to a Question.

as interpretation actualizes the meaning of the text for the present reader."[22] Bakhtin, on the other hand, argues that "to understand, it is immensely important for the person who understands to be *located outside* the object of his or her creative understanding—in time, in space, in culture."[23] The reason for this is because nothing new arises from the appropriation of information. It acts merely as a transaction where one person gains something already extant from another. Bakhtin argues that a dialogue between cultures brings something new into the world. "We raise new questions for a foreign culture," he writes, "ones that it did not raise itself; we seek answers to our own questions in it; and the foreign culture responds to us by revealing to us its new aspects and new semantic depths."[24] In other words, the final goal of hermeneutics is not to equalize, as Ricoeur argues, but to add.[25]

Dialogue is not confined to the moment. When Bakhtin suggests that dialogue is unfinalizable, he argues that even if the conversation partners cease participating in a dialogue, the dialogue can still continue even into perpetuity. In fact, the dialogue has no discernible beginning and so its unfinalizability refers to both sides of the time line of the dialogue. To understand this eternity of dialogue in the Bakhtinian sense, one presupposes the concept of utterance as basic unit of speech. Bakhtin explains this most comprehensively in another late essay called "The Problem of Speech Genres."[26] In this essay he explains that the utterance is the "real unit of speech communication" as opposed to the sentence, since the sentence

---

22. Ricoeur, *Interpretation Theory*, 31–32.
23. Bakhtin, "Response to a Question," 7. Emphasis in original.
24. Ibid.
25. Bakhtin reveals in an early essay, however, that though the goal of hermeneutics is to remain outside the object of understanding, one may need to appropriate the text in an earlier stage. Thus, Ricoeur's goal is an early step in Bakhtin's larger goal. In a passage that seems to describe the method of the young man's interpretation of the book of Job in Kierkegaard's *Repetition*, Bakhtin writes:
"Let us say that there is a human being before me who is suffering.... What I have to do is to experience and consummate him aesthetically.... The first step in aesthetic activity is my projecting myself into him and experiencing his life from within him.... I must appropriate to myself the concrete life-horizon of this human being as he experiences it himself.... During the time I project myself into him, I must detach myself from the independent significance of all these features that are transgredient to his consciousness. ... But in any event my projection of myself into him must be followed by a *return* into myself, a *return* to my own place outside the suffering person, for only from this place can the material derived from my projecting myself into the other be rendered meaningful ethically, cognitively, or aesthetically" (Bakhtin, "Author and Hero in Aesthetic Activity," 25–26).
26. Bakhtin, "Problem of Speech Genres."

often obscures genre and other contextual elements that help in the discernment of meaning.[27]

One major distinction between the utterance and the sentence that is important for this description is that an utterance has no real limit in length, superficially. That is, an utterance can be as short as a grunt or as long as a novel.[28] Thus, our case study, the book of Job, acts as an utterance in this paradigm. As Barry Sandywell states, "the concept of *utterance* also includes the congealed 'products' or material deposits of past acts of dialogue—the artifacts, practices, commonsense, philosophical doctrines, written texts, and institutions that make up the operative contexts of a living culture."[29] Therefore, the book of Job and, for our purposes here, interpretations of the book of Job in subsequent epochs act as different utterances in the same dialogue.

This point, that a dialogue can contain such large and seemingly closed-ended utterances, reflects the importance of addressivity in Bakhtin's thought. Addressivity, in fact is "a constitutive feature of the utterance; without it the utterance does not and cannot exist."[30] Every utterance arises from a previous utterance and anticipates another. In the case of Job, one might argue that the book of Job might be responding to different utterances. Some argue that the book attempts to answer the retributive theology of the Deuteronomist or perhaps it is an Israelite response to other ancient Near Eastern wisdom writings. One might argue that the "final," canonized form of the book responds to earlier manifestations of the book of Job that now figure into the final form. Consider the Elihu speeches that some later author wrote before the book's eventual canonization. Whatever the case, the book of Job did not rise up and, in Bakhtin's words, "disturb ... the eternal silence of the universe."[31] It instead responded to earlier utterances. The interpreter, then, must view an utterance as one voice in a dialogue, "a response to preceding utterances."[32]

Likewise, an utterance gives rise to responses. Bakhtin writes, "Each utterance refutes, affirms, supplements, and relies on the others, presupposes them to be known, and somehow takes them into account."[33] Thus, an

27. Ibid., 71.
28. Morson and Emerson, *Mikhail Bakhtin*, 125–26.
29. Sandywell, "The Shock of the Old," 203.
30. Bakhtin, "Speech Genres," 99.
31. Ibid., 69.
32. Ibid., 91.

33. Ibid. Consider also these quotes by Bakhtin in other essays: "every literary work *faces outward away from itself*, toward the listener-reader, and to a certain extent anticipates possible reactions to itself" (Bakhtin, "Forms of Time," 257). Emphasis in original. "The word in living conversation is directly, blatantly, oriented toward a future

ancient text is not a standalone document. It has antecedents and responses that also come into play in its meaning.

This brief summation of Bakhtin's theory of the utterance in a dialogue does not warrant, on its own, attention to the other utterances in relation to a given ancient or biblical text. However, it supports the practice in some way since it shows that the history that precedes a text is not the only element that exists in the textual dialogue. The text continues to develop as the dialogue continues. Bakhtin explains how this can be the case in some of his other works that deal with his theory of time, one of which comes in his discussion of the chronotope.

The Chronotope and the Nature of Time

Bakhtin describes the chronotope as a way of representing time and space in a novel, but his understanding of time in general is implicit in his discourse.[34] One element of time that bears importance for this defense of reception history does relate to Bakhtin's favoring of the novel as an important development in literary history. Because the novel exhibits the quotidian better than other artistic forms, it is a superior medium in temporal representation. In describing the chronotope in Goethe's works, he sees "essential traces of human hands and minds that change nature, and the way human reality and all man has created are reflected back on his customs and views."[35] The importance of this representation of humanity's ability to affect change on the future reflects Bakhtin's vision of the world as one in which one's activity in this world matters, thus relating to ethical responsibility and creative works, both.[36]

Related to the notion that actions in the present bear consequences in the future is the idea that historical events are not arbitrary but that history is a process where past, present, and future are linked together.[37] Thus, it follows that each utterance in an unfinalizable dialogue maintains some

---

answer-word: it provokes an answer, anticipates it and structures itself in the answer's direction. Forming itself in an atmosphere of the already spoken, the word is at the same time determined by that which has not yet been said but which is needed and in fact anticipated by the answering word. Such is the situation in any living dialogue" (Bakhtin, "Discourse in the Novel," 280).

34. See Bakhtin, "*Bildungsroman*," and Bakhtin, "Forms of Time" for Bakhtin's full discourses on the chronotope.

35. Bakhtin, "*Bildungsroman*," 32.

36. Morson and Emerson, *Mikhail Bakhtin*, 397. See also Bakhtin, *Philosophy of the Act*.

37. Morson and Emerson, *Mikhail Bakhtin*, 405.

importance in the development of meaning. Previous receptions in the history of interpretation of a biblical text are not random aberrations but necessary links in the history of the text—that is, necessary to the existence of the text we have at present time.

As the text as utterance proceeds through time, interacting with other utterances in the eternal dialogue, it experiences various chronotopes in what Sandywell calls the "heterotemporality of social existence."[38] The nature of history means that different people in different times and cultures experience the world in different ways. When these people are readers of the same text, the meaning of the text is enriched even beyond the knowledge or ability of the original author or readers.[39] At the very least, the readers are enriched by the multitude of meanings discovered in the text.

By understanding time and text in this way, the importance of the reception history of a text becomes self-evident. By relying merely on the interpretation of the text in its own world and the contemporary world, a large swath of its meaning falls by the wayside. In other words, the biblical text as we receive it today is not the biblical text that was read at its inception or canonization. Even supposing that we have somehow recovered the original autograph of the text does not mean that the utterance is the same as it was in its own epoch. The dialogue it has been participating in over the centuries has changed it and enriched it in that more of it is available for the modern reader to interpret. It has grown over time as readers excavate the buried meaning. Thus, part of our goal in biblical interpretation should be to interpret the dialogue which incorporates the text while we interpret the text.

Bakhtin claims that the utterance is an unrepeatable linguistic unit.[40] As it enters into different contexts, though it may contain the same words in the same order as before, it changes. This is the case for a single reader since the reader reacts differently to the second utterance than to the first.[41] It follows that it is the case with different readers as well. The book of Job carries with it a different meaning to a first-century Jew than it does to a twenty-first-century North American. A medieval Italian will also have read a different utterance than either the ancient Palestinian or modern Westerner.

---

38. Sandywell, "The Shock of the Old," 197.

39. Morson and Emerson, *Mikhail Bakhtin*, 429. In Bakhtin's own words: "The work and the world represented in it enter the real world and enrich it, and the real world enters the work and its world as part of the process of its creation, as well as part of its subsequent life, in a continual renewing of the work through the creative perception of listeners and readers" (Bakhtin, "Forms of Time," 254).

40. Bakhtin, "Problem of the Text," 108.

41. Morson and Emerson, *Mikhail Bakhtin*, 126.

Thus, even if the hermeneutical goal were to understand the ancient text as an ancient reader might, the quest would be futile.

Great Time

Near the end of his career Bakhtin adds to his understanding of time and the chronotope in his "Response to a Question from the *Novyi Mir* Editorial Staff," in which he gives his opinion of contemporary Russian literary and cultural studies.[42] In this essay, he presents his most sustained description of the concept of great time. Unfortunately, the brevity of the essay still requires much speculation and deduction on the part of the reader to understand the full significance of this concept.

Great time does arise sparsely throughout his later works, including in the essay "Toward a Methodology for the Human Sciences,"[43] where he compares great time to small time. Small time, he describes as "the present day, the recent past, and the foreseeable [desired] future." Great time, on the other hand is "infinite and unfinalized dialogue in which no meaning dies."[44] Thus, great time houses all interpretations of a text, while small time has a limited scope and falls short in what it can provide the interpreter.[45]

Great time, therefore, relates to that interconnectedness described in much of Bakhtin's discussion on time and dialogue. In fact, Sandywell calls Great Time "the temporal equivalent of 'polyglossia' at the level of cultural traditions. . . . The 'polyglot We' of great time includes anonymous others who reach back into the sources of cultural creativity and possible interlocutors solicited by future acts of interpretation."[46] Great time, then, relates directly to Bakhtin's theories on time and dialogue.

The general meaning of great time as Bakhtin describes it is the idea that "works break through the boundaries of their own time, they live in centuries, that is, in *great time* and frequently (with great works, always) their lives there are more intense and fuller than are their lives within their own time."[47] He gives several examples of this phenomenon in his writings.

---

42. Bakhtin, "Response to a Question."

43. Bakhtin, "Methodology," 169. Note, however, that the Bakhtinian authorship of this "essay" has come into question in recent years. The words most likely are Bakhtin's, but the various paragraphs are likely not in chronological order (Shepherd, "A Feeling for History?" 35)..

44. Bakhtin, "Methodology," 169.

45. See Langleben, "M. Bachtin's Notions of Time," 181.

46. Sandywell, "The Shock of the Old," 208.

47. Bakhtin, "Response to a Question," 4. Emphasis in original.

He argues that Shakespeare "has grown because of that which actually has been and continues to be found in his works, but which neither he himself nor his contemporaries could consciously perceive and evaluate in the context of the culture of their epoch."[48] In another essay, untranslated at the present time, he says that "Homer, and Aeschylus, and Sophocles, and Socrates, and all the ancient writers and thinkers remain, with equal entitlement, in great time . . ."[49] Presumably, he would say the same about Goethe, but instead with Goethe he praises him for having incorporated this thought in his work. Goethe views the past as resounding in the present, "taking on complex new layers of significance in each historical epoch."[50]

Great works, therefore, outgrow their own epochs. To focus entirely on the culture they represent is to ignore a great portion of their lives. As Bakhtin writes, "trying to understand and explain a work solely in terms of the conditions of its epoch alone, solely in terms of the conditions of the most immediate time, will never enable us to penetrate into its semantic depths."[51] They gain new meanings over time and require interpreters to harvest these meanings.

Bakhtin uses an agrarian metaphor in his *Novyi Mir* essay as well, but in doing so reminds us that the eternal dialogue stretches backward. He states that "great literary works are prepared for by centuries, and in the epoch of their creation it is merely a matter of picking the fruit that is ripe after a lengthy and complex process of maturation."[52] This statement reminds us that the great work responds to what comes previously. If the reception history of a text is a relatively untapped resource in biblical studies, that does not obviate the need for historical criticism. In fact it suggests that reception history is a component of historical criticism. The text responds to history and anticipates response in the future. It picks the ripe fruit and then plants more for future respondents.

That the fruit is ripe relates to the way Bakhtin views creativity. Creativity is constant and responds to immediate opportunities and needs.[53] The book of Job is a product of its culture and epoch as much as it is a product of its author or authors. Thus studying the book of Job requires studying its history and epoch. However, the book of Job's appearance in

48. Ibid.

49. Reproduced partially in Shepherd, "A Feeling for History," 33–34.

50. Lindsey, "The Problem of Great Time," 325.

51. Bakhtin, "Response to a Question," 4. We can presume that the "immediate time" he mentions in this essay is similar or the same as the "small time" mentioned in "Methodology for the Human Sciences."

52. Ibid.

53. Morson and Emerson, *Mikhail Bakhtin*, 414.

the world spurs the creativity of its readers. It contributes to the immediate culture and future ones as well. It continues to live in its own residues which necessitate creative response.[54] Modern interpretations of the book of Job, therefore, could not exist without those that had come previously. To understand how we arrived at our conclusions requires the knowledge of the previous generations' contributions.

Looking at an image of a text in great time, one sees a dialogue of a series of utterances. The subject of the dialogue is the text, but the text is also an utterance. Some of the utterances give rise to the subject and others respond to it. Each of these utterances are also products of their own chronotope, and thus, contain their own "outsideness," which allows for newness in the dialogue. When discussing the role of the readers in this dialogue, Morson and Emerson write:

> [Readers] can take maximal advantage of the differences and of their outsideness by an act of creative understanding that is truly dialogic in the best sense. Readers may make the differences an occasion for exploring the potential of the work in a way not available to its original author and readers, and so become enriched by something truly in the work but needing their own special experience to provoke.[55]

The picture here is that the reader, though creative in one sense, does not create meaning, as in the reader-response criticism of Stanley Fish. Rather, he or she unlocks meaning inherent in the text. The dialogue, therefore, is necessary to extract meaning.[56]

Summary of Bakhtin's Arguments for Reception History

To be sure, Bakhtin does not directly advocate the incorporation of reception history into the interpretive process. However, his descriptions of time

---

54. Ibid., 229. See also Bakhtin, "*Bildungsroman*," 36, where he writes, "The ghostly, terrifying, and unaccountable in it were surmounted by the structural aspects, already disclosed by us above, which are inherent in this way of visualizing time: the aspect of an *essential link* between the past and present, the aspect of the *necessity* of the past and the necessity of its place in a line of continuous development, the aspect of the *creative effectiveness* of the past, and, finally, the aspect of the past and present being linked to a *necessary future*." Emphasis in original.

55. Morson and Emerson, *Mikhail Bakhtin*, 429.

56. Relatedly, Shepherd writes that "what is missing in Fish's formulations is the acknowledgement of and insistence on the social and historical constitution of prior meaning which makes Bakhtin's model so persuasive," invoking the chronotope in his assessment of reader based theory. (Shepherd, "The Authority of Meanings," 141).

and the interpreter's hermeneutical goals seem to warrant the inclusion of reception history in the exegesis of an ancient text. Before continuing with an evaluation of Bakhtin's theories and the problems that might arise from them, let us review the various reasons for incorporating the history of interpretation based on Bakhtin's dialogical theories.

Firstly, the dialogue the interpreter has with a text did not start with the interpreter's impetus. In the case of the book of Job, the dialogue has been ongoing for more than two millennia. Important points have arisen in that long period that one need not forget. It is also likely that earlier interpreters have raised points that modern interpreters will raise independently. This, however, cannot be guaranteed and there is no reason, anyway, to reinvent the wheel.

Secondly, in arguing that the hermeneutical task should not require the modern interpreter to renounce his or her own culture, epoch, or context, but to "raise new questions for a foreign culture, ones that it did not raise itself,"[57] Bakhtin advocates a creative understanding of the text. What this also does, however, is place the modern interpreter in the same situation as the earlier interpreters in their own epoch and culture. The modern interpreter may conceivably be more able to enter into the mind of the author through the knowledge gained throughout history—knowledge of ancient culture, rhetoric, philology, etc. Since this should not figure into the goal, however, the earlier interpreters can remain in the dialogue without a temporal hierarchy silencing them. Great time democratizes interpretation. Of course, priority will be given in the end to that interpretation that can speak best into our own culture and epoch, but earlier interpreters should become partners in this quest.

Related to this second point is the realization that the goal of earlier interpreters of biblical texts fit much more closely to Bakhtin's stated desires than most modern methods. Rather than focusing on what the text might have meant, pre-modern exegetes were more intent on seeking answers to their own epoch's questions.

Thirdly, the "sclerotic deposits" of the ancient text as utterance that litter the time-space of the eternal dialogue have been picked up by other interpreters along the way.[58] That is, their creative reading has unlocked meaning and they, in turn, have deposited their own sclerotic deposits for us. Bypassing what has been left for us in the dialogue means a loss of data.

Lastly, by bypassing the millennia of data left for us by pre-modern exegetes, we also short circuit the dialogue. The interpretation of the text we

57. Bakhtin, "Response to a Question," 7.
58. Bakhtin, "Discourse in the Novel," 292.

have received is the result of centuries of small discoveries, betraying the prosaic nature of historical activity. The gradual nature of the eternal dialogue reminds us that others have trod before us. Without their work, the modern interpreter must begin at the beginning. We do not stand on the shoulders of giants so much as we stand on the shoulders of those standing on the shoulders of others with very few giants among us. This requires a humble posture, but it is also empowering. We recognize that very little of what we do can be considered groundbreaking or trailblazing. On the other hand, minor additions to the knowledge of a text are necessary for the continuing dialogue. Each voice in the dialogue affects change. This is empowering for us and also important for the voices that have gone before us. William Lindsey describes great time as "time in which the past inhabits the present in voices that did not have their full say in the past and time in which the future enters the present proleptically, insofar as it opens space here and now for voices that otherwise would have no opportunity to speak."[59]

The above, admittedly, acts more as a defense for and theory of the incorporation of reception history into the practice of biblical studies rather than as a prescription for how one might integrate the two practices. Bakhtin, to my knowledge, does not offer a method of interpretation,[60] though in practice biblical scholars have been using earlier receptions of biblical text selectively since the medieval era.[61]

Questions remain, though, as to how far one is willing and able to take the logical conclusions of Bakhtin's theories of time seriously in this regard. One issue that might hinder the historical critic from using the interpretations of a biblical text from previous epochs actually relates to the change that has come about through history. Would those who have participated in this dialogue actually agree with their own exegesis if given the knowledge that we have received by benefit of time? That is, would recent discoveries or linguistic developments that illumine our knowledge of the text have an important effect on earlier exegetes if they were given the information we have received by benefit of our place in history? Would this problem then preclude using these aspects of their exegesis that do not hold up to modern knowledge?

---

59. Lindsey, "The Problem of Great Time," 324.

60. A method of interpretation, after all, would look a great deal like a system, which Bakhtin criticizes. It would also seem to hinder creative response within the dialogue.

61. Patristic studies are plentiful among certain confessional groups, of course. Other scholars have tapped into more recent receptions in different ways. In the case of Job, Clines refers to Kierkegaard's *Upbuilding Discourses* to aid in his interpretation of Job 1:21 (Clines, *Job 1–20*). More recently, Susannah Ticciati has used Barth's interpretation of Job as a starting point for her own theology (Ticciati, *Disruption*). Newsom highlights other examples (Newsom, "Reconsidering Job," 175–77).

Obviously, one cannot incorporate the interpretations of all exegetes throughout history of a given biblical text. The number of interpreters of the book of Job, for example, is so vast that allowing all to speak into our own work would be counterproductive.[62] One will also find that one cannot reconcile the various readings of a text. However, the existence of irreconcilable views does not preclude dialogue, nor does it justify the silencing of earlier writers or views. Likewise, dialogue would not seem to mean passive acceptance of the interpretation.[63] Bakhtin, instead, seems to be advocating the acceptance of other readers in history into the conversation, or, perhaps advocating the interpreter's involvement in the conversation that has been ongoing already.

JOB AS SCRIPTURAL UTTERANCE

When dealing with a passage from the Bible, one encounters another set of layers or voices in this dialogue, for the canon of Scripture itself is a reception of previous utterances. The book of Job preceded the canon and perhaps the dialogues of the book of Job preceded the book of Job. The receptions of Job encountered in this book complicate the dialogue even further since they treat the book of Job as an utterance in the larger biblical canon rather than an utterance that stands on its own.

Consider Kierkegaard, Vischer, and Barth's interpretations in comparison to Kant's. One major difference between Kant's interpretation of Job and the three interpreters that lie at the centre of this project, besides the obviously huge difference in length, is his view of the Bible. Kant certainly did not hold the Scripture in as high regard as the others. More importantly, however, is the fact that he fails to mention any other biblical texts in his discourse on Job as both Barth and Vischer do. Kierkegaard also appears not to raise other texts during his discourse on Job in *Repetition*, but as I shall argue, his publishing *Fear and Trembling* on the same day as *Repetition* but under a different pseudonym shows he sees the need to read those two texts in proximity—two texts which include lengthy exegeses of the *Akedah*

---

62. See again, for instance, Vicchio, *Job in the Medieval World*; and Vicchio, *Job in the Modern World*. There is very little room in these surveys of Job in the history of interpretation for analysis or engagement with the texts.

63. For a potential example of passive acceptance (or perhaps more likely, a clever avoidance of conflict with authorities), note the final line in the prologue to Thomas Aquinas's *Literal Exposition on Job*. In discussing his goal of expounding the literal sense of Job rather than a spiritual or mystical sense, he writes, "Blessed Pope Gregory has already disclosed to us its mysteries so subtly and clearly that there seems no need to add anything further to them" (Aquinas, *The Literal Exposition on Job*, 69).

and Job. Kierkegaard also elsewhere waxes about the authority of all texts in the canon, so we need not belabor the point.

We will, in their respective chapters, give each interpreter their due. In these early stages, however, it behooves us to generalize Kierkegaard, Barth, and Vischer as exegetes who hold the biblical canon in a higher authority than many other scholars of their eras. All three recognize the importance of historical criticism and do not often begrudge those who practice the more *wissenschaftlich* aspects of biblical studies. However, the results of those studies make up only minor portions of their own exegesis and certainly do not satisfy them as the ends of biblical study.

Of course, their attitudes toward the Scriptures, though idiosyncratic in some respects, reflect the norm over the course of the history of biblical interpretation. Most exegetes utilize some manifestation of theological exegesis and generally treat the Bible as a whole rather than a mere anthology of disparate texts. However, I do not want to take this for granted. In the current epoch, the norm in academia still finds much to scorn with theological exegesis, canonical approaches to exegesis, as well as the reception history of biblical texts. In the following section, I continue to lay the hermeneutical groundwork for approaching the book of Job in these respects, continuing to use Bakhtin as an aid in the undergirding. Kierkegaard, Vischer, and Barth are not grand proponents of the reception history of biblical texts for exegesis, but they do approach texts theologically and with attention to the canon. Bakhtin's theories, which help defend the use of reception history also aid in defense of proto-canonical approaches—especially his theories of the utterance versus the sentence.

The Utterance Versus the Sentence

In some of Bakhtin's later essays he incorporates his earlier misgivings about Kant's desire for objective analysis in ethics, illustrated in his tract "Toward a Philosophy of the Act," into his more mature work on literary theory. Bakhtin expresses a frustration towards modern linguistic analysis because it focuses too much on the objective data found in the sentence.

His problems with the sentence, best exemplified in his essay "The Problem of Speech Genres" are that these basic units of communication lack much of the intangible information that makes up a dialogue. To begin to rectify the problem of the abstract and objective data that cannot take into account aspects of genre like irony, Bakhtin proposes using the "utterance" as a unit of speech instead.

Read Him Again and Again

One cannot measure an utterance in the same way as one measures a sentence.[64] While a sentence generally consists of a subject and a predicate, an utterance can consist of any number of combinations of words. Indeed, an utterance need not consist of any words at all, for a grunt can communicate more than a long string of words in certain contexts. One very telling difference between an utterance and a sentence is that a sentence is repeatable while an utterance is not. The same sentence in different contexts makes for different utterances. Despite being verbally identical, two utterances actually carry different contextual meanings while the sentences carry the same abstract meaning.[65] To show the significance of this for a biblical passage, let us see how one might view a single verse from Job as multiple utterances when it is repeated in different contexts. "I am not at ease, nor am I quiet; I have no rest; but trouble comes," says Job in 3:26 concluding his first speech.[66] The verse as recorded in the Leningrad Codex expresses anguish in typical Hebrew parallelism. As a sentence, one has much to explore. Three parallel clauses—a negation followed by a first person singular *Qal qatal* intransitive verb—give way to a fourth clause with a third person positive transitive verb that rhymes with the previously thrice repeated negation *lo'* and an abstract subject.

However much the sentence expresses, it does not explain much without viewing it in its larger context. The entire utterance takes up the entire chapter where the reader gets more of a sense of what has led to this finale of misery. But even in the context of chapter 3 Job's specific misfortunes remain a mystery. Some scholars devoted to the *Wissenschaft* of the text might resist seeing chapter 3 in the context of the whole book of Job. There are many reasons to believe that the prologue to Job and the dialogues do not share the same author or era of production. In this context, the dialogues of Job and his friends remain mute regarding the cause of Job's exasperation. On the other hand, the larger context in which chapter 3 falls can include the first two chapters, which lay out the cause of Job's suffering, both the heavenly motivation and the physical stripping away of Job's family, possessions, and health. If the sentence that concludes chapter 3 has these first two chapters as its context, the grammar of 3:26 does not change but the utterance does.

This generates little controversy. However, Barth and Vischer in particular, read the book of Job not merely as a whole utterance, but also in the

---

64. Even the sentence, however, confounds. Many linguists have argued how one determines the limits of the sentence. See Ricoeur, *Interpretation Theory*, 7.

65. Morson and Emerson, *Mikhail Bakhtin*, 126–27.

66. לא שלותי ולא שקטתי ולא-נחתי ויבא רגז

Job in Great Time

context of the biblical canon. In this case, Job 3:26 not only gains specificity from its proximity to Job 1–2 but also ironically foreshadows Christ's resurrection after Jesus experiences a similar turmoil to Job during his incarnation and passion.

Viewing the utterance in this larger context does not negate the validity of the more grammatical-critical reading; it merely points to the importance of the subjectivity of the individual reader. One who accepts the Christian canon as a single secondary genre made up of multiple primary genres like Job chapter 3 will react differently to Job 3:26 than someone who views all utterances in the Bible as singular and disparate.[67] The final form of the book of Job (if one can even use such a phrase, considering the unfinalizability of any utterance in the hermeneutic of Bakhtin) is less a product of an author, or even a redactor, as it is an occurrence in the course of an ongoing dialogue.

What Bakhtin's musings on great time imply and what he discusses more explicitly in his essay on speech genres is the dialogical nature of all utterances. Each utterance responds to a previously uttered statement and also anticipates future responses.[68] Bakhtin writes, "each utterance refutes, affirms, supplements, and relies on the others, presupposes them to be known, and somehow takes them into account."[69] Noting that Job does not appear as if from nowhere, we must acknowledge that it enters great time in response to previous utterances. These previous utterances may include the work of the Deuteronomist or the sage of Proverbs as is often surmised. Bakhtin, however, implies that it anticipates responses as well. This is easy to imagine. Consider the arguments of the friends. They not only express the likely sentiments of many sages within their own tradition, but also lend the potential arguments of other future sages to the argument in order to flesh out the meaning of the book of Job as a whole.

However, despite anticipating the response, it does not obviate response. The dialogue continues. In some ways, we see a response in the New Testament. Though mention of Job in the New Testament is rare or even

---

67. Bakhtin discusses the difference between a primary speech genre and a secondary speech genre in Bakhtin, *Speech Genres*, 72 ff. In the case of the book of Job, chapter 3 would be a primary genre as would chapters 1–2; the book as a whole would be a secondary genre incorporating multiple primary genres. I am suggesting that the Bible itself can also be a secondary genre made up of many primary genres.

68. Similarly, Ricoeur writes, "My experience cannot directly become your experience. An event belonging to one stream of consciousness cannot be transferred as such into another stream of consciousness. Yet, nevertheless, something passes from me to you. Something is transferred from one sphere of life to another." Ricoeur, *Interpretation Theory*, 16.

69. Bakhtin, *Speech Genres*, 91.

debatable, what is not debatable is that the authors of the New Testament and the authors of Job share a literary culture where the themes that arise in both utterances relate to one another in various ways. Perhaps one could think of the authors as attendees at a dinner party sitting on different ends of the table. They may not respond directly to one another, but all those seated around the table assure that the themes of the conversations overlap in some respect. Perhaps they even overhear the other's words, which influence their own thoughts.

Before moving on, one might note that much of what came above can be buttressed further by some of Kierkegaard's own ideas that emerge in his book *Repetition*. Besides containing much of his work on Job, *Repetition* also introduces the category of repetition. I deal with the category of repetition at length in chapter 3, but some things deserve mentioning here in the context of reception history of a biblical text.

Consider first, the word repetition, which has a specialized meaning in the work of Kierkegaard. In its most basic form, repetition suggests taking something that occurred in the past and bringing it into the present. Kierkegaard seems to suggest that it goes into the future as well, but clearly a forward moving focus is implied in some way. When the young man "repeats" the book of Job in the second half of *Repetition*, he moves the book of Job into the present.

One might protest the semblance of repetition with Bakhtin's theory of the utterance. Recall that an utterance is unrepeatable, which seems to fly in the face of the very idea of "repetition." However, as will become obvious later, some scholars have problems with the translation of the Danish word *Gjentagelsen* as "repetition" and believe that a better translation might be "resumption"[70] or "retaking"[71] since it has more to do with the existential reality of the interpreter than the text itself. Jolita Pons begins her exploration of Kierkegaard's hermeneutics with a discussion on the use of biblical quotation and the nature of quotation in general. She notes that, apropos to Bakhtin's theories on the utterance, "a verbally exact quotation that would seem to be a perfect repetition is ambiguous, because it is not clear whether it can keep its integrity in the new context."[72] Clearly, the young man's interpretation of Job reflects this ambiguity.

Also, what will become more evident when we look more closely at *Repetition* and the interpretation of Job within the book is that when the young man does appropriate the book of Job into his own life, he does not

70. Croxall, *Kierkegaard Commentary*, 128–29.
71. Mooney, *Selves in Discord and Resolve*, 28.
72. Pons, *Stealing*, 14.

attempt so much to enter into the mind of Job or the author(s) of the book of Job as he attempts to bring Job into his own mind.

The young man's goal does in some ways seem to fit Ricoeur's goal, as mentioned above, of the hermeneut over Bakhtin's. The young man does not seem to want to locate himself outside the text, but Bakhtin writes of the importance of being located "outside the object of his or her creative understanding—in time, in space, in culture," and the young man does remain in his own time, space, and culture as will become evident in chapter three. Notably, once the receiver appropriates the text into his life, in the hermeneutics of Kierkegaard, the text does not transform, but is the agent of transformation. Iben Damgaard observes that in the upbuilding discourse that discusses Job, which Kierkegaard published the same year as *Repetition*, the good reader of Job should transform the text into action (and could not interpretation be included under the label action?).[73]

Perhaps one will argue that Kierkegaard and the young man take things too far. There may be a place for ostensible objective analysis that bypasses the history of the text in great time. However, any analysis of any text from the past will need to take the text out of its own context in order to analyze it. Pons writes:

> Quotation introduces an object into circulation. This object might acquire a new value from that which it originally had. Because quotation detaches fragments of text from their respective contexts and attaches them to other contexts, there arises a tension between their independent value and the sense that the quotation might have had in its original context.[74]

Pons is discussing quotations of text, which may be very brief, but they also may be very long. On the surface there is a difference between a quotation used to defend one's own opinion, as someone may do with the platitudes Polonius recites to Laertes in *Hamlet*, and a commentary of a biblical book in the Old Testament Library, but the tension exists in some form in both examples.

Kierkegaard embraces the inevitable. The history of Job interpretation shows how the book's meaning is dependent at least partially on the context of the interpreter him or herself. Those who attempt to gain a pure and objective interpretation of the ancient book will be partially hindered by the distance between the interpreter and the context of the original text but also he or she will be hindered by the impossibility of escaping one's own context. The reception history of a biblical text is an important component of the meaning of the text for all the reasons cited above, but it also is

73. Damgaard, "'My Dear Reader': Kierkegaard's Reader," 101.
74. Jolita Pons, *Stealing*, 9.

important because once a person in the present makes a final claim on the meaning of the text, the present becomes a part of that reception history. The text appropriates each successive attempt at interpretation as it moves through great time.

Inherent in the movement through great time is an assumption of the unity of time itself. Each utterance responds to a previous utterance and so each utterance relates in some way to other utterances in the dialogue. It goes without saying that all utterances in the dialogue are connected. This same theory of utterances' relation to the unity of time lies behind typological interpretations of biblical texts, for typological interpretation assumes unity in the temporal. The typological imagination of Kierkegaard, Vischer, and Barth in their interpretations of Job follows.

THE TYPOLOGICAL IMAGINATION IN THE JOB OF KIERKEGAARD, VISCHER, AND BARTH

A single term that adequately describes the confluence of exegetical methods found in these different but related interpretations of Job will fall short. I use the term "typological" as a descriptor, noting that it falls under the broader category of allegory.[75] Barth's and Vischer's Christological interpretations of Job bear little resemblance to Gregory the Great's use of allegory and, perhaps Christological might act as a better adjective when discussing Barth and Vischer than typological, for it merely suggests that one somehow employ Christ in his interpretation. It also seems to allow one some freedom in that employment. However, using Christological would obviously exclude Kierkegaard's interpretations from the discussion even though I contend they belong.

When we look at Kierkegaard's interpretations below I will note how *Repetition*, in particular, relies on both allegory and a typological understanding of history. While many have disputed the identification of typology with allegory, other major voices have maintained that one should view typology as a subsection of allegory.[76] Henri de Lubac, in his dispute with Jean Daniélou over the nature of allegory and typology, asserts that "allegory had traditionally been a broader term, containing typology as one element among others."[77] Indeed, Erich Auerbach notes that "Tertullian uses

---

75. Note that I use the phrase typological interpretation and figural interpretation interchangeably, usually based on who I am quoting—*figura* being the Latin equivalent of the Greek *typus* (see Auerbach, "Figura," 47–48).

76. Dawson, *Allegorical Readers*, 16.

77. Cited in Boersma, *Nouvelle Théologie and Sacramental Ontology*, 182.

allegoria almost synonymously with *figura*, though much less frequently."[78] Two considerations arise when deriving what allegory indicates. The first aspect of allegory one must acknowledge emerges when examining a very general definition of allegory based on its etymology. As David Dawson explains, the origin of the word allegory derives from the Greek words *allos* (other) and *agoreuo* (to speak in the assembly, to proclaim), thus allegory is something other than what is proclaimed in public.[79] That is, an allegorical reading can offer something other than the "literal" meaning of the text, but it might also provide a new meaning to a text other than the accepted reading. In any case, the allegory or allegorical reading only exists in the presence of a "literal" meaning.[80] Dawson also proposes that allegory or "interpretations and compositions designated as 'allegorical' must have a narrative dimension."[81] The use of a metaphor becomes allegorical when the metaphor extends over the course of a narrative.[82] Examples of allegory, therefore, include *The Pilgrim's Progress*, which tells the story of a spiritual journey using material objects.

If one uses these two descriptions as a rubric for identifying allegory, then typological interpretation does seem to fall under the heading of allegory, too.[83] How typology distinguishes itself under most definitions of allegory is its relationship to history. In typology, the type precedes the antitype so that the antitype fulfils the type in some way. While allegory in general can find parallels between two disparate, discontinuous texts, typology argues for a particular philosophy of history in which a character or event prefigures a later fulfillment, usually in the person or work of Jesus Christ.[84] Hans Frei describes allegory in part as "the attachment of a temporally freefloating meaning pattern to any temporal occasion whatever, without any intrinsic connection between sensuous time-bound picture and the meaning represented by it."[85] Though "the line between allegory and typological or figural interpretation was often very fine," Frei writes, "when the temporal reality of an earlier instance was dissolved in favor of its meaning . . . the

78. Auerbach, "Figura," 47.
79. Dawson, *Allegorical Readers*, 3.
80. Ibid., 7.
81. Ibid., 3.
82. Ibid., 5–6.
83. In the same passage as the one cited above, Auerbach notes that "*allegoria* could not be used synonymously with *figura* in all contexts, for it did not have the same implication of 'form'; one could not write that *Adam est allegoria Christi*" (Auerbach, "Figura," 48).
84. McNeil, "Typology."
85. Frei, *Eclipse*, 29.

application of that meaning remained riveted to a temporal occurrence."[86] Therefore, C. S. Lewis's *The Lion, the Witch, and the Wardrobe* qualifies as allegory and not typology since Narnia exists outside of the realm of the historical time-space continuum. Typology is a type of allegory in which the repeatability of events in different contexts contributes theologically to one's understanding of a future-directed history.

We will have to look at each of the individual Job interpretations in order to see how the different texts by Kierkegaard, Vischer, and Barth fit under the above understanding of allegory and typology. At first glance, Barth and Vischer seem very intent on practicing allegorical interpretation. However, Vischer especially has a complicated relationship to allegory, typology, and spiritual interpretation of biblical texts. Henri de Lubac writes:

> The exegesis of a Karl Barth, a Roland de Pury, a Wilhelm Vischer, are reminiscent in many ways of the exegesis of the early Fathers. Their vehement rejection of the ancient word "allegory," though, is not uniquely attributable to the ambivalences of this word, to which we have already referred. It is derived from their difficulty in recognizing a real progress in the order of knowledge from one Economy to the other.[87]

Whether or not they practice allegory or typology while shunning the terms is up for debate.

Vischer's Allegorical Imagination Applied to the Book of Job

Vischer essentially equates typology as it had been understood historically with allegory, arguing that using the method of typology in Old Testament exegesis relates to transposing the literal sense of the text in figures and symbols of Christ.[88] Vischer claims to oppose typology as employed in this way because the word was made flesh and transposing the literal into the figurative spiritualizes the fleshed word, reversing the text as it was given to the church. It imposes a meaning onto the text rather than accepting what the text wants to say.[89] His rejection of typology and allegory must surprise those accustomed to thinking of Vischer as an allegorical reader who seems to transpose the literal meaning of Old Testament texts into something that refers to Christ.

86. Ibid., 30.
87. De Lubac, *Scripture in the Tradition*, 77.
88. Vischer, "La Méthode," 120.
89. Ibid., 121.

Job in Great Time

James Barr and Brevard Childs had a brief but spirited back and forth on the use of allegory in modern biblical exegesis where they broached the work of Vischer.[90] Childs holds that Vischer's approach equals allegory[91] and Barr counters with a rather extensive essay showing that Vischer's method runs counter to allegory and instead is an idiosyncratic literal approach fuelled by a high Christology.[92] It seems certain that Vischer would agree with Barr, noting his harsh words reserved for allegory and typology, though he would obviously not have agreed with Barr's final negative assessment of his work.

Barr's description of Vischer notes the propensity to quote reformed theologians, including and especially Luther and Calvin, but almost no scholars from earlier than the reformation like Origin or other fathers, which would go far in showing his lack of interest in allegory.[93] Indeed, Vischer often cites historical critics positively including Wellhausen in his Job discourse. Barr's final analysis of The *Christuszeugnis*, in particular, claims that Vischer fails to offer a "sound explanation of how [his Christological conclusions] had been reached in the first place or of why they should be accepted other than because the reader personally liked them."[94] Comparing the *Christuszeugnis* with Vischer's later essay on exegetical method, one would have to concede to Barr's assessment to some degree. Vischer's method does seem to advocate a plain sense reading of the Bible that incorporates a good understanding of the biblical languages. The exegesis of the Bible, in fact, should proceed with the same method as that used in the interpretation of other human-written texts in antiquity.[95] The sense that responds to the Holy Spirit, he contends, is the literal sense.[96]

On the other hand, how one might arrive at interpretations that find Jesus in the Old Testament often seem like flimsy word association in the *Christuszeugnis*. Rendtorff gives an example in Vischer's reading of Genesis 1 in which Vischer explains that the light that God calls forth in 1:3 "is—the

---

90. See Barr, "The Literal," 3–17; Childs, "Critical Reflections," 3–9; Barr, "Wilhelm Vischer and Allegory;" and Barr, "Allegory and Historicism," 105–20.

91. Childs, "Critical Reflections," 4.

92. Barr, "Wilhelm Vischer and Allegory," 44.

93. Ibid., 42. On the other hand, Frei provides several examples of Calvin and Luther using a typological interpretation. His descriptions of Calvin's exegesis, particularly, mirror much of what Barr says about Vischer (Frei, *Eclipse*, 19–28). However Frei argues convincingly for Calvin's "unquestioned assumption of a natural coherence between literal and figural reading," where Barr accuses Vischer of merely misreading the literal meaning of the text (ibid., 27).

94. Barr, "Wilhelm Vischer and Allegory," 54.

95. Vischer, "La Méthode," 109.

96. Ibid., 121.

expression can no longer be avoided if we are to expound our text fathfully [sic] and guard it against every kind of speculative misinterpretation—'the glory of God in the face of Jesus Christ' (2 Cor. 4:6)."[97] Rendtorff finds this makes Vischer's method obvious:

> He interprets a central concept in the Old Testament text by way of a New Testament quotation in which the same word appears, related to Christ; and then he expands the Christological aspect, a detailed quotation playing a central role (in this case Calvin, but more frequently Luther or Hamann). So here, on the basis of the keyword "light" in Gen. 1:4, he develops in essentials the beginnings of a Christological theology of creation.[98]

Rendtorff's criticism is helpful in understanding Vischer, but does lack mention of the likely reason that Vischer went to 2 Corinthians 4:6 first before looking at other New Testament passages that contain the word light in relation to Jesus Christ. The author of 2 Corinthians specifically alludes to Genesis 1:3, 4, saying, "For it is the God who said, 'Let light shine out of darkness,' who has shone in our hearts to give the light of the knowledge of the glory of God in the face of Jesus Christ." Vischer follows this up with several New Testament passages on light (among them Heb. 1:3, 1 Tim. 6:16, 1 John 1:5, and James 1:17), but the passage he goes to first has an explicit intertextual relationship with the passage he intends to interpret.

It should also be noted that Rendtorff's and Barr's treatments of Vischer makes the *Christuszeugnis* seem as though Vischer sees Jesus in every passage of the Pentateuch. This is not, however, the case. The book, instead, reads like a brief commentary on the Torah with the occasional, sometimes eye-opening, discovery of Christ's existence in the Old Testament, as in the example above. "The Witness of Job to Jesus Christ" is even more modest. Christ makes no appearance in Vischer's mini-commentary other than in a single parenthetical comment until his exegesis of the entire book is complete. After assessing the epilogue, Vischer concludes that "the Book of Job points beyond itself."[99]

Primarily, the book of Job points beyond itself to the culture that gave birth to the story, a culture in which the crucifixion and resurrection of Jesus Christ also arises. Vischer takes care not to claim the conclusion to the book of Job acts as an allegory or type to Christ, but skirts close enough to that claim that his English translator inserts the idea into the essay. Vischer uses the terms *Zeichen*, *Gleichnis*, and *Vorbild* to describe the relationship

97. Vischer, "The Witness of Job I," 44.
98. Rendtorff, *Canon and Theology*, 80.
99. Vischer, "The Witness of Job II," 148.

Job in Great Time

of Job to Jesus, translated into English as "type," "parable," and "type," respectively.[100] Despite Vischer's protesting the use of the words allegory and typology in his later essay, his final three pages of his Job essay fit leading definitions of the typology.

Typology is a rhetorical technique and a philosophy of history and Vischer's observation of literary parallels between the book of Job and the Gospels fits that description well.[101] When one arrives at the end of the book of Job, he notes that the book does not straightforwardly answer the question posed at the beginning of "whether there is a man who fully corresponds to the good Will of the Creator and justifies His work of Creation."[102] Rather, the book changes the question along the way and ends up pointing back to God. Job's speeches turn the Satan's question back onto God, thus pointing the book beyond itself, thus Vischer argues for a rhetorical thrust to the parallels.

Vischer ends by comparing Job's story to major events in the Gospels. God restores Job's life, which foreshadows the more dramatic resurrection of Christ. The Greek translation of Job adds that Job will rise again, strengthening the resurrection parallels. Before Christ's resurrection, Jesus also is tempted by Satan, tested by his friends, declared in the wrong as evidenced by Judas's betrayal, and seemingly forsaken by God. Through all of this, Jesus also remains steadfastly obedient to God. Vischer does not find Jesus in the story of Job so much as finds Job in the story of Jesus. The Job event—though Vischer does not claim it to be an historical event—finds its final fulfillment in the Christ event.

Vischer writes in the first pages of the *Christuszeugnis*, "The two main words of the Christian confession 'Jesus is the Christ' . . . correspond to the two parts of the Holy Scriptures: the New and the Old Testaments. The Old Testament tells us *what* the Christ is; the New, *who* he is. . . . So the two Testaments, breathing the same spirit, point to each other."[103] Despite Vischer's claims to the contrary, his description of the canon has much in common with the patristic exegesis that he has difficulty accepting.

De Lubac, in describing the spiritual exegesis of the fathers, writes,

> the objective continuity of figure and reality is well-translated, on earth, by continuity of awareness. . . . It is there that the entire dialectic of the two Testaments is drawn tightly together: the

---

100. Ibid., 147–48.
101. See Frye, *The Great Code*, 80. See also Frei, who specifies the importance of the temporal in the utilization of typology on several occasions. (Frei, *Eclipse*, 2, 29, 34).
102. Vischer, "Witness of Job II," 148.
103. Vischer, *The Witness of the Old Testament to Christ*, 7.

Read Him Again and Again

> New Testament in its entirety is brought forth by the Old, while at the same time the Old Testament in its entirety is interpreted by the New.[104]

De Lubac's aphorism describes Vischer's canonical theory seemingly better than Vischer himself. De Lubac himself, following Emil Brunner, criticizes Vischer's own description as "overshooting the mark," because it "becomes absolutely true . . . only after the event, only at the moment when the event is perceived, only when the Old Testament, thanks to this recognition of Christ, begins to be read in the spirit of the New."[105] Any reader of Vischer's interpretation of Job would recognize that, though de Lubac's description finds the mark somewhat in the *Christuszeugnis*, the criticism does not hold in the Job interpretation. The book of Job receives Vischer's full attention, with little to no distraction from Christological claims or interjections from the New Testament. Rather, "The Witness of Job to Jesus Christ" fits better into de Lubac's above description since Vischer merely highlights parallels between the story of Job and the Gospels. One finds it difficult to determine which story bears witness to which, the reason being that they each bear witness to each other. Vischer pivots off of Duhm's observation that the story of Job resembles some of Shakespeare's plays, suggesting that the book of Job "has a genuinely Israelite and biblical touch, and may be compared with the empty tomb of the Crucified One in the Gospels."[106] The thrust here is not that Jesus is present in the book of Job, but that the story of Job and the story of Jesus point to each other through culture and canon.

The result of Vischer's particular typological interpretation at the particular era that he produces such texts subverts the dominant reading of his day, another indication that his interpretive method might qualify as a type of allegory. Dawson argues that "religion, especially in the guise of a sacred text, can function as a counterhegemonic force, and, further, that allegory has been one of the principal means by which such challenges have been mounted."[107]

Dawson explains his theory with an example:

> If I draw on Platonic theories of the soul's origin and destiny in order to read this biblical story allegorically as an account of the

---

104. De Lubac, *Scripture in the Tradition*, 40. Cf. Frei, *Eclipse*, 2, who writes, "The customary use of figuration was to show that Old Testament persons, events, and prophecies were fulfilled in the New Testament. It was a way of turning the variety of biblical books into a single, unitary canon, one that embraced in particular the differences between Old and New Testaments."

105. De Lubac, *Scripture in the Tradition*, 78–79.

106. Vischer, "Witness of Job II," 148.

107. Dawson, *Allegorical Readers*, 9.

soul's ascent from bodily distraction to mental purity, I may do so because I want to reinterpret Plato's account by placing it within a scriptural framework. But in so doing, I may in fact subtly alter the meaning that Plato's account has on its own terms by making the once-eternal soul now directly created by God.[108]

One can see how Vischer's Christological interpretation of Job might fit this pattern as well, given the political and theological currents occurring in Germany in contrast with Vischer's own at the time of his writing. By drawing on the story of the gospels to help explain the story of Job, he "subtly alters the meaning" that Job has on its own terms. However, keeping in mind that in the Job interpretation especially, Vischer mainly points to the similarities between the two texts' narratives; he is also explaining the story in the Gospels by drawing on the story of Job. The dominant reading of the Gospels at the time found little relationship with them to Old Testament texts and Jewish culture. Vischer alters the meaning of the gospel story by placing it within Old Testament framework. Because of the reciprocal relationship between the testaments, he also alters the meaning of the book of Job, placing it within the framework of the story of Jesus Christ. The book of Job points beyond itself to the gospel of Jesus Christ. Job's devotion to God in the midst of great physical and social suffering reminds the reader of Christ, but Vischer, in making this case, forces the reader to see Jesus in the light of Job. The book of Job, as a text prior to the New Testament, in some ways subordinates the Gospels. Referring to his example on Plato, Dawson writes, "one might not only declare that Scripture rather than Plato offers the most persuasive description of the soul's transformation, but also insist that Moses preceded Plato and that Plato derived all his best insights from original Mosaic wisdom."[109] Might this not be said about Vischer's essay as well? Since Job preceded Jesus and is useful in describing the person and work of Jesus, one must at least grant that Job, as well as the Old Testament, needs a place at the table of Christian theology.

Of course one could argue that primacy works the other way as well and based on Vischer's later work one might be able to make that argument rather strongly. Emil Brunner criticizes the *Christuszeugnis* for what he perceives as Vischer taking into account . . .

> only the unity, and not the variety of the revelation in the O.T. and the N.T.: owing to this he obscures the historical character of the revelation by the orthodox view of a revealed doctrine (Christology). Out of the correct theological statement that the

108. Ibid., 11.
109. Ibid.

> Revealer in the O.T. is the same in the N.T., he derives an erroneous principle of exposition: that the O.T. in all its parts bears witness to this Revealer: Christ.[110]

Brunner remains sympathetic to Vischer's protest against "evolutionism," which would replace the Old Testament witness with the New Testament, but finds equally problematic what he views as Vischer dehistoricizing the Bible, suggesting, perhaps, that Vischer uses allegory, but not typology. He argues that the New Testament witness introduces something new to the Old Testament. When Vischer finds Jesus present in the Old Testament then primacy is given to Jesus, which would subvert the plain meaning of the text. Vischer "know[s] beforehand what the text ought to say. [He does] not 'expound' the text, but [he] 'read[s] *into*' it what [he] choose[s]."[111]

Readers of Vischer's exposition on Job, however, will recognize that Brunner's criticism does not apply to that essay however much or little it might apply to the *Christuszeugnis*. The book of Job receives Vischer's full attention until the end of his exposition of chapter 42. Though he might overshoot the mark a few years later with his more famous book that Rendtorff will claim has "had its day,"[112] "The Witness of Job to Jesus Christ" is a somewhat modest recognition of parallel stories, but it took a bold voice with a unique typological imagination to make the observation in the era and culture that he did.

At the very end of the essay, Vischer reassures his readers that though their lives have come after Christ, in contrast to Job, Job remains a witness to Christ for the believer. God's activity in the world holds importance throughout time. Vischer's philosophy of history weighs Job's witness as equal to those who come after, who have had full knowledge of Christ's witness. The character of Job resembles Christ and, thus, by observing the responses of Christ and also of Job in the face of trials by friends, angels, and God, one may grasp an idea of the normative response to trials in one's own life. Job, therefore, is a witness to Christ because he acts similarly to Christ when faced with similar trials.

---

110. Brunner, *Revelation and Reason*, 82.

111. Ibid.

112. Rendtorff, *Canon and Theology*, 87. "It is noticeable that, although at first the book was enthusiastically received—the first volume went through six editions in Germany between 1934 and 1943—it was just as swiftly forgotten, and there was no new edition after the Second World War."

Karl Barth's Typological Reading of Job

Barth and Vischer have plenty in common regarding their reading of Job, which should come as no surprise to those who know their common history. They both, as Swiss reformed scholars in Germany, left for Basel during the rise of National Socialism. Barth's Christological interpretation also bears a resemblance to Vischer's, though it takes quite a different form. Vischer's essay reads more like a commentary of the book of Job which concludes with a comparison between the story of Job and the story of Christ. Barth's, on the other hand, breaks the book of Job into four thematic sections for individual analysis.

The first section looks at Job in the prose tales in chapters 1, 2, and 42. The second looks at Job in the poetry of chapters 3–31. The third looks at God's response and the fourth at Job's three friends. Between each of these sections Barth discusses the doctrine of Christ as a response to "the falsehood and condemnation of man." To be sure, within these sections, the image of Job conforms to a picture of Christ to the point that one can look at the book of Job and find parallels to the Gospels. Barth claims it would be "difficult to read the Book of Job attentively without being aware of the fact that the figure of Jesus Christ as the true Witness unmasking the falsehood of man is delineated in it in distant, faint, fragmentary and even strange yet unmistakeable [sic] outline."[113]

For Barth, Job acts as a witness to Jesus Christ because one sees Job in two forms—the pure form of the prose tale and the more complicated historical form of the poetry. Jesus, likewise, presents himself in two forms. First, Barth notes his pure form in which Jesus is intimately and uniquely connected to God. "God exists in a relationship to Him and He to God which has no parallel on either side, which distinguishes Him from all other men."[114] Barth shows how Job's relationship to God fits this description, if not so radically as Jesus, and if lacking the saving significance of Christ's.[115] Secondly, though Christ exists in this pure form, he presents himself to humanity in the Gospels where the pure form is hidden and concealed in his suffering state. "Passion was the action in which in His existence the name of God was hallowed, His kingdom came, His will was done on earth as in heaven; the action in which God reconciled the world to Himself in the humiliation of the Son of God and exaltation of the Son of Man."[116] In the

---

113. Barth, *CD IV.3.1*, 384.
114. Ibid., 379.
115. Ibid., 388.
116. Ibid., 389.

same way, Job undergoes grave suffering, cursing his day and undergoing ostensible abandonment by God. Throughout Job's contention with God, he remains true to the deity. His pure form of the prologue, though obscured through his harsh words, remains throughout the narrative.

In this way, Barth's Christological exegesis resembles Vischer's, but it leans heavier on the Christology. Barth's main purpose in this section of his *Dogmatics is to* exposit the doctrine of Christ. His exegesis of the book of Job, though substantial in length and significant in its own right, mainly serves to illustrate Christ's role in the doctrine of reconciliation. Vischer, as argued above, works in reverse—the gospel of Jesus Christ primarily acts as an illustration to bolster the importance of the book of Job.

Barth's typology goes beyond the comparison of Job to Jesus, however. Job does resemble Christ in his relationship with God, but as he reminds his readers occasionally, Job is not Jesus Christ. Christ's special relationship to God the Father adds another layer of comparison to the typology of Job and the gospel. Just as Job has a pure form in the prologue and epilogue, which is obscured in the poetic sections, so does God. We read about God in his heavenly court, surrounded by his angels and in his omnipotence allow for Job's suffering. In the poetic section, this power is obscured to the point that Job does not recognize God. When Christ appears in his obscured form, "as the wholly Rejected, Judged, Despised, Bound, Impotent, Slain and Crucified," "He unmasks us as liars."[117] In the book of Job, it is God, not Job, who unmasks the friends as liars. God appears in the obscure form of Job's suffering and Job's friends cannot recognize God in that form. They remain steadfast in their faithfulness toward their previous understanding of God's pure form, while Job remains steadfast in his faithfulness to God in whatever form God appears, even if Job feels God abandons him in that form.

Christ, in his suffering earthly form, appears as a stumbling block to the Jews and as foolishness to the Greeks. Christ, then, appears in the book of Job not only as Job but also as God. Barth does not explicitly state this position, but insinuates it through the language used to describe God's appearance to Job and his friends in the poetry. Barth makes clear that "Job is not Jesus Christ,"[118] but leads the reader to conclude Christ's presence in God's character in the book without affirming or denying the connection.

Barth's Job does not correlate directly with Jesus Christ as overtly as Vischer's Job does, but a narrative dimension does emerge as do other typological elements that would suggest that Barth's reading might also qualify as allegory. The person of Jesus seems representative in both Job

117. Ibid., 390.
118. Ibid., 388.

Job in Great Time

and Job's God, which is clearly more than mere metaphor. To Barth, the person of Jesus Christ in some ways contains the narrative of the book of Job. Also, like Vischer, Barth does not refer to the Fathers, but like the ancient exegetes, he "organizes all of revelation around a concrete center, which is fixed in time and space by the Cross of Jesus Christ"[119]—the ultimate manifestation of God's revelation.

Lastly, as described by de Lubac again, by referring back and forth between the doctrine of the reconciliation of Christ and the story of Job as told in the Old Testament, Barth comments "on the New Testament through the Old, and then on the Old through the New."[120] When Barth introduces his interpretation of Job, he suggests that "it would not be difficult to illustrate this line of thought [on the freedom of God and man] both in general and in detail from the pages of the New Testament. . . . But this would take us far afield, and might involve mere repetitions of exegetical proofs already adduced. . . . And I will admit that secondarily I have had before me in this field a noteworthy figure in the witness of the Old Testament . . ."[121] Later in the section the above introduces, Barth brings in the New Testament to help with his interpretation of Job, writing, "As a remarkable Edomitish outsider, he belongs to the context of the witness of the history of Israel which is only moving towards the history of Jesus Christ . . . and with suitable qualifications Job may thus be called a type of Jesus Christ, a witness to the true Witness."[122] Job, therefore, helps explain Jesus Christ, but Barth exposits the book of Job in the context of the witness of the history that finds its culmination in Jesus Christ, fitting Barth quite well into the tradition of spiritual interpretation that arose in the figural imagination of the early Fathers.

Barth may avoid and perhaps reject the term allegory and its derivatives in his theological interpretation, but much of his exegesis of Job certainly qualifies as typological interpretation as well in its broader terms. Of course, Barth does not merely reproduce the interpretations of the early church fathers, but brings some of their goals in exegesis into a modern, post-enlightenment context. Barth does not reject the discoveries made by his contemporaries, but does not allow them to overshadow the meaning of the book of Job in the context of biblical history either.

Obviously, Barth's typological reading of Job bears little in common with Kierkegaard's, whose *Repetition* carries nary a mention of Christ outside of a recognition of his followers. However, *Repetition* and the category

---

119. De Lubac, *Medieval Exegesis. Vol 1*, xix.
120. De Lubac, *Scripture in the Tradition*, 9n.12.
121. Barth, *CD IV.3.1*, 383.
122. Ibid., 388.

Read Him Again and Again

of repetition flesh out a future-directed typology that complements the figural imaginations of Barth and Vischer.

Kierkegaard's Typological Reading of Job in Repetition

Though Kierkegaard's interpretation of Job lacks the Christological aspect of Barth's and Vischer's, it bears witness to an allegorical and typological imagination. In fact, *Repetition* in particular contains three distinct aspects of allegory related to Kierkegaard's reading of Job.

First, the story of the young man in *Repetition* is not merely an interpretation of Job, it is an allegory of Job. The young man represents Job and Constantin Constantius represents the friends. The young man's story is essentially a repetition of the story of Job. In this case, *Repetition* works as allegory but not typology since the narrative lacks the temporal relation with the biblical story. I will describe the details of the allegorical representation of Job in *Repetition* in chapter 3 in more detail.

On the other hand, the character of Job seems, to Kierkegaard, to have a typological relationship with the character of Abraham. Multiple times does Kierkegaard place the two characters beside each other. He published *Fear and Trembling* and *Repetition* on the same day in 1843 and many years later he compares Job's loss and Abraham's willingness to give up Isaac and contrasted their "Jewish piety" with Christianity's call to voluntarily forsake all and follow Christ.[123]

Kierkegaard does not, however, compare Job to Jesus in the ways the two later interpreters do. Nevertheless, his typological understanding of the text anticipates and perhaps informs Vischer and Barth, which brings us to the most significant aspect of typology in *Repetition*. The category of repetition contains implicitly within it a future directed typology born partly out of a Bible-instigated theology. Frye holds up *Repetition* as "the only study I know of the psychological contrast between a past-directed causality and a future-directed typology."[124]

---

123. Kierkegaard, *Christian Discourses*, 185–86. Kierkegaard, of course, breaks no new ground by paralleling Abraham and Job. Chapter 18 of the second century BCE book of Jubilees inserts a satanic character next to God as Abraham stretches out his hand to slay Isaac, a scene reminiscent of the wager between the Satan and Yahweh over Job. When Yahweh wins the wager, the prince Mastema is put to shame (18:9, 12). Other rabbinic texts from antiquity elaborate even more on this relationship, expanding the story of the wager over Abraham. For a recent discussion of this arguing for another second century BCE conflation of the two stories see Vermes, "Isaac, the First Lamb of God," 62–67.

124. Frye, *Great Code*, 82.

Job in Great Time

The name alone explains much of what constitutes typology in narrative. The antitype quite obviously repeats many of the aspects of the type. In the Job interpretations of Barth and Vischer, Jesus seems to repeat the experience of Job's suffering and dialogue with his friends and God. However, as will be detailed in chapter 3, the Kierkegaardian category of repetition has a much more specialized sense than a mere repeating of events.

When Kierkegaard contrasts repetition with recollection, he endorses a future focus. Recollection brings about despair, as illustrated by Constantin's recollection of his childhood at a farce. The young man, likewise, focuses on the ideal image of his beloved, inspired by his own recollection, which leads to suffering and disillusionment about his own life. The young man experiences repetition when he focuses on what has yet to come. The divine repetition comes about partly through this future focus.

One might note that any interpretation of an ancient text requires some recollection. To understand Job, after all, requires one to look back in time. However, the interpretation of Job in both *Repetition* and the upbuilding discourse defers the focus back to the activities of the interpreter. The purpose of the upbuilding discourse is to inspire the reader to act. The young man, likewise, interprets the book of Job through appropriation. As he moves forward in the book, he moves forward in his life. The character of Job is projected forward in time, not unlike the character of Job in both Vischer and Barth's versions. Thus, repetition embodies typology as made manifest in biblical interpretation. Auerbach observes:

> Figural prophecy implies the interpretation of one worldly event through another; the first signifies the second, the second fulfils the first. Both remain historical events; yet both, looked at in this way, have something provisional and incomplete about them; they point to one another and both point to something in the future, something still to come . . .[125]

Recall the above discussion of reception history using the literary theory of Bakhtin. The general thesis that biblical scholarship should necessarily include the history of the Bible's interpretation leading up to the present era complements especially Kierkegaard's forward focused category of repetition. The Bakhtinian defense of reception history projects an ancient text forward as it grows in great time. At each successive interpretation, the text undergoes a repetition. As the interpreter of the text in the current era, reading through these successive interpretations throughout history shares much in common with other studies of typology—for instance, studies of the use of the Old Testament in the New Testament, which are many

125. Auerbach, "Figura," 58.

and varied, and certainly include the more noteworthy works of Wilhelm Vischer.

In all cases, the interpreter sees how the earlier text projects itself into the future, thus growing in great time. The text, therefore, is not static but future-directed. The text itself, if one might conflate the narratology of Bakhtin and the philosophical theology of Kierkegaard, does not control its own "repetition" in the way that Constantin and the young man wish to do in *Repetition*, but experiences repetition outside of its own control.

Kierkegaard's category of repetition, then, undergirds the typological readings of Barth and Vischer, and not only in the way described above. In all three interpretations, the text of Job defers some meaning to the future. Vischer clearly finds meaning in the book of Job that impacts the meaning he finds in the Gospels. Barth, likewise finds meaning in Job that impacts Christian theology as a whole. In all three, their interpretations of Job are meant to impact their readers' lives in significant ways. This may seem like a rather mundane "discovery" but it places these three scholars in somewhat unusual places in their fields and in their eras and cultural contexts. Vischer, after all, was attempting to study the Old Testament in a cultural context that seemed to think the Old Testament had little to no impact on its readers' lives. It had become a document void of meaning to the Christian. By showing its relation to the New Testament and to the life of Christ, Vischer attempts to show the book of Job's relation to the Christian life. Barth and Kierkegaard, as well, turned to the book of Job as a text that might help them in the edification of their readers. Job, in both interpreters' texts, acts as an illustration supporting a larger thesis. Barth has Job in his mind as he expounds upon the reconciliation of God in the doctrine of Christ and Kierkegaard's young man turns to Job in his letters to Constantin in order to buttress claims about his own personal journey. By referring to Job as a way to support a larger thesis, the interpreter implies a figural understanding of the book of Job.

Kierkegaard's book *Repetition*, promoting the forward moving category of repetition, also contributes to Barth's reading of Job as Barth approaches the book of Job in great time. Kierkegaard's reading of the book of Job alters its meaning in the chronotope. Barth even admits that his interpretation of Job is quite dependent on Kierkegaard and Vischer—two of his major points on Job come directly from them. Without Vischer and Kierkegaard's insight, Barth might not have much on Job to present. Even considering his dependence on them, he does show some disagreement, especially with Kierkegaard. Not all of his disagreement is warranted, however, and he may share more in common with Kierkegaard than even he realizes, due to complications that *Repetition*'s pseudonymous authorship creates.

If Kierkegaard, Vischer, and Barth are participating in a dialogue, it is necessary to understand how that dialogue transpires. Before moving to Kierkegaard, the next chapter will track Job through Christian readers up to Kierkegaard.

2

Gregory, Aquinas, Luther, Calvin, and Kant on Job as Predecessors to Kierkegaard, Vischer, and Barth

THE INTERPRETATIONS OF JOB by Kierkegaard, Vischer, and Barth are distinctively Christian interpretations. The typological imagination that each employs fall in the Christian tradition, Christ being the anti-type for Job in both Barth's and Vischer's work and Kierkegaard positing a typological theory that supports their reading. All three interpretations, however, depart in extraordinary ways from other major Christian interpreters. The purpose of this chapter is to examine some of the most important and dominant precedents regarding Job in the Christian tradition. Because the most important aspects of the Job of Kierkegaard, Vischer, and Barth are their typological imaginations and their vision of the book of Job as one documenting God and Job's free devotion to each other, I confine most of my discussion to the earlier interpreters' incorporation of those elements.

Needless to say, a survey of all Christian interpretations of Job goes beyond the scope of this book, as does examinations of Jewish interpretations. While there is much to admire in the various Jewish interpretations from antiquity up until the Enlightenment, it seems as though their views had little impact on the readings of the three main scholars in this current study. Instead, I focus on Gregory the Great's *Moralia*, Thomas Aquinas's *Literal Exposition on Job*, the preface to Luther's translation of Job, Calvin's *Sermons* on Job, and Immanuel Kant's essay "On the Failure of All Attempted Philosophical Theodicies."

We will see five strikingly different views of Job—striking because four of the scholars share similar views on the authority of Scripture. Kant, whose theology and view of Scripture do not fit as snugly within orthodox Christianity as the other figures, has ideas that became highly influential in Western thought and were certainly familiar to Kierkegaard, Barth, and Vischer if his interpretation of Job was not explicitly so.

GREGORY THE GREAT'S JOB

Gregory's *Moralia*, as one might expect, reads very differently than a modern commentary on Job. In order to understand better how he reaches the conclusions he does, it helps to know what he thinks of the Bible and how he reads it. One will note that he has a high view of the Scriptures, calling them "a letter of the omnipotent God to his creature."[1] As for who the creature is, of course this might include any human. However, the proper place to read and interpret the letter from God is the church.[2] The authors of the text act, in some way, as conduits for the word of God. In the preface to the *Moralia* itself, Gregory explains inspiration thus:

> Blessed Job also, being under the influence of the Holy Spirit, might have written his own acts, which were, for that matter, gifts of inspiration from above, as though they were not his own; for in so far as it was a human being, who spoke things which were of God, all that he spake belonged to Another, and in so far as the Holy Spirit spake of what is proper to a human being, it was Another that gave utterance to the things that belonged to him.[3]

None of this should surprise anyone with even cursory knowledge of the history of biblical interpretation. Gregory's hermeneutic begins to emerge as more original when he discusses the Bible's effect on the reader. Scripture, he explains, acts as a mirror to the reader's "inward face". In the Bible "we learn the beauties that we possess; there we are made sensible what progress we are making, there too how far we are from proficiency."[4] If Gregory sees this as such an important aspect of the Bible, his decision to

---

1. Kessler, "Gregory the Great," 1344. See also Schreiner, *Where Shall Wisdom*, 25.
2. Kessler, "A Figure of Tradition," 146.
3. Pope Gregory I, *Morals*, Pref. 1.3.
4. Ibid., 2.1.1.

focus his entire commentary on a book of the Bible around the morals that one can glean from the text should not surprise.

Also important in this description of the Bible is Gregory's focus on the interiority of the Christian. The outward face of a person differs from his inward face. The text of the Bible has an outward letter and an inward spirit.[5] The spiritual and physical natures in the world at large differ greatly in Gregory's hermeneutic.[6] Thus Gregory, following Origen, believes that behind the literal text lies a spiritual meaning, which the responsible exegete must discover.[7] This is especially true for the Old Testament, which prophesies the revelation of Christ in the New Testament.[8] The nature of the Bible necessitates for Gregory a threefold order of exegesis—an interpretation of the historical aspects of the text, an interpretation of the allegorical aspects, and a moral interpretation.[9]

Gregory understands that under this rubric one must still entertain certain compromises. In an epistle to Leander discussing the *Moralia*, Gregory explains some problems in holding to the rubric too tightly. Regarding the importance of the literal aspects of Job 31:16–20, he writes that "if these words [Job's oath concerning his responsibility to the poor] be violently strained to an allegorical signification, we make void all his acts of mercy."[10] He likewise warns against the isolated use of the literal interpretation when he notes that "doubtless whereas the literal words when set against each other cannot be made to agree, they point out some other meaning in themselves which we are to seek for."[11] Thus because Job's outburst in chapter three seems to contradict the narrators declaration in 1:22

---

5. Kessler, "A Figure of Tradition," 140–41.

6. Note also that his propensity for allegorical interpretation extends to the secular world, which one should read like the Bible (Kessler, "Gregory the Great," 1342).

7. Ibid., 1350.

8. Schreiner, *Where Shall Wisdom*, 23.

9. While Gregory does not abandon the theory of this threefold interpretation in the *Moralia*, in practice, he only ostensibly sustains this for a few chapters of his work on the book of Job. By the middle of the book, the labels drop and he combines the method under the same heading.

10. Pope Gregory I, *Morals*, Epistle 4. Katharina Greschat writes of Gregory's hermeneutic as it emerges in the preface: "*Der Schriftinterpretation kommt demnach die Funktion eines Bindegliedes zwischen den Notwendigkeiten dieser Welt und dem Streben nach der Ewigkeit zu*" (Greschat, *Die Moralia*, 52).

11. Pope Gregory I, *Morals*, Epistle 3. One should note that Gregory's interpretation of the Song of Songs does not entertain notions of the literal meaning since, in that book, "God descends to the language of human love in order to inflame and to exalt man to the divine love" (Kessler, "Gregory the Great," 1343).

that Job did not sin with his lips, Gregory seeks something other than the literal meaning.[12]

What this rubric must eventually lead to is the moral interpretation. Gregory was a scholar, but his exegesis was not merely academic. As papal Deacon and later Pope, he was also a pastor and so he emphasizes the need to conform one's actions to the Holy Scriptures to the end that even one who has not read the text could understand the Bible through the actions of him who has.[13]

Gregory's general scriptural hermeneutic is made manifest in the *Moralia*, which touches on all aspects of the Christian life, leading one scholar to call it a "Christian encyclopaedia not in a logical but biblical form."[14] Despite its immense scope, the *Moralia* does sustain a few ideas throughout its hundreds of thousands of words. Namely, Gregory focuses on the suffering of the righteous by way of allegorizing the character of Job as a type of Christ *and* the church.

As with many interpreters—including Calvin, Kant, and Kierkegaard—Gregory's biography seems an important impetus for him to write a major work on the book of Job.[15] However, unlike the others we will look at, the suffering Gregory experienced was not social but physical.[16] Gregory does not carry the opprobrious animosity towards Job's friends that Kierkegaard does, especially, since he identifies more with Job's skin conditions than his loss in social status. More importantly, Gregory views suffering itself not

---

12. Pope Gregory I, *Morals*, Preface 7. See also Schreiner, "Role of Perception," 91.

13. Kessler, "Gregory the Great," 1340. De Lubac cites a poem by Sixtus of Siena which divides the four senses of Sacred Scripture by the work of different fathers. Gregory's emphasis on morals was seen as his specialty, while other fathers filled important roles in the other senses: "Under the guidance of Jerome you will learn history derived from Greek and Latin sources. / Origen and Ambrose will lay open allegories and anagogy. / Chrysostom and Gregory will set forth the senses that are apt to form morals . . ." (de Lubac, *Medieval Exegesis*, 4).

14. Kessler, "A Figure of Tradition," 140.

15. Greschat, *Die Moralia*, 47–48.

16. Gregory writes in his opening epistle: "For many a year's circuit has gone by since I have been afflicted with frequent pains in the bowels, and the powers of my stomach being broken down, makes me at all times and seasons weakly; and under the influence of fevers slow, but in constant succession, I draw my breath with difficulty; and when in the midst of these sufferings I ponder with earnest heed, that according to the testimony of Scripture, *He scourgeth every son whom He receiveth*; the more I am weighed down by the severity of present afflictions, from my anticipations for eternity, I gather strength to breathe with so much the better assurance. And perchance it was this that Divine Providence designed, that I a stricken one, should set forth Job stricken, and that by the scourges I should the more perfectly enter into the feelings of one that was scourged" (Pope Gregory I, *Morals*, Epistle 5). So Gregory even feels that he has an advantage in his interpretation because of his sufferings.

as a problem to overcome, nor as an evil.[17] This likely stems partly from his allegorical interpretation, viewing Job as a type of Christ and Christ as someone the church should strive to be like.[18] If Christ is the pinnacle of humanity and his sufferings carry such special significance, then suffering in itself may not be something to overcome but to endure or even to embrace. Susan Schreiner notes three spiritual realities that Gregory sees arising from suffering as self knowledge, freedom, and perception.[19] By self knowledge, Gregory means that the sufferer turns inward and can focus on the depth of his sin. Gregory also indicates that suffering acts as a chastening of the sufferer, writing, "For unless a grain of mustard seed be bruised, the extent of its virtue is never acknowledged. For without bruising it is insipid, but if it is bruised it becomes hot, and it gives out all those pungent properties that were concealed in it. Thus every good man, so long as he is not smitten, is regarded as insipid, and of slight account."[20]

If suffering leads to introspection and chastening, then one might desire suffering over well-being. In fact, tranquility bears a danger that suffering does not in that it makes one complacent with earthly desires. In Gregory's dualism, the Christian should desire not earthly things but heavenly ones, thus suffering actually frees one from that attachment to the physical world. When our present life oppresses us, it shows "the way of liberty, while it tortures."[21] Of course Gregory's belief that suffering leads to freedom and that tranquility leads to bondage stems partly from Jesus, who preaches a kingdom where the last shall be first and the first shall be last and the monarch of that kingdom has a crown of thorns and hangs on a cross rather than sits on a throne. Thus, the paradox Gregory perceives has biblical precedent.

Despite the *Moralia*'s silence in the critical era, Gregory's influence does stretch over the centuries and seems to affect Kierkegaard, Barth, and Vischer in many ways, albeit likely indirectly since they never cite him. Many aspects of the *Moralia* touch on themes that the later scholars find embedded in Job

---

17. Schreiner, *Where Shall Wisdom*, 27.
18. Pope Gregory I, *Morals*, 1.24.33.
19. One can argue that really perception is so intrinsically connected to self-knowledge and freedom (in that one's freedom depends on his perception) that perception itself does not merit its own category. However, Schreiner's thesis on the reception history of Job is that the theme of perception or human understanding ties together the various precritical interpretations of the book of Job. The early interpreters seem all to be asking how a sufferer can perceive God's providence in his life (Schreiner, *Where Shall Wisdom*, 19).
20. Pope Gregory I, *Morals*, 2.6.
21. Ibid., 26.13.21.

as well, namely, allegory and freedom. Concerning allegory, though Vischer will verbally reject the allegory of the patristic era embodied by the *Moralia*, he and Barth both fall into the tradition sustained by Gregory but largely abandoned in the Reformation and in the Enlightenment in that they find much in the book of Job to compare to Christ. However, Barth and Vischer's interpretations of Job would still offer much in the way of exegetical insight into Job without their parallels to Jesus—their parallels making up a small portion of their work. With the *Moralia*, on the other hand, allegory and tropology are such important aspects that one could hardly imagine it without those elements of exegesis. His entire scheme hinges on seeing how the literal Job refers to the allegorical Christ, who in turn instructs the church in how to act. Thus, some of the moral teaching in Job Christ passes on. Though it does appear in the section of his *Church Dogmatics* on the Reconciliation of Christ, Barth's interpretation of Job could stand alone. Vischer's interpretation does rely more on how Job and Christ share a one-to-one relationship. However, even Vischer's "Job as Witness to Christ" has a striking paucity of mention of Jesus through the majority of the text compared to the Christ-soaked *Moralia*. This difference extends beyond the superficial, as will become more evident in the section on Vischer. Briefly, one can note differences in the assumptions with which the two interpreters begin. Regarding Gregory, he develops a system of exegesis that incorporates the methods of Augustine and Origen, two already well-respected exegetes. Gregory is also writing for monks as apocrisiary for the Pope and abbot of St. Andrews monastery, so his authority is well established.[22] Vischer, on the other hand, writes in a hostile environment of scholars who not only likely see Christological typology of the Old Testament to be anachronistic, but he also writes in a political environment which holds all things Jewish in a hermeneutic of suspicion at best and which is blatantly anti-Semitic at worst. Vischer's program does not begin with the assumption that the Old Testament prophesies Christ, but he uses Christ to promote the Old Testament.[23] Nevertheless, Vischer's attempt to link Job with Christ does have precedent with Gregory in some way.

Gregory and all three of the later interpreters also discuss freedom in the text of Job. Again, however, their emphases differ. Freedom in Gregory is contingent on the Augustinian metaphysic that he espouses.[24] Suffering

---

22. Schreiner, *Where Shall Wisdom*, 4.

23. More will be said on this in the chapter on Vischer.

24. R. A. Markus argues that Gregory's allegorical hermeneutic corresponds with his metaphysic. He writes that "Gregorian religion was in every way a religion of detachment: scriptural in its substance, it detached the reader from the letter of the Scripture, helping to detach him, at the same time, from the world he was to read in its light" (Markus, *Gregory the Great and His World*, 50).

brings freedom because it causes the sufferer to look to a place different than the physical world. Thus the freedom that dominates Gregory's interpretation focuses on the liberation of the human from sin and even from the world.[25] Kierkegaard, Vischer, and Barth, however, focus their attention on the freedom of God in God's interaction with creation in general and humanity in particular. In Vischer and Barth, especially, Job 1:9 acts as the hermeneutical lens through which they view the rest of the book, and they understand that verse to raise the question of whether God has the freedom to act outside humanity's expectations as well as whether a human can express a disinterested devotion to God. Gregory does not entertain that thought and spends a relative little time discussing that verse.[26]

THOMAS AQUINAS'S JOB

Roughly six and a half centuries after Gregory composed his *Moralia* Thomas Aquinas wrote his *Literal Exposition on Job*, a commentary that more closely resembles a modern commentary in several ways. For one, Thomas relies mainly on expositing the words of the text without attempting to reveal any allegorical dimensions of the text. He explains his motive in avoiding the allegorical interpretation partially in his prologue where he commends Gregory's disclosure of Job's "mysteries" to the point that he, Thomas, need not "add anything further to them."[27] For the most part, Thomas abides by his rule. However, he does betray this in his interpretation of the second half of Job 19, a passage of high relevance to his overall interpretation of the book of Job.[28] In this section, Thomas views the redeemer in the famous passage Job 19:25 ("I know that my redeemer lives") as the resurrected Christ who would grant resurrection to all of humanity in the end times. This somewhat unusual passage in the otherwise "literal" reading of Job contains two of

---

25. ". . . Gregor wolle seine Leser mit den *Moralia in Job* einzig und allein zur *contemplatio* des Göttlichen anleiten, damit sie sich mit Hilfe der Schriftmeditation schon hier immer weiter von dieser Welt lösen und auf dem Weg zur Ewigkeit voranschreiten können" (Greschat, *Die Moralia*, 244).

26. "Whereas God is a just and a true God, it is important to enquire how and in what sense He shews that He had afflicted Job without cause. For because He is just, He could not afflict him without cause, and again, because He is true, He could not have spoken other than what He did. So then that both particulars may concur in Him that is just and true, so that He should both speak truth, and not act unjustly, let us know, that blessed Job was both in one sense smitten *without cause*, and again in another sense, that he was smitten not without cause" (Pope Gregory I, *Morals*, 3.3.3).

27. Aquinas, *The Literal Exposition on Job*, 69.

28. Indeed Susan Schreiner calls it Thomas's "hermeneutical key to the book" (Schreiner, *Where Shall Wisdom*, 74).

the more important aspects of Thomas's reading of Job—that Job is in the right because he has faith in God's providential activity and his belief in the resurrection of the dead.

Of these two themes, Thomas explicitly holds that the book of Job is about providence,[29] but Thomas's belief in the resurrection is intrinsically related to how God provides for humanity—a debt he owes to Maimonides.

Thomas's focus on the literal interpretation of Job as opposed to the spiritual meaning differs from Gregory not merely because he did not want to reinvent the wheel. The difference stems also from differences in their hermeneutics, which in turn stem from differences in their ontologies. While Gregory's dualism gives him the impetus to look behind the physical reality to the spiritual meaning behind that reality, Thomas's Aristotelian ontology focuses on the visible realities before him, which he understands as "good and true and beautiful in themselves."[30] One must take care to note that the word sense (*sensus*) refers to what we might term "authorial intent," thus, Thomas perceives metaphor and other figures of speech as metaphor and figures of speech on top of their actual literal meaning. He derives meaning from the conventions of language rather than from importing spiritual truths from the life of Christ or the church. As clarification, note that from Job 19:9, when Job accuses God of taking "away the crown from [his] head," Thomas describes that as Job announcing the loss of his dignity rather than a physical crown.[31] This explanation gets at the heart of the argument rather than the grammar.[32]

Thomas's hermeneutic, as many biblical hermeneutics, contains the complicating fact that biblical books have two authors—the human author and the divine author.[33] While non-biblical books can only have a literal sense, the divine origins of the Bible can allow for typological and spiritual meanings beyond the literal sense.[34] Thus, Job can prophesy Christ in chapter 19 despite the centuries dividing them because God authors both the Old and New Testaments.[35] As Yocum states it, "the meaning of the literal text may go beyond what the human author understood. In addition to this, while human authors use words to signify things God, the Creator of all things, may use those things signified by the words of the text to signify other things."[36]

29. Aquinas, *The Literal Exposition on Job*, 68.
30. Healy, "Introduction," 8.
31. Aquinas, *The Literal Exposition on Job*, 265.
32. Froehlich, "Christian Interpretation," 542.
33. Schreiner, *Where Shall Wisdom*, 71.
34. Froehlich, "Christian Interpretation," 545.
35. Yocum, "Aquinas' Literal Exposition on Job," 26–27.
36. Ibid., 26.

Read Him Again and Again

Two things in particular draw Thomas's tendency toward spiritual interpretation. First, as Gregory employs the spiritual dimension in Job when the book seems to contradict itself, Thomas similarly believes that when the literal sense of Scripture "appears to be claiming something clearly untrue, its divine author must intend a meaning other than the apparent."[37] Second, he willingly compares Job to Christ and often refers to the New Testament when interpreting the Old Testament and also utilizes the help of earlier authorities within his traditions in order to present an interpretation "more familiar and approachable to his Christian reader."[38]

Though Thomas has a willingness to draw upon these earlier traditions, he also employs a later medieval "scholastic method" of interpretation that helps explain his conclusions and occupation with certain aspects in the book of Job.[39] This method requires the three elements of reading (*lectio*), disputation (*disputatio*), and preaching (*praedicatio*).[40] In particular, Thomas sees disputation as important in the book of Job since he views the friends' debates with Job as a medieval disputation.[41] This focus on the developing argument between Job and his friends arises from Thomas's focus on the literal sense of the text. Gregory's focus on the allegorical aspects allows him to ignore the finer points of the arguments since they deferred their meaning elsewhere.[42]

In this extended debate, Thomas sees the argument develop linearly, but it eventually reaches a stalemate, which necessitates the Theophany.[43] In fact, despite the physical suffering and loss of family and property that Job experiences, Aquinas seems to point to the result of the debate itself as an aspect of Job's suffering on top of his material losses. The social suffering that Job perceives trumps the physical suffering that spurred the debate in the first place.[44] The debate, perhaps, has gone beyond mere *disputatio*, since Job accuses the friends of persecuting him like God:

---

37. Healy, "Introduction," 17.

38. Yaffe, "Interpretive Essay," 11. Note here that Vischer might owe more to Aquinas than to Gregory, despite appearances and, perhaps, preconceptions. However, even here there is likely no direct line of comparison, but rather a common spirit that Aquinas and Vischer share.

39. Kretzmann, "Introduction," 5.

40. Healy, "Introduction," 12.

41. Stump, "Biblical Commentary and Philosophy," 260.

42. See Schreiner, *Where Shall Wisdom*, 73.

43. Ibid., 74.

44. Thomas determines this by the order of Job's reparations in chapter 42. He writes, "Now chief among Job's adversities, as it were, was that he had been deserted by his friends; therefore, the remedy for this adversity is put first when *Now there came*

as if to say: The persecution from God is sufficient for me, but it would be your place rather to offer consolation. Now he shows how they were persecuting him, adding *and glut yourselves on my flesh?*, a question which properly pertains to disparagers who are said to feed on human flesh inasmuch as they are delighted by the infirmities of others.[45]

This is not to say that Aquinas minimizes the afflictions instigated by the Satan under God's allowance. The suffering Job receives from his friends is unnecessary, for the most part, which explains God's rebuke of Eliphaz, Bildad, and Zophar. However, Thomas does see a purpose in the suffering Job receives from God.[46] Partly, the purpose is to vindicate God in his wager with the Satan. God uses the suffering to declare Job's virtue.[47] However, Thomas also implies that suffering chastens the sinner, a common sentiment among Job interpreters.[48] The suffering of Job, therefore, relates to Thomas's major theme of God's providence in the book of Job.

In the prologue to Thomas's commentary, he writes that:

> the diligence of later philosophers examining the truth with sharper insight has shown with evident proofs and arguments that natural things are controlled by providence; for one would not find such a reliable course in the movement of heaven and of the stars and in the other effects of nature unless all these things were ordained and governed by some supereminent intelligence.[49]

Because the world is ordered towards the will of God, one must conclude that the suffering of individuals must also have that orientation. However, different views of providence may have different theories as to how the

---

to him all his brothers and all his sisters and all who knew him before." Here is also a reference to Job 19:13 (Aquinas, *Job*, 472). In his discussion of chapter 19, he notes that Job, when listing his afflictions, mentions firstly his loss of honour and glory in verse 9 (ibid., 264). He notes that in verse 22 Job views the debate as a type of persecution on top of God's affliction (Aquinas, *Job*, 268).

45. Ibid., 268.

46. On 1:20–21, Thomas writes, "For it would not be pleasing to God that anyone suffer adversity except for the sake of some good coming from it" (ibid., 89).

47. Ibid., 92.

48. Stump, "Biblical Commentary and Philosophy," 263. See also Yaffe, "Interpretive Essay," 24. Note, however, that Thomas does not emphasise the chastening nature of suffering as previous interpreters. Schreiner, in fact, argues that Thomas shifts "away from the therapeutic notion of suffering . . . to questions about providence . . ." (Schreiner, *Where Shall Wisdom*, 55).

49. Yaffe, "Interpretive Essay," 67.

suffering fits into God's plan. Job's friends, according to Thomas, view the world as predictable and ordered with one to one correspondence between sin and suffering.[50] However, this view does not account for the complexity of the world—that evil itself somehow fits into God's order. In the end, God's declaration that Job had spoken rightly while his friends had not derives from the friends' "perverse dogmas" associated with their simplistic understanding of providence.[51]

The missing element in the friends' dogmas turns out to have been a belief in the resurrection. Job's faith in the afterlife, expressed in his speech in chapter 19, suggests that he believes God would justify the apparent injustice of his suffering eventually.[52] His friends, on the other hand, cannot reconcile the apparent incongruity between Job's suffering and his claims of innocence; they have no belief in a future life of reward and punishment contingent upon the deeds in the present life.[53] Thus the problem posed in the book of Job, a problem which God does not address directly, relies on a prophetic pronouncement by Job that Aquinas interprets as reference to Christ.

There are, of course, several problems with Aquinas's overall interpretation that go beyond the scope of this book. Most problematic is the notion that the book of Job does not clearly contain passages that refer to a resurrection of the dead and contains others that seem to deny it altogether (of the latter, we will examine below). Chapter 19 is notoriously difficult to interpret, so to base one's exegesis of the whole book on that passage seems a bit dubious, today.[54] However, granting that chapter 19 may allude to an afterlife, it does seem that Aquinas's interpretation of Job's suffering might merely extend the parameters of God's justice to fit the friends understanding of providence. That is, the friends perceive that Job must have sinned because he has been punished instead of rewarded. However, Thomas argues that Job has not yet received his reward, a reward that likely looks similar to the friends' understanding, but presented in a different time. If the doctrine of resurrection does not appear in the book of Job, a more complex hermeneutic must be employed to explain how one can utilize the doctrine of resurrection in a book that does not contain it or determine a very different interpretation of the book as a whole.

---

50. Schreiner, *Where Shall Wisdom*, 75.

51. Aquinas, *Job*, 214, 471. See also Stump, "Biblical Commentary and Philosophy," 262.

52. Ibid., 76.

53. See Ibid., 73.

54. Chapter 19 was seen as a high point in Job for many years, though.

In light of this important aspect of Thomas's interpretation of Job, let us look at the similarities between Thomas's interpretation and those of Kierkegaard, Barth, and Vischer. For the most part, these later interpretations do not share much in common with Thomas. Thomas's reluctance to incorporate Christological readings into his commentary, due to his goal of describing the literal sense means a general paucity of typological comparisons of Job and Christ. Even his interpretation of chapter 19 does not compare Job to Christ. Rather Job declares a faith in Christ apart from himself.

As mentioned above, Thomas views the argument between Job and his friends developing linearly, which requires at least a qualified belief in the unreliability of the friends' arguments. As we will see below, Calvin seems to have a difficult time viewing the friends' claims as open to doubt. In this way, Thomas anticipates the later scholars in a way that bypasses Calvin, one of Barth and Vischer's heroes. It also bears a resemblance to the Socratic irony that Kierkegaard relies on so heavily.

Another instance that bears a resemblance to the Socratic irony that Kierkegaard employs, but in a much smaller scale, is Thomas's exposition of Job 10:21, where Job says, "before I go, and do not return, to the shadowy land covered by the mist of death." Thomas, here, would seem to encounter a problem that would dismantle his entire exegesis of the book. Job fairly clearly seems to deny the possibility of an afterlife. However, Thomas interprets this as Job appropriating the position of his adversaries in the debate. Thomas writes:

> one should say that he is speaking in the manner of a debater—according to the opinion which his adversaries hold—before the truth is manifested. Now below Job will manifestly indicate the truth of resurrection; therefore, in all the preceding passages he speaks of resurrection supposing the opinion of those with whom he was debating, who did not believe that there was another life except this one, but [did believe] that men are either punished or rewarded in his life alone for the good and the evil deeds which they do.[55]

Akin to this is Kierkegaard's hermeneutic of appropriation, whereby the interpreter assumes the role of the character who one wants to understand. Thomas's use of this method, however, seems less a purposeful interpretive strategy than a way to sustain his overall thesis of Job without foregoing the passages that seem to undermine it.

---

55. Aquinas, *Job*, 192. See also Thomas on 7:11 and 23:3. Cf. Schreiner, *Where Shall Wisdom*, 80.

Thomas's departure from Gregory's reading is not limited to his lack of allegory or irony. His literal interpretation and his focus on the disputation in the dialogues also depart from Gregory's understanding of Job's suffering. Gregory's own physical ailments along with his flattening of the arguments in the poetic sections led him to prop up the physical suffering of Job as the main problem to solve. Thomas, as mentioned above, views Job's social situation as the main cause of Job's suffering. This he shares with the later scholars, in particular with Kierkegaard. Like Kierkegaard, Barth, and Vischer, Thomas is much more critical of the friends than Gregory and sees them as exacerbating the problems initiated in the prologue.

The main themes that tie together Kierkegaard, Barth, and Vischer are those of freedom and trust in God. Thomas's Job does contain aspects of freedom that relate to the later interpreters, however, they are quite muted for various reasons. In fact they are muted partly because of the type of faith that Job has. Thomas's Job has a much greater confidence than the Job most people see.[56] His faith in the resurrection of the dead means that he seems to see his suffering as an element in a system.[57] This is radically different than the Job of Barth (as well as Vischer and Kierkegaard). Barth sees God as completely free from universal systems. With Barth, it is God alone that Job must trust and not a doctrine separate from God, like resurrection. God's freedom means that Job may not receive reparations in the afterlife and so Job need not display the confidence that Thomas bestows upon him. Schreiner describes Thomas's Job as not finding "deliverance *from* history but rather faith in the ultimate order *of* history."[58] When God afflicts Job, it is not without reason, but

> without a reason which is manifest and perceptible by the afflicted man. For if the afflicted man were to perceive the reason why God is afflicting him and that the afflictions are useful to him for his salvation, it is manifest that he would believe that he had been heeded, but since he does not understand this, he believes that he has not been heeded.[59]

---

56. Stump, "Biblical Commentary and Philosophy," 261.

57. Note here a similarity between Thomas's Job and the Abraham described in Hebrews 11:17–19. Thomas would not be the first, nor the last, to imply a comparison of the plight of Job to that of Abraham in the *Aqadah*. See, for instance, how Kierkegaard compares the two in the next chapter. Curiously, Thomas makes no explicit mention of the binding of Isaac in his entire *Literal Exposition on Job*.

58. Schreiner, *Where Shall Wisdom*, 89.

59. Aquinas, *Job*, 174.

Thomas's Job, therefore, looks quite different from the later interpreters that we will encounter. His guiding principles stemming from his prejudgments make this so. On the other hand, his interpretation does share some features with the later Lutheran and Calvinist scholars that they do not share even with Luther and Calvin.

LUTHER ON JOB

Though Barth's and Vischer's reformed tradition grants them some inevitable similarities to Calvin, whom we will examine presently, they, along with Kierkegaard, are also firmly placed in the tradition of Martin Luther. Luther influences all three in several areas and his influence certainly extends to the three interpretations of Job, especially Kierkegaard's. However, Luther does not present his readers with an extended interpretation of Job of his own. The preface to his translation of Job provides us with only a little evidence of how he might have interpreted the book of Job in a commentary, lecture, or sermon.

In his preface to the book of Job, Luther makes a few points that are relevant to the interpretations of Kierkegaard, Vischer, and Barth. He claims the book "deals with the question whether misfortune comes from God even to the righteous."[60] Of the friends, Luther claims that they have a "worldly and human idea of God and his righteousness, as though he were just like men and his justice like the justice of the world,"[61] which applies well to Vischer, especially, who proposes that the friends imagine that Job takes God to court, but that Job recognizes the futility of such a worldly exercise.

Regarding Job's sinlessness Luther seems to grant that Job did not deserve the initial suffering he received from God, but spoke wrongly in his complaints about the suffering.[62] Luther's conclusion regarding the plot of

---

60. Luther, *Word and Sacrament I*, 251.
61. Ibid.
62. Ibid., 252. Vicchio misreads this interpretation from Luther. He quotes Luther as saying that God torments Job "without cause," but forgets to give this much weight in his interpretation of Luther (Vicchio, *Job in the Medieval World*, 179). This is par for the course with Vicchio, who also suggests that "Luther does not believe, as the omniscient narrator of the book of Job does, that Job is 'blameless and upright.' Luther sees Job's angry, iconoclastic remarks about God to be evidence that the patriarch from Uz is not sinless." The quote from Luther that inspires this remark reads, "To be sure, when Job is in danger of death, out of weakness he talks too much against God, and in his suffering, sins. Nevertheless, Job insists that he has not deserved this suffering more than others have, which is, of course, true." Luther does not contradict at all the description of Job in the first lines of the prologue. He instead insists that Job sinned "in his suffering," which clearly comes after the narrator describes Job as blameless. The narrator barely

the book is that "God alone is righteous, and yet one man is more righteous than another, even in the sight of God."[63]

Luther views the hiddenness of God's grace as an important theme in the book of Job and also, like Calvin, omits any explicit comparison between Job and Jesus Christ. Glatzer notes that Luther does not mention how the book might preach Christ, an important aspect to Luther's Old Testament hermeneutic,[64] which seems to have directly influenced Vischer in his Old Testament exegetical method.[65] Luther's Job, therefore, may not have influenced Vischer or Barth directly, but their similar worldviews may have contributed to the later interpreters' interpretations despite the relatively small one in Luther's corpus.

On the other hand, Luther makes a small but significant comment that may have influenced Kierkegaard's Upbuilding Discourse on Job. Luther claims that the book of Job may best be understood by those "who experience and feel what it is to suffer the wrath and judgment of God, and to have His grace hidden from view."[66] As we will see, one of Kierkegaard's purposes in the discourse is to convince the reader how he or she might relate to Job's sufferings. Job's sufferings under the wrath of God may seem extraordinary to the casual reader, but Kierkegaard claims that we have all experienced something in our lives that relate to Job.

CALVIN ON JOB

Calvin's reading of Job, despite Vischer's and Barth's indebtedness to Calvin in so many other ways, departs from many of the aspects that connect Kierkegaard, Barth, and Vischer—aspects that even medievals and moderns share. For instance, Calvin eschews typological interpretation, particularly Christological interpretations. When he does compare Job to another biblical character he goes to David,[67] but even to David he seems drawn because of his ambivalence towards the righteousness and humility of Job—something with which he does not have a problem with respect to David. Calvin's reading also seems devoid of any recognitions of irony—a quality obviously present with Kierkegaard, but also in Barth and Vischer in that they

---

speaks at all about the morality of Job once the dialogues begin, which is where Luther claims Job speaks wrongly.

63. Luther, *Word and Sacrament I*, 252.
64. Glatzer, *The Dimensions of Job*, 32.
65. See Wilhelm Vischer, "La Méthode."
66. Luther, *Word and Sacrament I*, 252.
67. Schreiner, *Where Shall Wisdom*, 96.

recognize the unreliability of the speeches by the three friends and Elihu. Calvin's literal method of interpretation, which holds him back from typology, also forces him to take the words of Scripture at face value. So even the words of the friends he accepts as God's word without a sense of irony. Of course this is ironic in itself because of God's pronouncement in 42:7 that they did not speak rightly of God, but Calvin downplays this ironic aspect. Regarding freedom, Calvin does recognize God's sovereignty, but actually seems to limit God's freedom in some ways through an *a priori* understanding of God as sovereign but not a tyrant.[68] However, Calvin does anticipate Kierkegaard, Barth, and Vischer in his reading of Job in other important ways—even in some that contribute to the three aspects we are exploring.

Much of Calvin's particularity in his interpretation of Job stems from his biblical hermeneutic. Like most, if not all, exegetes, his understanding of the nature of the Bible leads him to interpretations of the text that other assumptions about Scripture might preclude. Regarding the book of Job, however, Calvin's readers must remember that, unlike many of his other works on Scripture, he did not leave us with a commentary on Job. Rather, Calvin produced 159 sermons. Though we should not make too many assumptions as to how a sermon or a lecture on Job by Calvin might differ from a commentary on Job, one can conjecture that the homiletic form might lead to certain difficulties regarding the text that might not arise in a full blown commentary. The book of Job seems especially susceptible to this since a preacher must preach on large swaths of text that, in the end, prove to be spoken by unreliable sources. Since most of Calvin's sermons are on sections that contain about five to ten verses per sermon, sometimes nine sermons in a row might be on the words of one of Job's friends. Calvin, therefore, gives them the benefit of the doubt and preaches on their speeches as if they contain God's word.

Calvin's second sermon on the friends' speeches presents a very good example of the problems that he encounters. In his fifteenth sermon on Job, he covers Job 4:6–11, where Eliphaz asks Job "who that was innocent ever perished?" Eliphaz clearly insinuates that Job has received suffering from God because he has sinned despite Job's claims. However, the prologue strongly suggests that Job suffers *because* of his innocence. This problem places Eliphaz's comments in this section into question. Calvin must, therefore, show care when commenting on Eliphaz's ostensibly theologically orthodox comments. The passage quoted above from 4:7 would seem to fit well into Calvin's theology, so preaching on this section alone creates a problem that might not arise in a commentary, which could more easily take into account the rest of

---

68. Helm, *John Calvin's Ideas*, 305.

the book. Calvin writes of this verse, "Eliphas . . . taketh here a good sentence, so as the reasons which he bringeth here against Iob are good and holie, not withstanding that the cace bee evill. And surely the principles that are sette downe here, are drawne out of Gods pure truth. By reason whereof it is as much as if the holie Ghost had pronounced this saying."[69] Thus, Calvin's belief that Scripture is God's Word complicates his reading of the passages by unreliable sources. Of course a high doctrine of Scripture does not preclude a recognition of the ironic element of unreliable sources as in such statements by Eliphaz. Nor does a recognition that the statements will seem awfully problematic by the time the reader reaches God's declarations in 42:7 preclude finding truths in the speeches of Eliphaz. However, one either must wonder if Calvin's reading of Eliphaz's statements as partially valid stems from the homiletic medium he employs or the fact that Eliphaz's statement matches so well with Calvin's theology. The fact that Eliphaz is declared wrong by God in the end seems like a call to put his words under a hermeneutic of suspicion.

Before delving too deeply into Calvin's interpretation of the friends, we should review some aspects of his general exegetical method to illumine how he might come to some of his conclusions about the friends as well as Elihu, Job, and God.

Calvin generally desires to mine the plain meaning of Scripture. One might suggest that he favours the literal meaning of the text, but this does not appreciate the nuance of his interpretation. He does pay attention to genre, rhetoric, historical context, and the author of the text, which are part of the literal meaning.[70] At the level of the sentence, Calvin takes care to recognize certain figures of speech such as metaphor.[71] On the whole, however, Calvin resists more elaborate interpretations such as allegory. For instance, regarding God's speeches on Leviathan and Behemoth, Calvin rejects the medieval reading that has those primeval creatures representing Satan.[72] Regarding other biblical books in his other works, Calvin rejects the notion that Genesis 3:15 refers directly to Christ's victory over Satan.[73] However, Calvin does not eschew all Christological exegesis, for instance, in some more generic prophesies like Isaiah 53, and reads the Bible as having the knowledge of Christ as its goal.[74] Thus, Calvin employs no hard and fast rules or method in his exegesis, however sober he is in his work. He

---

69. Calvin, *Sermons on Job*, 66.
70. Opitz, "Calvin's Exegesis," 440.
71. De Greef, "Calvin as Commentator on the Psalms," 86.
72. Schreiner, *Where Shall Wisdom*, 142.
73. Opitz, "Calvin's Exegesis," 449.
74. Steinmetz, "John Calvin as an Interpreter," 285. Opitz, "Calvin's Exegesis," 447.

cares, in general, about drawing out a "useful teaching" from Scripture, so his sermons on Job should hold to that theory.[75]

Nevertheless, Calvin's attempt to mine teachings from Scripture, in what qualifies as a somewhat objective standpoint for a person who holds the Bible in a high regard, does not mean he does not remain susceptible to his own prejudgements regarding the message of Scripture. As suggested by his previously quoted comments on Job 4:7, Calvin's theology seems to guide his reading of Job as much as Job forms his theology. Eliphaz's words, taken on their own without knowledge of God's pronouncements of Job in the prose sections, do ring true to Reformed ears. The sinful nature of humanity is the main cause of evil and misfortune in the world. Eliphaz, therefore, presents a strong case for why Job experiences his own suffering. The cause and effect relationship between well being and relative sinfulness presented in Deuteronomy supports this notion. Calvin cannot merely dismiss the words of the friends since they adhere so well to his own theology. On the other hand, because God rebukes them in the end, Calvin must find them at fault for some reason.[76] He concludes that their speeches are, for the most part, right, but in their posture towards Job one can find fault.[77]

Calvin has less of a problem justifying the words of Elihu. Since God does not rebuke Elihu directly in the epilogue, Calvin views Elihu as presenting the orthodox position without reservation. Susan Schreiner refers to Elihu as "Calvin's mouthpiece" and that "Calvin's interpretation of chapters 32–37 offers a straightforward presentation of his real attitude toward Job and his friends."[78] When Elihu claims that God "does not let the wicked live; He grants justice to the lowly" (36:6), Calvin reassures his parishioners that God's providence is relatively predictable in that sin has earthly consequences and justice is something upon which one can count. One suffers in order to lead one to recognize one's sins and repent.[79] Because Elihu plays such a small part in the interpretations of Barth, Vischer, and Kierkegaard,

---

75. Ibid., 441. See also Steinmetz, "Calvin as Interpreter," 291.

76. Clines, "Job and the Spirituality of the Reformation," 71.

77. Schreiner, *Where Shall Wisdom*, 99. See also Vicchio, *Job in the Medieval World*, 188. One should note here that the book would hardly work without at least somewhat persuasive rhetoric on the behalf of the friends. If they spoke in what one could perceive on the surface as fallacious and unorthodox then the debate between the friends and Job would not sustain the reader's interest. The tension that grows as Job remains intractable despite his potential heresy and blasphemy only to withstand the scrutiny of God in the end makes for a book so compelling that it has remained a classic for millennia. One can hardly fault Calvin for his attraction to the friends' arguments. That he maintains his ambivalent stance towards their speeches is another matter.

78. Schreiner, *Where Shall Wisdom*, 132.

79. See ibid., 133.

we need not explore too much of Calvin's view of him. It should be enough to recognize the importance Elihu figures in Calvin's sermons and that this stems partly from what he says, but also it seems that Calvin's comprehensive reading of the book of Job results in his favoring Elihu over the rebuked friends and the borderline blasphemous Job.

Lastly, with Elihu, Calvin can safely endorse the view that suffering can chasten or teach without having to excuse the words for their eventual rejection by God.[80] In summary, Elihu, out of all of the characters, poses the fewest problems for Calvin precisely because his speeches invite no references outside of themselves. Calvin can take what Elihu says at face value since God does not rebuke him or even mention him. Of course, Elihu poses problems to later interpreters because of his dubious inclusion in the book itself. The doubt that many have regarding Elihu's origins arises mainly *because* no other character seems to recognize his presence. Other cases can be made disputing his inclusion such as vocabulary and poetic style, but his mysterious presence, or lack thereof, in the story triggers suspicion. Calvin's hermeneutic and historical context frees him from having to make a critical assessment that might lead to excising Elihu from discussion. On the contrary, Elihu becomes the hero of the book.

Of course, the likely hero is instead the titular character, but Calvin finds that Job's words make him uneasy. Calvin cannot deny that Job is in the right, but must qualify this final assessment with some harsh words directed towards Job. He gives less weight to God's approval in 42:7 as do his predecessors like Gregory.[81] Regarding Job's comment in 9:17 that God multiplies wounds without cause, Calvin writes,

> It seemeth very rude geere. For that God should torment men after a sort without cause, it is not only simple uniustice, but such a crueltie as he were not to be taken any more for iudge of the worlde, but rather for a tyrant. It seemeth that Iob blasphemeth God here in saying that he was smitten and wounded without cause. But if we remember what hath bene sayd: we shal know his meening and what he speaketh. For the holy Ghost hath guydeth and governed him in his tung, to the intent that wee should have an instruction that might be much to our profite. Iob then first sayeth here (according to his naturall understanding) that God smiteth him without cause. And afterwarde moreover let us marke that these wordes *without cause* have respect to the apparent & open knowledge of men. I have told you heretofore, that Gods Iustice is knowne two wayes. For sometimes

80. Ibid.
81. Ibid., 108.

God punisheth the sinnes that are notorious to the worldward.
Ye see that God chastizeth such a one.[82]

Calvin reveals much of his interpretation of Job in this small passage. Rather than allow for Job to say that God wounds him without cause, a theme that Vischer will tackle many years later at great length, Calvin admits that this sounds like blasphemy but that the Holy Spirit led Job for our sake. That is, Job's ostensible blasphemy profits the reader by example. More importantly to the ongoing exegesis of Calvin, we can excuse Job because he presents his own experiences as he perceives them. Schreiner's book deals with this idea in great depth and though at times seems to overstate her case, one can easily find her thesis about Calvin's interpretation of Job compelling. Her basic thesis as it applies to the above quote argues that Calvin does not actually believe that God acts without cause, but only that in our human capacity we perceive that God acts without cause. This allows Calvin to maintain a position closer to the friends than Job, but excuse Job of blasphemy because from his perspective, Job has every right to think that God has hurt him for nought.[83]

Within this idea that Job's perceptions somewhat excuse his comments lies a sentiment by Calvin that suffering can have the purpose of teaching and chastising. Since the prologue rules out the possibility that God is punishing Job for sins, Calvin allows for another reason for suffering.[84] Unlike the Calvinists Vischer and Barth, Calvin does not spend much time wrestling with the idea of God inflicting Job for nought. As evident in the passage quoted above, he thinks that that idea makes God out to look like a tyrant. While Barth will wax rhapsodic on God's freedom and the importance of it in his theology, Calvin takes care to mitigate God's freedom with God's other characteristics.[85] The overarching mitigating characteristic is justice. However, because of Job's and our human perception, God's justice does not always reveal itself.

The hiddenness of God and its effect on Job's perceived suffering is a regular theme in Calvin's sermons. Like the later interpreters we will eventually examine, Calvin perceives that the suffering that Job experiences results less from the loss of property, family, and health described in the prologue

---

82. Calvin, *Sermons on Job*, 163.

83. Schreiner, *Where Shall Wisdom*, 100, 23–24. Schreiner writes, that "on the basis of Job's friends, Calvin can argue that as a 'general rule' a direct cause exists between suffering and sin." Later she reiterates that Calvin "wrestles openly with the danger that the book of Job contradicts the Book of Deuteronomy." She states, that "we can detect Calvin's continual uneasiness with the possible tension between Job's laments and the Law. His sympathies often gravitate toward the friends."

84. Ibid., 116.

85. Ibid., 119.

but more from the torturous feeling that God is unreliable or absent after his losses.[86] The friends, so self-assured, do not recognize Job's suffering to this extent because they understand the justice of the world to be visible and palpable. What Job begins to reveal is a hidden justice—what Calvin calls God's double or secret justice. The justice that the friends presume active in the world is one upon which humans can reasonably rely, but God employs a secret justice that proves imperceptible in our limited state. What this implies, and what Calvin discusses explicitly throughout his sermons, is that the theme of providence that Aquinas finds so prevalent in the book of Job, Calvin finds too. Job's travails, as torturous as they seem, need not lead one to believe that God is a tyrant or unreliable. Rather, one must trust that the doctrine of providence will win out in the end. Justice will prevail, but in the meantime, the mystery of God's providence may confuse and lead to the feeling of uncertainty.[87]

To summarize for our purposes, we will look at the prevailing themes of our three main interpreters of Job and how Calvin's interpretation leads to or anticipates the later scholars, notably in the aspects of typology and freedom.

First, Calvin's literal approach to the Scriptures resists allegory. As noted above, he rejects traditional readings of the Behemoth and Leviathan as representative of Satan. He also resists Christological readings of passages that traditionally lead in that direction. Consider his sermons that include chapter 19:25. Throughout history, Christians have read the "redeemer" in this famous passage as prefiguring Christ and have felt the freedom to embellish on that reading. However, Calvin quotes the passage in his sermon as "I know that my God is alive . . ."[88] He does not deny, of course, that God will make himself manifest in the person of Jesus, but nor does he hint that Job prophesies the future incarnation. As we shall see, despite Barth and Vischer's juxtaposition of Job and Christ, neither do they see Job prophesying in that way.

Where they differ more so, especially regarding Vischer, is the character of Job as prefiguring Christ. Calvin's objection towards Job's words would seem to lead to his resistance to this typology. On the other hand, Calvin does not reject all typological readings in the book of Job. Rather than the typical Christological readings of the premodern era, however, Calvin somehow moves toward a reading that incorporates King David into the narrative of Job. Part of this seems to have to do with Calvin's affinity towards the Psalter.

---

86. Ibid., 104.

87. Clines, "Job and the Spirituality of the Reformation," 66.

88. Calvin, *Sermons on Job*, 336. This translation may be a conflation of the ideas found in the Hebrew text and the LXX, which reads οιδα γαρ οτι αεναος εστιν.

In a way, this makes sense because the Psalter, like the book of Job, is divinely inspired, but often out of words from the heart of a suffering human. The difference is that David as psalmist and in the narratives in 1 and 2 Samuel consistently confesses to his sins—something Job rarely if ever does. It is through his comparisons with David that Calvin can move to Christ in his sermons. For Calvin, David is a type of Christ. As head of the community in Israel, David is an image of Christ.[89] So it is through David, not Job, that Calvin can talk about Christ. However, all three suffer at the hand of God, so they all have something in common. Calvin's uneasiness toward Job hinders his ability to make a direct leap to Christ and so he goes through a more humble character with whom Calvin feels more comfortable.

Calvin resists the possibility of granting God the vast freedom that Barth and Vischer grant. Calvin seems to have difficulty reconciling God's freedom with his justice. The laws that God sets up seem to limit God's freedom in some ways for Calvin. Although this is not a typical view of Calvin, the freedom of God does seem limited in his interpretation of Job, seemingly because of his discomfort with Job's borderline blasphemous remarks that butt up against the comments by Job's friends, which sound more respectful of God. By favoring the friends and Elihu over Job, Calvin opens himself up to the criticism that Barth, Vischer, and Kierkegaard level at the friends and their own critics—the friends and those who resemble them are putting the system of God's justice above the person of God, thereby subjecting God to his own law. In the end, he has more in common with Barth than not, but Barth seems more willing to enter the darker places than Calvin does. Calvin seems somewhat timid when it comes to challenging God's relationship between justice and freedom.

KANT ON JOB

Let us now turn to Immanuel Kant's interpretation of Job, which takes up a small portion of a short essay he wrote in 1791 called "On the Failure of all Attempted Philosophical Theodicies."[90] Its size precludes an extended meditation on his discourse, but his approach and what he says merits mentioning in the context of our larger program. The conclusions at which he arrives anticipate Kierkegaard, Barth, and Vischer in important ways, and it seems likely that Kierkegaard was familiar with the essay. Kant's approach to Job and his theories about Job's integrity share much in common with Kierkegaard's interpretation in *Repetition*. Also when one notes the timing

89. Opitz, "Calvin's Exegesis," 450.
90. Kant, "Theodicies," 283.

of particular remarks by Kierkegaard that mirror Kant's musings in this essay, one may conjecture, as Ronald Green does, a direct link between Kant's essay and Kierkegaard's book.[91]

Like many who gravitate towards the book of Job, Kant seems to have identified with Job's suffering. Unlike Gregory the Great, however, who experienced physical suffering, Kant experienced a social suffering at the hands of his critics in a way similar to Kierkegaard's.[92] A. L. Loades indicates that Kant's essay in part takes aim at a pastor and minister of justice named J. C. Wöllner, who put out a series of edicts that institutionalized certain understandings of Lutheran orthodoxy by the state and made vulnerable some whose own interpretations fell into suspicion. Since Kant himself "was unlikely to accommodate his thinking so [sic] the prevailing spirit of the State or to ecclesiastical dogmatism in any form," he penned his essay, clearly siding himself with Job, insinuating that Wöllner and his followers represent Eliphaz *et al.*[93] He, like Kierkegaard, elevates Job in relation to Job's friends because of the pronouncement made by God in Job 42:6 about their relative virtue.

Though his reading of Job shares these similarities with Kierkegaard, the vehicle with which he drives his interpretation more resembles Barth's. After presenting his reasons for why philosophical theodicies fail, Kant turns to the story of Job to buttress his thesis.

Kant's essay, which acts as a rebuke of Leibniz's conviction that we live in the best of all possible worlds,[94] begins by defining theodicy as "defences of the highest wisdom of the Creator against the complaints which reason makes by pointing to the existence of things in the world which contradict the wise purpose." God's advocate, in order to justify God in the face of these complaints must prove the purpose of "what one deems contrary to purposefulness," that it is "an inevitable consequence of the nature of things," or that some being other than God is the responsible agent.[95] His main argument as to why philosophical theodicies fail is based on his belief in the unknowableness of God and thus, the unknowableness of the truth of the theodicy. This does not mean that the problems need remain irresolvable.

---

91. Green, *Kierkegaard and Kant*, 22–24.

92. Loades, *Kant*, 38–42.

93. Ibid., 40. See, for instance, Kant's veiled, yet blistering, critique of the religion-edict when he writes that "if Job were to appear before some tribunal of dogmatic theologians, some senate or inquisition, some worthy presbytery or some high consistory of today (with the exception of one), he probably would have met with a worse fate" (Kant, "Theodicies," 293).

94. Lamb, *The Rhetoric of Suffering*, 65.

95. Kant, "Theodicies," 283.

He merely suggests, like Calvin, that we may never know the solution. In a line reminiscent of the spirit of Job 28, Kant states,

> there is a task which our attorney does not need to undertake, that is to prove the highest wisdom of God by what is learned from experience in the world. This he could not do at all, for it requires omniscience to recognize in any given world (as known in experience) such perfection that one could say of it with certainty that there could not be any greater in the creation and government of the world.[96]

Theodicy can only speculate on the justification of the divine. It does not truly defend God but rather one's preconceptions of God—it overreaches reason.[97]

Kant, however, does believe that an authentic theodicy remains a possibility as opposed to the doctrinal theodicies that inevitably fail. Kant turns to Job as an example of authentic theodicy. Job's perceptions of his suffering, coming from his honest and immediate views of his own personal fate strike Kant as an adequate example of theodicy. The ends of it are not to bolster a universal truth at the expense of a suffering individual but to bolster the suffering individual.[98]

The rest of the essay goes through a number of proposals as to how one may justify misfortune in the world under the watch of a benevolent Creator. Kant finds each argument lacking, invoking at times language reminiscent of Job himself. He discusses the incommensurability between crime and punishment in the observable world. Upon the observable world, a common theme in biblical Wisdom literature, Kant limits his reasoning. This disjunction between empirical data and convincing theodicies is where Kant bases most of his conclusions about the failure of theodicy.

The main theme running through Kant's meditations on Job is the importance of a free conscience with respect to morality. Kant describes Job as "healthy, rich, free . . . he lived in a happy family, had good friends, and above all . . . he was at peace with himself and had a good conscience. All these blessings, except the last one, were taken away from him by a terrible fate sent to try him."[99] Job, Kant surmises from the text, continues to speak

---

96. Ibid., 284.

97. Mittleman, "The Job of Judaism and the Job of Kant," 39.

98. As discussed below, Kant seems to avoid the frame narrative of Job in his exposition, perhaps because the folk tale puts into question his analysis of philosophical theodicies. The heavenly wager could be used to elevate a universal truth. On the other hand, Kant does not suggest that this doctrinal theodicy is necessarily false, only that it is unprovable. Job and his friends never know for sure the root of Job's suffering so the authentic theodicy is the only true option.

99. Kant, "Theodicies," 291.

his mind even after the fate that befell him. This explains his outspokenness throughout the dialogues. Job acts not as an iconoclast or with impatience as much as he speaks his mind with confidence. His sincerity certainly trumps anything else he might say or do. Thus, Kant suggests the eventual failure of all theodicies since the only right thing to say in a situation like Job's is what the sufferer feels at that precise moment.

To illustrate this in more detail, Kant contrasts Job's behavior with his friends' reactions to Job's outspokenness. Kant recognizes the friends' belief in retributive justice, which mitigates their responses to his sufferings, aggravating Job more because they do not perceive his sincerity. The arguments of either side do not impress Kant as much as the posture of the individuals making the arguments.[100]

Though the topic of the conscience does not loom large in Kant's works, nor in perceptions of his work, the importance of the conscience in ethics does arise in his important work *Religion within the Limits of Reason Alone*, which he wrote two years later in 1793.[101] The importance of the conscience in Kantian ethics stems partly from moments of doubt—when reason alone may not have the capability of deciding an ethical dilemma. The conscience then acts as a guide.[102] Kant seems to elevate the conscience, at times, to a level higher than faith.[103] In *Religion*, he defines the "future judge" "at life's close" as "his own awakening conscience, together with the empirical knowledge of himself which is summoned to its aid."[104] This description corresponds well to the Job in "On the Failure of All Attempted Philosophical Theodicies." One reason Kant views the conscience this way is that if a "question is addressed to the judge *within* a man he will pronounce a severe verdict upon himself; for a man cannot bribe his own reason" the way he can attempt to mollify an outside judge "with prayers and entreaties, or with formulas and confessions in which he claims to believe."[105] Thus, the conscience supersedes even God. Because Job speaks honestly about

---

100. "The crucial point about Job's discussion with his friends was the character which they exhibited when they reasoned with him" (Loades, *Kant*, 41).

101. Kant, *Religion within the Limits*, 70–72, 173–78. For an extended discussion on the role of conscience in Kant's work, see Timmermann, "Kant on Conscience," 294–309.

102. Ibid., 306.

103. Mittleman, "Job of Judaism," 40. Mittleman writes, "Sincerity stands in for or replaces faith, at least the faith that is a conviction of the existence of things unseen."

104. Kant, *Religion*, 71.

105. Ibid., 72.

his own perceptions, Kant views him highly. When Job confesses his lack of wisdom about unknowable things, Kant views him as a hero.[106]

Kant further breaks down the difference between Job and his friends, saying that Job uses practical reason while the friends use speculative reason. Presumably, he means that Job bases his arguments on empirical data, though he remains the only observer of the data, while the friends ratiocinate based on an *a priori* understanding of how the moral world operates. Kant's interpretation displays a keen awareness of the story, but seems not to grasp all that is at stake.

Glaringly absent is any mention of Job's devotion to God, but this may stem from Kant's understanding of faith. At the heart of Vischer and Barth's interpretation, and implied in Kierkegaard's as well through his novelistic style, lies the wager between the Satan and God in 1:9. The Satan asks God if Job fears God for nought. This effects Job's loss of all he has. Kant expresses Job's loss in the passive voice, relegating God's activity to the background and seeming to negate the Satan from the story altogether. Though he does not say so, it seems likely that Kant does not consider the folktale element of the book of Job at all, referring only to the dialogues between Job, Job's friends, and God. He also says nothing regarding the final scene, referring to the denouement as God's assurance of Job's piety rather than his restoration.

Kant hints at how Job's devotion to God may play into his reading of the story in the final paragraph of his analysis. Kant concludes the section by introducing Job's faith, but faith in what, he remains a bit vague. After God has pronounced Job right as compared to his friends, Kant writes:

> The faith which arose out of such unusual answers to his doubts, that is, which arose simply out of the conviction of his ignorance, could arise only in the soul of a man who in the midst of his most serious doubts could say, "Until the hour of my death, I will hold fast to my piety" (27,5–6) With this resolution Job proved that he did not base his morality on his faith but his faith upon his morality. In this case, faith, however weak it may become, is a truer and purer one; this kind of faith is not found in a religion that cultivates self-interest and seeks favours, but in a religion of good behaviour.[107]

With this chiastic remark, Kant betrays his understanding of the divine and cryptically affirms Job's devotion to God that he seems to overlook when setting the scene of the story of Job. Job's morality, conscience, and faith all act as strands of the same knot. Job's free conscience reflects his piety, which

106. Mittleman, "Job of Judaism," 40.
107. Kant, "Theodicies," 293.

acts as a window to God. Sincerity, Kant claims, is the basis of every virtue as well as the main requirement of faith.[108] Job, then, in his sincere objections to his lowly state, displays a virtue and, in effect, a devotion to God that the friends cannot claim because of their unbecoming flattery.

Job's devotion to God seems almost able to exist without need for God at all. Kant focuses almost entirely on conscience. However, God does play an important role in his analysis. God honors Job "by showing him the wisdom of his creation and its unfathomable nature."[109] Note that the nature of creation remains unfathomable even after God tells Job of it. God shows "to Job an ordering of the whole which manifests a wise Creator, although his ways remain inscrutable for us . . . even more in the connection between this order and the moral one."[110] God's ways lie beyond our knowledge and so Job's strategy of honesty and sincerity proves the better route than his friends' attempts to appease the Creator with their human reason.

In the end, Kant does anticipate Barth, Vischer, and Kierkegaard in various ways. For instance, he touches on the freedom of Job and God in the story. Kant's few quotes of the text of Job include 23:13, which declares God "unique," a reflection of Barth's visions of God's wholly otherness that match Kant's musings on the unfathomability of God's wisdom. God "does what he wants," Job continues, which Kant uses to argue for the doctrine of "unconditioned divine decree."[111] Job, likewise, speaks freely of his condition and God's involvement in it. While his friends "spoke as if they were overheard by the Almighty . . . and as if they cared more for winning his favors by passing the right judgment than for saying the truth. The dishonesty . . . contrasts with Job's free and sincere outspokenness . . ."[112] Job's freedom and inhibitions in utilizing his freedom in Kant's assessment anticipate one of the angles that Kierkegaard, Vischer, and Barth approach the book of Job.

We might also note that his method of approaching Job, as illustration for a larger project, reflects Barth's springboard approach to the text. As noted above, Kant potentially shares a formal relationship with Kierkegaard through the latter's own study. This comes through in many respects in Kierkegaard's work, but regarding Job, both Kant and Kierkegaard note the importance of subjectivity in the story. The important aspect of Job's character is his personal conscience and not the objective ratiocinating of the friends. With Vischer, Kant also notes the importance of morality in the story, but whereas Vischer

108. Ibid., 294.
109. Ibid.
110. Ibid.
111. Ibid., 292.
112. Ibid.

notes that God's goodness is a goodness beyond good and evil, goodness for Kant marks the one consistent aspect of theology.

One must not, however, overstate the analogous relationship between Kant and these later thinkers. The differences, in the end, outweigh the similarities. Most of these will become clearer in the later chapters, but a few are obvious enough to state here. Regarding Barth especially, Kant, though he does not display a strong faith in the powers of human reason to locate God compared to others, does elevate reason above that of Barth, who eschews all natural revelation. Barth places all initiative for humanity's faith in God in God's realm. Barth, of course, shows much more interest in Christ than Kant, as does Vischer. Kant, in fact, does not mention Christ in his essay.

This regard for God's initiative in the book of Job and beyond relates to the pride of place in which the three later writers view the Scriptures. One need not explore the finer points of Kant's view of Scripture for this project. In fact, he says very little regarding the authority of the Bible in his illustrative use of the book of Job other than that he finds his theory on theodicy "expressed allegorically in an old Scripture."[113]

Concerning this last comment, one notes that despite the close identification of allegory with medieval biblical interpretation, Kant does not shy away from allegory at all. Besides finding his theory on theodicy expressed allegorically, he also finds himself represented allegorically in the character of Job and Wöllner and his followers represented allegorically in the characters of Job's friends. He also regards Genesis 2–6 as an allegory of the history of humanity in his essay *Muthmaßlicher Anfang der Menschengeschichte*.[114] Thus allegory actually is an important aspect of Kant's hermeneutics, but it differs much from the typological imagination of Barth and Vischer in that he uses biblical stories to illustrate abstract concepts or as historical antecedents while Barth and Vischer focus on God's activity in some stories of his special revelation as parallel in others. The vastly different theologies separating Kant and Barth and Vischer seem to lie at the root of their different incorporations of typology or allegory.

CONCLUSION

Though these five interpretations of the book of Job bear little resemblance to each other, they all remain important contributions to the dialogue of Job in the chronotope. The book of Job changes slightly after each interpreter since their influence has impact on the dialogue even if the next interpreter

113. Ibid., 291.
114. Reventlow, "Towards the End of the 'Century of Enlightenment,'" 1038.

seems to approach Job anew. The five approach the text differently and come away with different results, but all contribute to the dialogue. Gregory begins heavy on the allegory, an element which all but disappears until Kant's essay during the Age of Enlightenment. When Kierkegaard arrives, he picks up where Kant leaves off though he fits much better in Luther's school. Even though he contributes to this dialogue like all those before and after him, his interpretation of the book of Job stands apart in many ways as a strikingly unique approach.

3

Each Time I Come to a Word, It Is Again Made Original

The Repetition of Job in Kierkegaard's Young Man

SØREN KIERKEGAARD IS NOT a conventional biblical scholar, to say the least.[1] Though some of his upbuilding discourses can act as small commentaries, he does not share the same interests in his interpretation as does one interested in the historical aspects of a biblical text. With regard to Job in particular, his method of interpretation often strays quite far from that of the conventional scholar. His most extended discourse on Job, one that works with the largest portion of the biblical book, is written under a pseudonym in the form of a series of letters in the second

---

1. Joel Rasmussen presents an overview of Kierkegaard's peculiar biblical hermeneutics. He writes, "Despite his biblical repertoire, however, Kierkegaard is not widely regarded as an important biblical interpreter, at least not among most biblical scholars. Whereas critical studies of nineteenth-century Scandinavian literature, of post-Kantian continental philosophy, and of modern Protestant theology regularly include considerations of Kierkegaard's works and influence, when one turns to intellectual-historical studies of the development of modern biblical interpretation, such works generally pass over Kierkegaard in silence ..." (Rasmussen, "Kierkegaard's Biblical Hermeneutics," 249–50). See also Lori Brandt's essay in the same collection of essays, where she writes, "Perhaps [Kierkegaard's] prolific use of Scripture has been overlooked because Kierkegaard made no claim to being an academic exegete and ignored many of the historical-critical interpretive practices that were emerging in his day as being too impersonal and thus unhelpful" (Brandt, "Kierkegaard's Use of the Old Testament," 231).

half of the book *Repetition*. Though there is much insight into Job from this discourse, his interpretation differs in key ways from his upbuilding discourse from the same year. The upbuilding discourse, a short, reflective commentary on a single verse, is written under the name Søren Kierkegaard. This discrepancy in "authorship" with regard to Kierkegaard's works in this period can be seen as artificial—perhaps what matters is only that the different texts are all penned by Kierkegaard. Certainly, the various publishers of Kierkegaard's works feel this way to some end, considering that his short works are rarely seen published alone in a single volume despite having different pseudonymous authors. For instance, Princeton publishes *Fear and Trembling* by "Johannes de Silentio" with *Repetition* by "Constantin Constantius." However, de Silentio and Constantius are not mentioned on the cover or title page. Oxford, likewise, publishes *Repetition* with *Philosophical Crumbs* by "Johannes Climacus." By ignoring the pseudonymity of Kierkegaard's works, one can easily mistake the varying works as requiring the same reading strategy. There is reason to believe that they can and should be read in conjunction, suggested by Kierkegaard's decision to publish *Fear and Trembling* and *Repetition* on the same day.[2] However, the difference in "authorship" should be taken into account when interpreting the books themselves. The use of multiple names by Kierkegaard is a key to understanding his works and is an important strategy that he employs in his own interpretation. It also may give insight into his feelings on authorship with regard to the biblical text.

The following chapter describes Kierkegaard's interpretation of *Job* in two works published in 1843. Because of his unique style, incorporating Socratic irony, one must learn to read between the lines of his assumed characters' words for his beliefs.[3] Also, despite the different pseudonyms employed, there is much one can learn about *Job* in *Repetition* by paying attention to *Fear and Trembling*. Yet it is also evident that Kierkegaard himself continues to see parallels between the characters of Abraham and Job in the respective stories upon which he reflects in his 1843 works. In a later

---

2. See especially Taylor, "Ordeal and Repetition." Taylor argues convincingly that both texts are meant to be read in conjunction and that *Fear and Trembling* sets up *Repetition*.

3. I use the word "belief" here, as opposed to "intent," because it seems clear that Kierkegaard's "intent" was what we have in the words published. However, he likely believed something different than those words expressed by Constantius, de Silentio, et al.

volume of discourses, published in 1848, Kierkegaard pairs the two Old Testament patriarchs as counter examples to Simon Peter in Matthew 19.[4]

Before delving further into Job and his potential relationship to Abraham in Kierkegaard's work, it is necessary to explore briefly how the Bible fits into Kierkegaard's program. The next section of the chapter will examine Job in Kierkegaard's discourse on Job 1:20–21. Before highlighting Job in *Repetition*, the chapter will explore the category of repetition. In the book *Repetition*, the character of the young man "repeats" the character of Job by appropriating the life of Job as his own. Thus, an exploration of Kierkegaard's interpretation of Job requires an exploration of this unusual hermeneutical method wherein the story of Job is repeated as an allegory of the young man's own life. As Iben Damgaard writes, "The young man is completely absorbed in Job's words. He surrenders himself to the text without reserve."[5] I will show that the young man takes this further than even Damgaard suggests by showing that the young man appropriates the lives of others into the lives of the characters in the book of Job.[6] The chapter finishes with an analysis of Kierkegaard's vision of Job, trying to bridge the ostensible gap between Job in the discourse and Job in *Repetition*.

THE BIBLE IN KIERKEGAARD

The Bible is an unquestionably important document for Kierkegaard's philosophy. Despite his era, champions, and sparring partners, Kierkegaard's "attitude towards God as both Ultimacy and Intimacy," as T. H. Croxall states in 1956, comes ultimately from his interpretation of the Bible.[7] This is undoubtedly the case, but not many, unfortunately, have ventured to explore Kierkegaard's method of interpretation since Croxall made that statement, Croxall included.[8] Determining Kierkegaard's method of exegesis is a difficult undertaking. He does not present an explicit hermeneutic and his

---

4. Kierkegaard, *Christian Discourses*, 185–87.

5. Damgaard, "My Dear Reader," 97–98.

6. Timothy Polk's assessment of *Repetition* also theorizes that the young man appropriates the character of Job and even suggests that Constantin Constantius typifies the friends, but again, does not go as far as I insist the book goes in appropriating the characters. See especially Polk, *The Biblical Kierkegaard*, 174.

7. Croxall, *Kierkegaard Commentary*, 34.

8. A very recent attempt to correct this omission in Kierkegaard scholarship and perhaps biblical scholarship as well is the two volume book *Kierkegaard and the Bible* (Damgaard, "Kierkegaard's Rewriting of Biblical Narratives." and Lee C. Barrett and Jon Stewart, ed. *Kierkegaard and the Bible: Tome II*). Two other important volumes are Pons, *Stealing*, and Polk, *Biblical Kierkegaard*.

pseudonyms do not use the Bible in the same way as he would promote under his own name. This will become evident in the below comparison of "Søren Kierkegaard's" upbuilding discourse and "the young man's" letters in *Repetition*. However, what seems to be the driving force of his biblical hermeneutic in his autonymous[9] and even many of his pseudonymous works is "a principle of imitation through imaginative identification."[10] This, of course, brings subjectivity into the foreground of interpretation, such that the various personalities will interpret different texts differently because of their own relationship with the texts.

Nevertheless, there are wrong methods of interpretation according to Kierkegaard. The first half of the nineteenth century in Europe presented one with a variety of methods and emphases in biblical interpretation.[11] One aspect that was gaining headway in the mainstream since Eichhorn's 1780 publication of *Einleitung in das Alte Testament* was historical criticism to which Kierkegaard was not opposed. However, he certainly held reservations regarding historical criticism. Of the many journal entries that he writes with respect to the Bible, one from 1848 illustrates his attitude towards Scripture well:

> A Reformation that removed the Bible would now, basically, have just as much validity as Luther's removal of the pope. All this about the Bible has given rise to a scholarly and legalistic type of religiousness, sheer diversion. A sort of "learning" in that direction has gradually found its way down to the commonest class and no human being reads the Bible humanly any more. If anything it is all too human to defer interpretation to human authorities. This causes irreparable harm; it becomes a refuge for excuses and evasions, etc. respecting existence, for there will always be something to check on first, always this sham that one

---

9. Autonymous works are those written in an author's own name.

10. Fishburn, "Soeren Kierkegaard, Exegete," 232.

11. For a brief description of the different emphases among Old Testament scholars during the era just before Kierkegaard, see Reventlow, "Towards the End." See also Rogerson, *Old Testament Criticism in the Nineteenth Century*. Mogens Müller has published a recent article that maps out the trends in biblical scholarship at the time of Kierkegaard and how Kierkegaard fits into the era, noting that "it must be admitted that Kierkegaard was not in any substantive way influenced by what was going on in this field" (Müller, "Kierkegaard and Eighteenth- and Nineteenth-Century Biblical Scholarship," 285). It is also unclear whether Kierkegaard was even familiar with the important names in historical criticism prior to his own study. He does not engage with the enduring figures of the time like Eichhorn, Gabler, de Wette, etc. There was no truly dominant approach to biblical criticism anyway. Whether comparing with neologists, rationalists, or other schools of thought, Kierkegaard does not seem to fit. He was a *sui generis* biblical interpreter.

must have the learning in shape before one can begin living—
which means one never gets around to the latter.[12]

Kierkegaard's vitriolic, perhaps hyperbolic, tone indicates his attitude towards the importance of the Bible. If one is to use it wrongly, it is best not to use it at all. The invective also hints at a biblical hermeneutic. One should use the Bible for living, or not at all.

With an understanding of this principle of imitation in mind, one notices another curious difference between his autonymous and pseudonymous works, namely his pseudonyms' preferences for the Old Testament. This is perhaps no accident. Just as he does not mean for his readers to stop at his pseudonyms' conclusions on the matters upon which they reason, he does not mean to read the Old Testament as the final say on the matters upon which it reasons. His pseudonymous writings lead his readers to the truth beyond what the narrators are saying. The narrators themselves are not aware, or at least do not understand, the actual truth to which Kierkegaard himself is pointing through them. Likewise, Old Testament characters point beyond themselves to the ultimate truth revealed in the New Testament. In *Repetition*, Constantin Constantius and the young man fumble their ways through ideas concerning the category of repetition. Constantin contradicts himself on occasion while the young man seems to develop his idea of the category over the course of nine months. The end product for the reader is a series of wrong answers and dead ends; we must recreate the category with what is left. It is repetition through apophasis.[13]

Kierkegaard's stated position on Scripture aligns well with his Socratic rhetoric. He writes in his journal, anticipating Barth, "the Holy Scriptures are the highway signs: Christ is the way."[14] If the goal of reading Scripture is for it to point one to Christ, the Old Testament, which does not mention Christ explicitly, plays a similar role to Kierkegaard's pseudonyms. The characters of the Old Testament act earnestly, but do not hold all of the necessary information themselves. Instead, they point the way through their lives to the life of Christ. In a Christian discourse of 1848, five years after the publication of *Repetition* and the upbuilding discourse on Job, Kierkegaard suggests that Job and Abraham fell short of the Christian ideal despite their admirable qualities. Job and Abraham put up "with an unavoidable loss in such a way that [they] not merely [do] not lose faith in God but believingly adore ... and extol ...

---

12. Kierkegaard, *Papers and Journals*, 343–44.

13. For an extended discussion on Kierkegaard's maieutic rhetoric see Evans, *Kierkegaard*, 24–45. For a similar discussion from a poststructuralist point of view see Poole, *Communication*.

14. From Kierkegaard's journals, quoted in Rosas, "Kierkegaard, Soren Aabye," 333.

His glory, that is Jewish piety."[15] The Jewish piety of Job and Abraham, despite falling short of the Christian ideal, according to Kierkegaard, nevertheless is important in pointing the way to the Christian ideal.[16]

If Kierkegaard feels this way about the Bible's authority, his attitude towards historical criticism should come as no surprise. In short, he sees historical criticism as a useful tool, but it should not remain the focus of one's Bible study. The problem that historical criticism creates is a dependence on objective scientific evaluation of the text, which lacks the reliability it presumes to have, for "even with the most stupendous learning and perseverance, and even if the heads of all the critics were mounted on a single neck, one would never arrive at anything more than an approximation."[17] The reliance on this illusory objective knowledge is destructive for two reasons. Because it is based on impersonal data, the results' relationship with subjective faith is dubious. This is the case for the person who had no faith to begin with and for the person who had faith already. Climacus writes, "faith does not result from straightforward scholarly deliberation, nor does it come directly; on the contrary, in this objectivity [of historical critical inquiry] one loses that infinite, personal, impassioned interestedness, which is the condition of faith."[18] On the other hand, for the person who had faith already, "he is rather in such a precarious position that much effort, much fear and trembling will be needed lest he fall into temptation and confuse knowledge with faith."[19] He takes issue with a method of interpretation that presumes that truth comes through objective knowledge rather than through subjectivity.

Kierkegaard responds to the dispassionate, scientifically-minded criticism with what seems like a polar opposite method that comes across in his pseudonyms as well as his own autonomous interpretation of Holy Scripture. Rather than remove oneself from the equation, he proposes reading the Bible as if it were a personal letter from God to the reader.[20] He writes in one of his journal entries, "Above all things read the New Testament without a

---

15. Kierkegaard, *Christian Discourses*, 186. As discussed below, Kierkegaard's position on Job and Abraham in this later discourse may not have been his position in 1843, but may have been a result of his literary evolution.

16. It is unclear whether Kierkegaard thought of Job as an ethnic Jew or not, but he did regard him as Jew*ish*.

17. Kierkegaard, *Concluding Unscientific Postscript I*, 24. N.B. The pseudonym for this work is Johannes Climacus.

18. Ibid., 29.

19. Ibid.

20. Rosas, "Kierkegaard," 331. See also Kallas, "Kierkegaard's Understanding of the Bible," 34. Both Rosas and Kallas quote the same Journal entry from 1850.

commentary. Would a lover dream of reading a letter from his beloved with a commentary!..." (*sic*).[21] Kallas calls this a "passionate" hermeneutic—one which calls for action upon reading the love letter from the beloved.[22] Rosas compares Kierkegaard's hermeneutic to reader-response theory and points to Kierkegaard's "various hermeneutical models" as a reminder of the "variety of possible readings of the Bible."[23] Kierkegaard likely does not limit this hermeneutic to the Bible, however. In the preface to 1843's *Two Upbuilding Discourses*, he writes of "that single individual whom I with joy and gratitude call *my* reader."[24] It is the individual who must interpret any text.

If there is any single method that Kierkegaard does promote and that is consistent with his claims of finding truth through subjectivity, it is the principle of identifying with the characters of the biblical texts. This is especially the case with the New Testament character of Jesus, but it is also the case with Old Testament characters, notably Abraham and Job. By identifying with the characters, the Old Testament changes for the reader from being an intractable legal document to a living guide. When the reader places herself in the sandals of Abraham, she puts herself into a position to meet God as the patriarch did. This is insinuated in *Fear and Trembling* by de Silentio.[25] Yet, in the end, the *Imitatio Christi* is the desired climax of this journey through the Scriptures. It is a logical progression, as suggested above, to move from the pseudonyms' preference for the Old Testament to the autonyms' preference for the New, because the pseudonyms exist in order to point the way to the truth.

One should also note the potential problem that arises in Kierkegaard's literary evolution. Five years after the publication of *Repetition* and *Four Upbuilding Discourses*, Kierkegaard published *Thoughts Which Wound from Behind—for Edification: Christian Addresses*.[26] In the second of these addresses, he attends to Matthew 19:27 in a similar fashion to his earlier discourses. In discussing the line, "Behold, we have forsaken all and followed thee," Kierkegaard brings up Job who says, "The Lord hath taken away," contrasting Job's passive loss to the voluntary forsaking of the Christian.[27] Job,

---

21. Dru, ed. *The Journals of Søren Kierkegaard*, 384. #1077 One will note that Kierkegaard here does not mention the Old Testament. As discussed below, Kierkegaard's evolution of thought includes his shifting positions on Christianity and Judaism. See note 198.

22. Kallas, "Kierkegaard's Understanding," 34.

23. Rosas, "Kierkegaard," 334.

24. Kierkegaard, *Discourses*, 5. Emphasis in the original.

25. Fishburn, "Exegete," 237.

26. Kierkegaard, *Christian Discourses*.

27. Ibid., 185–86.

therefore, like Abraham, displays a Jewish piety and not a Christian piety. Kierkegaard's negative opinion of Job does not emerge in the publications of 1843, so this paragraph of 1848 surprises the reader. It is not my intention to ignore this seeming anomaly in Kierkegaard's discussions of Job, but since this passage comes after *Repetition* and the earlier discourse, and since it does not play into later discussions of Job by Barth as do the earlier publications, I do not want to dwell much on the passage. Tadayoshi Hayashi attributes the discrepancy between the later vision of Job and the earlier ones to an evolution in thought regarding Kierkegaard's understanding of the Old and New Testaments and, likewise, his understanding of the distinctions between Christianity and Judaism.[28] Lori Brandt, however, does note that "though Old Testament references taper off in his later works, [Kierkegaard] continues to draw on the stories and paradigms contained in the Old Testament for inspiration and direction for human life, from Job to Abraham to David."[29] Nevertheless, he does favor the New Testament over the Old because he naturally, as a Christian, views "Christ as the ultimate paradigm for Christian living."[30] With these principles in mind, we move to the text and character of Job in Kierkegaard's work. Before proceeding to the pseudonymous *Repetition*, however, it is prudent to look first at the brief discourse that Kierkegaard published in the same year.

JOB IN "THE LORD GAVE, AND THE LORD TOOK AWAY; BLESSED BE THE NAME OF THE LORD"

Roughly two months after publishing *Repetition*, Kierkegaard published a book of four "upbuilding discourses." The first of these four discourses is a brief commentary on Job 1:20–21. Despite its later publication date and its smaller scope, it may be wise to examine this discourse before moving to *Job* in *Repetition*. The reason for this is that Kierkegaard's purpose in this later text is much more direct than in the pseudonymous *Repetition*. The discourses in general also give a better indication of his hermeneutical method for written texts.[31] Beyond this, it is also an important document because, like *Fear and Trembling*, it intends to give hope to the inconsolable, again showing a connection that Kierkegaard sees between Abraham and

---

28. Hayashi, "Kierkegaard über Hiob," 71.

29. Brandt, "Kierkegaard's Old Testament," 247.

30. Ibid., 231.

31. See Delecroix, "Quelques Traits," 243. Delecroix writes that the autonymous *Discourse* "est un exercice de lecture et de compréhension de la Parole."

Job.³² This discourse was published under his own name and, according to his preface, has a homiletic thrust.³³ However, his populist intentions do not stop him from inserting his more complex ideas concerning subjective reflection and recollection. They are more hidden, seeming more like part of the background rather than the focus. The focus of the discourse is the text itself and what it can do to edify the readers.

The discourse, despite opening with all of Job 1:20–21 as an epigraph,³⁴ focuses mainly on the last proverb that Job pronounces (1:21b). What results is a very close reading with which Kierkegaard wants his readers to identify in order to understand their own faith in God. The first verse and a half are somewhat peculiar to Job's condition at that stage of the narrative and not easily applied to the common nature of Kierkegaard's probable readership. The last proverb, however, has a much more universal thrust and Kierkegaard shows how it is applicable to anyone who reads them.

The applicability of the phrases and one's ability to identify with Job's condition may not seem likely to Kierkegaard's readers at first. But Kierkegaard, through typical irony, shows just how universal this phrase is. He begins by discussing Job as a teacher, but also as one whose actions correspond to what he says.³⁵ Through this activity Job can encourage people who now experience trials. The record of Job's life is not just an interesting story. It rather allows the character of Job to live on as a pedagogue to those who are experiencing trials.

At this point, Kierkegaard makes a surprising move, suggesting that this phrase may not be so universal. Reflecting his dependence on Martin Luther, he writes, "Only the person who has been tried and who tested the saying in being tested himself, only he rightly interprets the saying."³⁶ While

32. Arbaugh, *Kierkegaard's Authorship*, 127.

33. Though he is careful not to call it a homily since he was not ordained to preach. (Kierkegaard, *Discourses*, 107).

34. Ibid., 109.

35. Ibid.

36. Ibid., 112. In Luther's preface to his translation of Job, he writes of the book as a whole, "It is understood only by those who also experience and feel what it is to suffer the wrath and judgment of God, and to have his grace hidden" (Luther, *Word and Sacrament I*, 252). Hendrix writes of Luther's hermeneutic, "there was for Luther a sense in which Scripture was not fully interpreted until it encountered and illumined the life of the addressee" (Hendrix, "Luther Against the Background," 236). See also Bruns, who writes of Luther's hermeneutics, "interpretation is an event that moves in two directions. It is not possible to interpret a text without being interpreted by it in turn" (Bruns, *Hermeneutics Ancient & Modern*, 156). Rasmussen also discusses briefly Kierkegaard's appreciation for Luther's hermeneutic, writing that "Kierkegaard was gratified to see in Luther a forerunner for his own well-known emphasis on subjectivity" (Rasmussen, "Kierkegaard's Biblical Hermeneutics," 256).

this at first seems preposterous, it is merely a rhetorical move by Kierkegaard, who, by the end of the discourse, suggests that all of us have indeed experienced trials analogous to Job's. Thus, when seen through these tried eyes, we are all capable of interpreting this hard phrase; all of us have been tried, so we are all capable interpreters.

Besides being a rhetorical strategy of Kierkegaard, positing a universality onto the text also reveals an important hermeneutical strategy that he upholds throughout the discourse and, indeed, throughout much of his interpretation of Job in *Repetition* as well.[37] The proper way to interpret the book of Job, according to Kierkegaard, is to identify with the character of Job. This goes beyond Job as well. The way to interpret Abraham is to identify with Abraham. That the method of interpreting Job is akin to the method of interpreting Abraham should not be surprising since, as stated above, this is a companion piece to *Fear and Trembling* more than it is to *Repetition*. This is evident in its main themes—faith and worship.

Kierkegaard does not discuss faith and worship alone, but in relation to those topics that arise in the phrase under discussion. He sees this phrase revealing Job's faith in the sovereignty of God and his worship through thankfulness for God's gifts. Considering Job's fate at the hands of natural and human antagonists, his speech strikes Kierkegaard as noteworthy.

Before exegeting the passage in question, Kierkegaard briefly sets the scene, recounting the moment Job hears about the fate that befell his children and property. Job's responds, "Naked I came from my mother's womb, and naked shall I return," putting no blame on God for his own misfortune. Despite his sorrow, Job responds with faith in God's plan.

The next brief section deals with the phrase "the Lord gave, and the Lord took away," which Kierkegaard claims focuses on thanksgiving for the gifts that God gave him. The key to the thanksgiving is the fact that Job not only forgets but is able to remember the gifts with which God has blessed him. This allows Job to detach himself from his loss but not from the memory of his loss. The honesty keeps a transparency between him and God, and the faith he has is for the true God; "the Lord, who had taken [his possessions] away, remained in his upright soul."[38] Kierkegaard presents two hypothetical situations that lead to pain or deceit and contrast with Job's reaction.

Kierkegaard next isolates the clause "the Lord took away" to show that Job is fully confident of the sovereignty of God rather than the mediating

---

37. In *Repetition*, however, he is less explicit about the need for this move. It comes out, instead, in his presentation.

38. Kierkegaard, *Discourses*, 118.

forces that he believes God uses to take away Job's family and possessions. The hypothetical person that Kierkegaard uses to illustrate what Job is *not* is hesitant about where to put the blame for his misfortune. Job has no room for the doubt displayed in the other potential responses because of his faith in the sovereignty of God, but it is also evident that Job is not concerned about the lost possessions if the alternative is a loss of God—that is, the true God who Job is sure is the agent of his current situation. When all material things are stripped from the situation, however important those things are, Job is able to be aware of God and cannot give God up. Though Kierkegaard does not mention Abraham in this section, it is very difficult not to notice the similarities between Job in this discourse and Abraham in *Fear and Trembling*, since both characters experience loss at the hands of God yet do not show anger but acceptance of their loss.

Though Job loses his material belongings, "the Lord did not take everything away, for he did not take praise away from him, and he did not take away peace in the heart, the bold confidence in faith from which it proceeded, but intimacy with the Lord was still his as before . . . and only praise was left and in it his heart's incorruptible joy."[39] Though Job experiences sorrow, he also experiences joy, for the source of Job's joy is God and God remains with him despite his losses.

This is what Kierkegaard seems to want to emphasize the most since he is most concerned with the pastoral application of the verse. He intends to build up his audience with Job as an exemplar. The finale of his discourse counters any hypothetical objection to Job as teacher. Kierkegaard lists many such hypothetical objections and follows them up immediately with ways in which Job is similar to these people: "Are you wise and sensible, and is this your comfort? Job was the teacher of many people. Are you young, and is youth your security? Job, too, was once young. Are you old, on the edge of the grave? Job was an old man when sorrow caught up with him."[40] In the end, Job's example is one that covers much ground. Most people, if not all, can identify with him and with his trials. In fact, freedom from trials is not something that one should desire since the fact of the universality of trials will loom over the one not tested. The psychological damage done to the one dreading future trials is worse than the damage incurred in the actuality of trials.

As far as a homily, Kierkegaard has done a fine job with this discourse. His rhetoric is typical of his ability to seize the reader's attention and, despite the discourse's autonomous authorship, he uses Socratic irony to allow

---

39. Ibid., 122.
40. Ibid., 124.

the reader to arrive at the desired conclusion regarding the interpretation of the text. This does not specify his method of interpretation, however, which remains difficult because of its genre as homily. What one can do is evaluate the conclusions and decide how accurate they are with respect to the text. It is safe to say that an evaluation of Kierkegaard's exegesis of Job 1:20–21 shows that he has contributed an important interpretation of this small section of *Job*. Kierkegaard's reading of Job's first pronouncement after Job's hearing of his tragedy does show much insight and creativity. By showing what Job does not say—"The moment the Lord took everything away, he did not first say, 'The Lord took away,' but first of all he said, 'The Lord gave'"[41]—Kierkegaard focuses on the significance of what he does say. By isolating the phrase from the rest of the text, he is able to focus on the piety of Job in that particular moment, which becomes an important teaching tool for Kierkegaard. When placed back in the context of the book as a whole, a new vision of Job emerges. This holistic Job is the one with whom the Young Man is able to identify in *Repetition*, and some of the themes of that book do present themselves in this later work.

Kierkegaard does not spend much space on verse 20 at all. His exegesis begins in earnest at verse 21b, first focusing on "the Lord gave." He sees Job's words at this juncture as referring to his thankfulness in this surprising time of loss. Rather than shrink from the shock of losing everything that he had, he recalls everything that the Lord had given him with enough gratitude that "it was as if it were not the Lord who took it away but Job who gave it back to him."[42] The key word, repeated several times throughout the section is "recall." He recalled God's goodness, his own prosperity, those who recollected him, his days of glory, and his own righteousness.[43] He has a long memory which leads to a farewell in which he lets everything go and the memory vanishes "like a beautiful recollection."[44] Recollection and memory emerge as very important concepts throughout Kierkegaard's works, and in *Repetition*, Constantin Contantius contrasts the categories of recollection and repetition. Constantin describes repetition as a recollection forward and calls it the Christian answer to the pagan recollection, so it is a little jarring to see this most righteous of all men, bar Jesus, being described by a concept that seems to carry less than positive overtones throughout the Kierkegaardian corpus.

41. Ibid., 115.
42. Ibid., 116–17.
43. Ibid., 116.
44. Ibid.

Kierkegaard's pseudonym William Afham actually uses various terms to describe recollection and distinguishes between memory (*Huskommelsen*) and recollection (*Erindringen*) in *Stages on Life's Way*.[45] In this work, "to remember" (*at huske*) is an indiscriminate act "in that it merely provides 'a mass of details'" while "to recollect" (*at erindre*) is "a cognitive act involv[ing] a reflexive relationship to the person doing the recollecting."[46] Recollection, thus, concerns itself with a specific task while memory is more general. Constantin contrasts recollection (*Erindring*) with repetition (*Gjentagelsen*), a subject upon which we will touch presently.

Note, however, that in the discourse, Kierkegaard uses a third term to describe Job's remembering (*mindes*). Kierkegaard uses *mindes*, likely, because the other two terms would sound out of place in a religious discourse.[47] In everyday Danish, the three terms are largely interchangeable.

Bearing in mind the lack of distinction between the various synonyms of memory, let us note another passage broaching the topic in another of Kierkegaard's publications from 1843, *Either/Or*. The section in this large work entitled "The Unhappiest One" discusses recollection fairly clearly.[48] The essay also makes implicit and explicit references to Job, suggesting that the topics discussed are not merely linguistically related, but also thematically.[49] The general idea of recollection in "The Unhappiest One" is that recollection leads to unhappiness because it focuses on the unreality of what has already past. One who recalls cannot be present to himself since his physical self exists in the present while the self is focusing on the past. This disconnect is the actual cause of unhappiness, but recollection and hope can lead to this absence from oneself. While hope in the future can also lead to unhappiness, recollection has a greater chance of doing so because the past has no chance of becoming present, while what one hopes for in the future can possibly become present.

So why is Job, who recollects so many things in the past, such an exemplar to Kierkegaard's *edifying* discourses if recollection is put in such a bad light? In the author's own words:

---

45. Stokes, "Locke, Kierkegaard," 657.

46. Ibid.

47. Personal email correspondence with Patrick Stokes and Niels Jørgen Cappelørn (21 December, 2009).

48. Kierkegaard, *Either/Or, Part II*, 217–30.

49. One should note also that the pseudonym Kierkegaard uses for "The Unhappiest One" is A, actually an indicator for an anonym. It is likely that this is the same anonymous "author" who penned the letters on Job in *Repetition*, usually known as the young man.

> If, generally, only the person who is present to himself is happy, then these people, insofar as they are only hoping or only recollecting, are in a sense certainly unhappy individualities. But, strictly speaking, one cannot call an individuality unhappy who is present in hope or in recollection. The point to stress here is that he is present in it.[50]

Job, in the moment that Kierkegaard sees as so important to build his audience up, is apparently present in his recollection. The author of "The Unhappiest One" goes on to describe the unhappiest one as

> one in which it is recollection that prevents him from becoming present in his hope and it is hope that prevents him from becoming present in his recollection. This is due, on the one hand, to his continually hoping for that which should be recollected; his hope is continually being disappointed, but he discovers that this disappointment occurs not because his objective is pushed further ahead but because he is past his goal, because it has already been experienced or should have been experienced and thus has passed over into recollection.[51]

It is no surprise, nor likely no problem, that Job is unhappy at that moment. It would be ethically and psychologically problematic if he were not. However, Job shows himself as an example by not hoping for what he recollects. Instead, he moves from recollection of the things the Lord has given him to acceptance that they are gone. Even in the dialogues, he does not hope for that which he recollects despite all of his complaints. He deals with the past in the present rather than hoping for it in the future.

These problems with recollection are discussed in the upbuilding discourse as well in the hypothetical situations that Kierkegaard uses as foils to Job's action. One person may recall the happy days but becomes impatient because that previous joy has "educated and developed him to perceive pain." This, according to Kierkegaard, is a problem with ingratitude and the mis-recollection of the past. He either felt he never appreciated what he had when he had it, or he recollected a distortion of the real past. Another person acts as if he did not lose anything. He avoids dealing with the loss. These two positions reflect the unhappy ones in "The Unhappiest One": the first is absent from himself through recollection, the second is absent from himself through hope. Job, by contrast, sees God as the agent of his past prosperity and gives thanks so that it is not a "restless memory" that runs

---

50. Ibid., 223.
51. Ibid., 225.

out of control.⁵² That is, he does not recollect or hope to the point of being absent from himself.

This explanation of Job's edifying activity comes from the mind of Kierkegaard, but it does encounter some problems. It does seem as though Job in the dialogues acts a bit differently than the Job of the prologue. Kierkegaard does incorporate the Job of the dialogue into his exposition but elides some important aspects of the dialogues. For instance, when discussing all of what Job recollects in his speech, Kierkegaard quotes from 29:8 and 29:13—"when the young withdrew out of respect for him, when the old rose and remained standing" and "the blessing of the abandoned was upon him."⁵³ This suggests that after recollecting these blessings and gifts from God he lets them go as explained above. However, in the book of Job, the character of Job follows up these memories with a speech that would suggest that he is focused on the recollection of or perhaps hoping for the past. Job 30:1 states, "But now they mock me, men younger than I, whose fathers I would have disdained to put with my sheep dogs." There is a sense of despair in Job's comments, comments that show how far he has fallen. Perhaps he does not pine for his former days of glory, but it seems questionable as to whether or not he has truly let go of the past. The majority of the dialogues present Job as less than accepting of his loss. He demands an explanation from God for his suffering, and one may wonder how much attention Kierkegaard pays to the whole book. However, this view of Kierkegaard's reading fails, for the most part, when one considers his other mentions of Job. The young man in *Repetition* is very aware of Job's speeches, and he paraphrases parts of Job's first speech in "The Unhappiest One."⁵⁴ Concerning the truly unhappy persons, he writes:

> we know a worse calamity [than death], and first and last, above all—it is to live[;] ... the unhappiest one of all would be the person who could not die, the happy one the person who could. Happy is the one who died in old age; happier is the one who died in youth; happiest is the one who died at birth; happiest of all the one who was never born.⁵⁵

In the end, the question of whether Kierkegaard misrepresents the dialoguing Job is debatable, but the impression he gives is, for the most part, an insightful and important consideration when evaluating the character of

---

52. Kierkegaard, *Discourses*, 118.
53. Ibid., 116.
54. Kierkegaard, *Either/Or II*, 221.
55. Cf. Job 3:3, 11–13 for the same sentiment from Job himself.

Job. Job never asks explicitly for everything back that he once had, though he is not nearly as reserved in his expression of loss as Kierkegaard seems to imply. A discussion of a key aspect in *Repetition* follows—Job's lack of pining for his lost possessions.

The next section of the discourse is, frankly, less fraught with difficulty. Kierkegaard discusses the significance of the phrase "the Lord took away" in isolation from the rest of the proverb, which is that Job, despite hearing about the mediating agents of Job's loss from the servants—Sabeans, lightning,[56] Chaldeans, a great wind—interprets the true agent as the Lord himself. The effect of this is two-fold. The first is the psychological effect on Job himself. His pronouncement is not a despairing one, but one that sees God. Job's faith in the wisdom of God is great. Rather than being impotent towards his well-being, hoping for what he used to have, he puts his trust in the Creator who bestowed the gifts to him in the first place. The result is that the gifts in which he found so much pleasure do not control him, but direct him to the one who gave them. Once they are gone, his focus is still on the giver of those gifts.

The second effect of this interpretation is political. By ignoring the Sabeans, the Chaldeans, and meteorological powers, he declares them impotent. They are not the controlling influences in the world, they are powerless; they would not have any power had the Lord not given them that power. Just as Job received freely from the Lord, these entities received all their power from the Lord. Thus, Job's faith in God's sovereignty is evident in his speech.

The last section of Job's proverb is about joy in the midst of trials. Kierkegaard does not deny the sorrow that Job must certainly experience, but he finds it noteworthy that Job praises the Lord's name. Though it seems as though God has taken everything from Job, he does leave him praise. Job displays an intimacy with the Lord that is not merely mediated by his possessions but is independent of what God had bestowed on him. In some ways, perhaps it is actually dependent upon what God had taken away from him.

What Kierkegaard has vaguely described in the person of Job at this moment is a repetition. Job's letting go of the past and relying on God for an undefined future is a key aspect of the religious movement of repetition. The next section will highlight these aspects of the category of repetition, a very difficult concept that seems open to many different interpretations. However, this seems par for the course on a concept that is dependent on "freedom."

---

56. Literally "fire of God/gods."

REPETITION AND THE CATEGORY OF REPETITION

After the publication of *Repetition* in 1843, a Professor Johan Ludvig Heiberg published a treatise "with primary emphasis upon the orderly repetitions of the movements of heavenly bodies."[57] In the treatise, Heiberg refers several times to Kierkegaard's previously published work. With characteristic exasperation, Kierkegaard wrote a reply explaining Heiberg's misunderstandings of repetition and accusing Heiberg of reading only half of *Repetition*. Kierkegaard never published his response to Heiberg, which may have something to do with his desire to remain invisible behind his pseudonyms. Though he wrote the open letter under the name Constantin Constantius, his own voice seems to come to the surface more often than his independently published pseudonymous works most often allow. He even points out the fact that his rhetorical style is maieutic and that the first half of the book "is always either a jest or only relatively true," which certainly disrupts the rhetoric itself.[58] Nevertheless, by revealing the man behind the curtain, Kierkegaard allows for a less speculative hypothesis of this notoriously difficult and elusive work. Before moving on to the meat of *Repetition*, it will help to point out some clarifications that Constantin lays out for Heiberg in this rather direct letter.

"Constantin" is quick to clarify that Heiberg's treatment of repetition in discussing the natural world is quite far off the mark. In fact, it seems quite opposite to the point that Constantin is trying to illustrate. Constantin never discusses repetition in nature, but "about repetition in the issues of freedom."[59] He repeats this in the second part of the open letter and explains the "history" of the concept of repetition. In this illustrative section, he anthropomorphizes the concepts of freedom and repetition to go through the stages of freedom in order to show that freedom will paradoxically seek out repetition. These three stages of freedom mimic the "three stages on life's way" that define much of Kierkegaard's work—the aesthetic, the ethical, and the religious.[60] Thus freedom, in the first stage (a), fears repetition "for it seems as if repetition has a magic power to keep freedom captive once it

---

57. Kierkegaard, *Fear and Trembling/Repetition*, 379.

58. Ibid., 303, 305. Note also the way he describes, in the body of *Repetition*, the "author" of *Either/Or*, who "is at times somewhat deceitful, not in the sense that he says one thing and means another but in the sense that he pushes the thought to extremes, so that if it is not grasped with the same energy, it reveals itself the next instant as something else" (*Fear and Trembling/Repetition*, 133).

59. Ibid., 297.

60. Ibid., 301–2.

has tricked it into its power."[61] It is in a state of desire which longs for the new. Repetition, however, appears in this stage and sends freedom into a state of despair, this equaling the aesthetic stage. The second stage (b) is freedom qualified as sagacity, which corresponds to the ethical. In this stage, "repetition is assumed to exist, but freedom's task in sagacity is continually to gain a new aspect of repetition."[62] This also proves difficult as repetition's relentless nature is not fooled by sagacity's ingenuity. This leads to the third stage (c), the religious stage, in which "freedom breaks forth in its highest form, in which it is qualified in relation to itself."[63] In this stage, "freedom's supreme interest is precisely to bring about repetition[;] . . . freedom itself is now the repetition."[64] Freedom, in a sense, needs repetition and will, despite all that is available to it, choose repetition. Thus, repetition in his book is "transcendent, a religious movement by virtue of the absurd" and different from the repetition in the natural world.[65]

Constantin also notes that repetition is a breaking of the past to infinite possibilities and that "eternity is the true repetition."[66] Mooney describes it as "getting our cognitive and moral bearings not through prompted remembering, but quite unexpectedly as a gift from the unknown, as a revelation from the future."[67] Repetition in the natural world is irrelevant to the philosophical category of repetition and distracts from it since one can predict with some certainty when something might repeat. The reader of *Repetition* concludes that the category of repetition only comes "when all human certainty is let go."[68]

61. Ibid., 301.
62. Ibid.
63. Ibid., 302.
64. Ibid.
65. Ibid., 305. The phrase, "by virtue of the absurd" appears often in *Fear and Trembling*, but also features in *Repetition* when Constantin introduces the young man's situation. He writes of the young man's potential for loving the girl, "He has now come to the border of the marvellous; consequently, if it is to take place at all, it must take place by virtue of the absurd" (page 185). In *Fear and Trembling*, de Silentio describes the "knight of faith" as making "one more movement even more wonderful than all the others, for he says: Nevertheless I have faith that I will get her—that is, by virtue of the absurd, by virtue of the fact that for God all things are possible" (page 46). The final phrase recalls Jesus's declaration that it is "easier for a camel to go through the eye of a needle than for the rich to enter the kingdom of God . . . but with God all things are possible" (Matt 19:23–25) The absurd, therefore, indicates an impossible situation where all hope is lost, where one must summon the "strength and energy and spiritual freedom to make the infinite movement of resignation" (page 47).
66. Ibid.
67. Mooney, "Introduction," viii.
68. Croxall, *Kierkegaard Commentary*, 141.

I say "the reader of *Repetition*" with some trepidation since the meaning of the book has eluded many, while some commentators, like Bigelow have concluded that "it is essentially undecidable whether or not we can understand repetition."[69] Poole is even less sure of repetition's graspability, determining after a lengthy interpretation of the book *Repetition* that "there is . . . no Kierkegaardian doctrine of repetition."[70] Poole's deconstruction of *Repetition* contains many important and compelling points and is instructive on the ironic hermeneutic of Kierkegaard, but strikes me as fallacious on two accounts. The first is that, though he rightly notes the shifting definitions of repetition throughout the book which make settling on its true meaning difficult,[71] he does not seem to take seriously that the book refers to itself as a "venture in experimenting psychology." That is, the book progresses to a conclusion after various hypotheses and theories regarding repetition are eliminated or debunked with evidence. The second is that, though Poole relies on postmodern theories regarding the text throughout his book, he seems fixated on how Kierkegaard's biography may have influenced the published form of the book. He calls the young man's eighth letter "inauthentic" since Kierkegaard manipulated the text after he had submitted the manuscript.[72] However, as I intend to show when we arrive at the eighth letter, this reveals the spiritual nature of repetition and effects how one reads the finale of Job as well. To raise questions of Kierkegaard's intention as an author bears some weight, perhaps, but his intention was clearly to publish the book in its final form. So despite Poole's certainty, a doctrine of repetition seems evident if ambiguous. One place to begin to understand it is to note how Constantin contrasts it with the Socratic category of recollection.

Note above how recollection and memory figure into Kierkegaard's interpretation of Job in the upbuilding discourse. Recall that Kierkegaard and his pseudonyms refer to recollection as pagan, pointing to Socrates's claim that truth exists inside everyone. For one to gain truth or learn truth, one must recollect what one already possesses.[73] Kierkegaard notes

---

69. Bigelow, *Kierkegaard and the Problem of Writing*, 167. See also Holm, "Kierkegaard's Repetitions," 16. Holm says that it is "impossible to purge repetition of its confusing rhetoric."

70. Poole, *Communication*, 82.

71. Ibid., 63.

72. Ibid., 73.

73. Evans, *Kierkegaard: An Introduction*, 59. See especially *Phaedo*, where Socrates explains through a series of syllogisms how the immortality of the soul, the continuity of opposites, and knowledge as recollection are all intrinsically related. (Plato, *The Last Days of Socrates*, 92–99).

that the Danish word *Erindring* literally means "internalizing," thus it does not exist externally.[74]

Repetition, by contrast, is external. It is also something that has not yet happened; it is future directed. Rather than looking inward toward what one already possesses, it requires external revelation.[75] The English word "repetition" does not contain this idea etymologically like the Danish word *Gjentagelsen*, which is why some scholars prefer a different English translation, like "resumption,"[76] or "retaking,"[77] and describing it as self-reception rather than self-choice.[78] Thus, the freedom that Constantin discusses in his response to Professor Heiberg is not so much a freedom of choice as it is a freedom from having to choose. The transcendence of repetition points outside oneself to something only a deity can provide, but it results in a wholeness of oneself.

Constantin in the book does not seem to grasp the externality of repetition through the course of his narrative. He wants to control repetition, but control exemplifies recollection. He recognizes that recollection and repetition are functional opposites, but does not discover that they are also opposites methodologically. Ironically, the one who eventually discovers repetition's actuality is the young man Constantin mentors. The young man's exemplar of repetition is the character of Job.

The Job discourses of the young man appear in the second section of the book. As Constantin suggests in his open letter to Professor Heiberg, the first half of the book is only "relatively true." It is a lengthy discussion of the concept of repetition, the situation in which the young man finds himself, and an attempt at repetition by Constantin that ends in failure. The themes that creep up throughout the first half have to do with motion, recollection, hope, Hegelian dialectic, infinite possibility and other motifs that are present throughout the works of Kierkegaard in that era of his writing. It would

---

74. Crites, "The Blissful Security of the Moment," 232.

75. We can see this reiterated somewhat in *Philosophical Fragments*, where "Climacus first develops what he calls the 'Socratic' view of the Truth and how the Truth can be acquired, a view that draws on the Platonic view that humans have an inborn knowledge of 'the Forms,' so that what we call learning is actually 'recollection.' . . . Climacus then pretends to invent an alternative to this view, using the tools of logic and the imagination . . . [which] centers on the idea that human beings have lost the Truth and can only regain it through a Teacher who is both divine and human, an incarnate deity. The Truth on this view must come to humans through a special kind of divine revelation, rather than through any human philosophy" (Evans, *Kierkegaard: An Introduction*, 110).

76. Croxall, *Kierkegaard Commentary*, 128–29.

77. Mooney, *Selves in Discord*, 28.

78. Mooney, "Introduction," xi.

go way beyond the scope of this book to discuss all of these issues, but they are all related to Kierkegaard's understanding of freedom.

The first section of *Repetition* begins with Constantin Constantius recalling an anecdote where Diogenes refutes the Eleatics' denial of motion by walking. This leads Constantin into a discussion of the possibility of repetition. The connections are not obvious between these two topics, but it becomes clear that motion is a key component to repetition in the mind of Constantin. In fact, the question of whether repetition is possible "practically immobilized" him, so he decides to experiment on the possibility himself by taking a trip.[79] At the end of the section, after conceding failure, the despairing Constantin announces that his new symbol is the coach horn. "A coach horn has infinite possibilities, and the person who puts it to his mouth and puts his wisdom into it can never be guilty of a repetition," he writes.[80] But a coach horn is also a symbol of motion. Repetition has paralyzed him and he desires freedom. "Farewell!" he exclaims to the "hope of youth" and, presumably, to the concept of repetition.[81] This, of course, drips with the irony that Kierkegaard loved, as he explains in the open letter that he must have resisted publishing because the irony would die with the public's knowledge of the letter. Constantin fears repetition almost as much as he does not believe in it. Though he searches it out, it seems that he never truly desires repetition in its religious sense. Perhaps he undertakes his experiment in order to prove it does not exist, for he seems desperately unaware of repetitions all around him throughout.

His experiment is to travel to Berlin for a second time, which will seem fraught with problems as a scientific experiment, the first indication of which is on the coach ride to Berlin. After a brief complaint about the discomfort one experiences riding on a coach, he recounts his last trip on the "end seat forward inside the carriage." It was an unpleasant ride, so "hoping at least to remain a limb on a lesser body, [he] chose a seat in the forward compartment. That was a change. Everything, however, repeated itself."[82] This last statement is difficult to take seriously. If there were a change, then there would have been no repetition. Thus, the experiment fails before it begins. Nevertheless, Constantin carries through and includes other dubious episodes that suggest that he is perhaps even oblivious to repetition. Consider that the time of year is not the same and thus the city of Berlin is acting in a different way than they had previously. He arrives in Berlin on the *allge-*

---

79. Kierkegaard, *Fear and Trembling/Repetition*, 131.
80. Ibid., 175.
81. Ibid.
82. Ibid., 151.

meine Busz und Bettag,[83] so the general ethos of the town was different than before. This would seem to prohibit repetition, "but this is of little concern to [his] project. This discovery had no connection with 'repetition,' for the last time [he] was in Berlin [he] had not noticed this phenomenon."[84] At this early point in the narrative, the reader should be aware of the flippancy of Constantin's experiment. He seems to dismiss certain aspects that might have been important.

The almost farcical attempts at his repetition continue even as he appropriately attends a farce at the theatre. As time proceeds his desire for repetition grows, but he is unable to make a religious movement. The repetition he desires is not the repetition that Kierkegaard promotes, but one that cannot be actualized. Constantin's understanding of repetition is false because it focuses too much on the ideal of the past—and in that Hegelian sense it is internalized as idealized. As Holm writes, "The backward direction [of recollection] . . . goes from real to ideal, from reality to language, or as Goethe terms it, from the particular to the universal. Conversely, the divine repetition and allegory share the foreward-going [*sic*] pace from respectively, the ideal to the real, and from language's 'base' to the reality."[85] In the end, Constantin will deem repetition impossible, but not before despairing once more of repetition itself. He does experience repetition at his home, but "of the wrong kind."[86]

Constantin's words contradict each other. There is no repetition, but there is repetition of the wrong kind. The words and actions of Constantin Constantius mean to point us ironically beyond him to the thoughts of Kierkegaard himself. The entire first half of the book is somewhat absurd. Even the play that Constantin attends is a farce, which is hardly an accident.

A farce is not repetitive but free. It inspires multiple interpretations by different individual audiences and different individuals within the audience. It follows no repetitive formula like a comedy or tragedy.[87] In short, it is absurd. And it is absurdity that is the vehicle for the true, divine repetition. The prototype of repetition by virtue of the absurd is Job, who receives everything back double despite his stance against God. The young man is aware of this in the character of Job. And the second half of *Repetition* contains the letters of the young man on this topic.

---

83. The universal day of repentance and prayer that prepares one for Advent.
84. Ibid., 153.
85. Holm, "Rhetorical Reading," 26.
86. Kierkegaard, *F.T./Rep*, 169.
87. Ibid., 160.

The young man's story begins in the first section of *Repetition*, but in some ways it precedes the book altogether. The young man and Kierkegaard have much in common, particularly in their romantic lives. Constantin meets the young man and learns that he has fallen in love with an unnamed woman. His love is overwhelming, but it soon becomes evident that the young man is in love with an idea and not an actuality. He still longs for the woman, but goes through suffering beyond that of ordinary heartbreak.

Constantin's advice is for the young man to transform himself into "a contemptible person whose only delight is to trick and deceive." He also tells him to be "inconstant" and "nonsensical."[88] Constantin, however, is the one who is inconstant in his understanding of repetition, as shown above. But Constantin accuses the young man of not believing in repetition at this point and wonders if he did, "what great things might have come from him."[89] Eventually the tables turn and Constantin is the one who denies that repetition exists while the young man is on the cusp of grasping it.

This table-turning occurs in the second half of *Repetition*. The section begins with Constantin describing the aftermath of his previous advice in the time elapsed. The young man had left the country in order to escape his troubles, but Constantin had feared him dead. One day, though, the young man sends Constantin a letter and follows that one up with several more, spaced about a month apart from each other. The letters do not invite correspondence, but are only one sided. The young man gives no return address and seems only to want to speak with no interruptions or advice. Constantin prints the letters and adds no editorial comments until after the last one. These letters contain the young man's interpretation of Job.

Though the young man's situation regarding the girl may seem trivial to the reader compared to Job's situation, the discrepancy does not stop the young man from identifying with Job. One will recall that this is in line with Kierkegaard's discourse published a few months afterward. Anyone can identify with Job, because everyone has gained and lost possessions. Burgess, in fact, views the young man as a good example of a Joban pupil as described in the discourse.[90] However, the young man goes beyond the prologue of Job and can compare himself with Job throughout the biblical book. His main desire is a repetition, something Constantin accuses him of not believing in. It is not altogether clear if the young man does believe in repetition, but it is what he desires. Just as Job receives everything back

---

88. Ibid., 142.
89. Ibid., 146.
90. Burgess, "Repetition - a Story of Suffering," 258.

double at the end of his eponymous book, the young man desires his life back at the end of his anonymous letters.

THE YOUNG MAN'S LETTERS

Constantin Constantius introduces the second section by analyzing the young man's main problem with the woman. Constantin does not think that the young man can win the girl back, thus only absurdity can accomplish this "repetition." The woman herself is not an actuality but has become an ideal in the mind of the young man, a "reflexion of motions within him."[91] Thus, the problem that must be reconciled is the split within the young man himself. Repetition is a re-taking of himself and this, it turns out, is too transcendent for Constantin.[92] At this point, Constantin compares himself and his mindset to that of philosophers and professors who think only in the immanent. The young man does not seek counsel from Constantin or other worldly thinkers, but from Job, "an unprofessional thinker."[93] Here is the first instance that Constantin and the young man will play roles in the Job narrative. Constantin, so the young man seems to think, shares much in common with Job's friends. He is earnest in his advice, but the advice does not meet the particularity of the young man. It is based too much on the universality of scientific thinkers. What Job experiences is absurd and the young man feels the same about his own experience.

This role-play will work itself out in the young man's letters. He sends a letter every month for about a half a year and each letter exemplifies a stage in the narrative of Job. The epistolary medium allows the young man to express himself through each stage using the emotion he is experiencing at that particular moment, rather than a long explanation from a singular point of view. That is, each letter has a different tone, which is important in understanding Kierkegaard's interpretation of Job. As the letters progress from one month to the next, one witnesses the slow transformation of the young man from aesthete to the beginning stages of the religious. There is trepidatious confusion at the beginning (prologue of Job) followed by rage (chapters 3–27) followed by a movement of faith at the end (chapters 29–31, where Job withdraws from dialoguing with his friends to plead his final defense to God) to wait for God to meet him in the thunderstorm (chapters 38–42). Kierkegaard's Job becomes evident throughout the series

---

91. Kierkegaard, *Fear and Trembling/Repetition*, 185.
92. Ibid., 186.
93. Ibid.

of letters and the young man exemplifies Kierkegaard's hermeneutic in a rather extreme way.

Delecroix argues, in fact, that the young man "fournit le texte kierkegaardien d'un authentique procès de lecture."[94] Delecroix lays out three principles of a Kierkegaardian understanding of a text through reading: 1) "Rejet d'une compréhension explicative . . . au profit d'une relation interne et ambivalente entre le lecteur singulier et le texte." Thus, one determines meaning through the rhetoric of a text rather than the elements. 2) "L'incertitude objective qui caractérise le sens du texte est en réalité l'avantage donné à l'émergence d'une véritable subjectivité qui, dans l'acte de trancher (du sens), se révèle à elle-même en même temps qu'elle choisit, par le biais de propositions le monde qu'elle comprend, la forme de son existence." 3) "Il y a . . . un moment où, dans l'opération de lecture, le sujet qui lit *est* ce qui est lu (le texte est, littéralement, *approprié*)."[95] The young man clearly follows these principles Delecroix proposes, particularly the third, when the young man is appropriated by the text of Job, as will be explained below. He will identify with the posture of Job rather than his literal message; he will appropriate those around him into the text's antagonists; and he will allow the text of Job to read him.

15 August

The first letter by the young man does not reference Job explicitly despite being the longest of his missives. Addressed to *"My Silent Confidant,"* it works mainly as an explanation of his current situation. He has left Copenhagen, symbolic of his absence to himself, and has forced Constantin into being silent by including no return address. The reader also begins to see the young man's displeasure in Constantin's friendship. Constantin's advice cannot relate to his current predicament.

Though the letter has no explicit reference to Job, it foreshadows the young man's imminent identification with the biblical character. It also alludes to Kierkegaard's comparison of Job and Abraham. At around the third page, while questioning Constantin's advice to sacrifice himself for the sake of the girl, the young man alludes to the trial upon which Job puts God while playing with the idea of becoming an unusual hero—"not in the eyes of the world but to oneself—to be able to appeal to nothing in defense against men but to live imprisoned within one's own personality, to have in oneself one's own witness, one's own judge, one's own prosecuting attorney,

---

94. Delecroix, "Quelques Traits," 251.
95. Ibid., 249–50. Emphasis Delecroix's.

and in oneself the only one."[96] Just as Abraham in *Fear and Trembling*, Job is a solitary figure. The crowd does not understand him. Thus the young man will eventually identify with Job. Unlike Abraham, Job tries to contend with his friends, who do not understand him. Abraham tells no one of his plans. Job must eventually lay everything into God's hands after his exasperating conversations while Abraham seems all too aware of the world's opinion before his trial begins. So the young man will identify with Job, not Abraham, since he has an analogue to Job's friends in Constantin Constantius.

The young man, in response to Constantin's advice remarks, "It is true, every word is true, but it is a truth so very cold and logical, as if the world were dead. It does not convince me, it moves me not."[97] Just as the friends rely on cold logic with Job's complaints, the young man sees Constantin doing the same with him. In both cases, the friends cannot see beyond their own knowledge. They have no imagination to see beyond the general consensus. The friends of Job cannot imagine that Job has done nothing wrong and yet still felt what they perceive is the wrath of God. Thus Job is all alone and must plead his case to God alone, the only one with the vantage point to rule in favor of such an absurd possibility. It is only a matter of time before the young man identifies with Job. Once he does so, he does not hold back.

19 September

The second letter is an extended identification with Job. In fact, though it is addressed to the same "*My Silent Confidant,*" Constantin plays no part in it. Throughout the letter, the second person is played only by Job himself. The young man's emotion comes to the fore right away as he repeats the name of Job three times: "Job! Job! O Job! Is that really all you said, those beautiful words: The Lord gave, and the Lord took away blessed be the name of the Lord?"[98] Perhaps Job repeated those words as a mantra. Perhaps he remained silent for seven days. The young man seems to be picking Job's brain so that he can enter it himself. Job's method of repetition becomes the young man's and faith becomes a possibility for the young man.

The young man is enraptured by Job's bravery in the face of God. Certainly this is more effective than comforting oneself with words one knows are not true. Thus the friends do not fear God so much as they are cowards before him. Job, on the other hand, truly fears God even while complaining, for he treats God as if he had his own personality rather than as an

---

96. Kierkegaard, *Fear and Trembling/Repetition*, 190.
97. Ibid., 191.
98. Ibid., 197.

impersonal force. The young man desires the same of himself and encourages Job to continue his complaints so that he may follow suit. He understands that his trial seems trivial compared to that of Job, but suggests, as does Kierkegaard in the upbuilding discourse, that "one who owned very little may indeed also have lost everything . . . he, too, has in a sense been stricken with malignant sores."[99]

This letter contains several explicit references to the dialogues of Job as well as Job's first words. The young man refers to Job's final defense of his ethical behavior in chapter 29, in particular: "You who in your prime were the sword of the oppressed."[100] He also references chapters 7 and 9, which are early defenses of Job. The sentiments of chapter 7 are evident in the young man's complaints. Job responds to his friends' explanations in chapter 6 with his own side of the story, but eventually changes his focus to God. His friends become invisible in the second half of the speech and his addressee becomes God. The young man has yet to reach this stage, but he has alternated from speaking to Constantin in the first letter to speaking directly to Job in the second, imitating Job's rhetorical technique. In the following letters, I contend that the young man will take over the personality of Job and instead of addressing him, address God as Job would have done.

11 October

Roughly one month after addressing Job directly, the young man begins to identify with him in a different way. The October letter is, like the others, addressed to *"My Silent Confidant,"* but the addressee in this letter does not seem to be Job and does not seem to be Constantius Constantius either. Taking his cue from Job, he addresses God. The "Silent Confidant" is the God who waits for 37 chapters to speak to Job. It is when Job is at the end of his rope, yet still maintains his innocence, that God speaks. Job pleads his case and sits and waits for God to speak and so the young man does the same.

The young man begins the letter with a series of questions that only God can answer. He asks, "How did I get into the world?"[101] Later he asks, "How did it happen that I became guilty? Or am I not guilty?"[102] He even seems to wonder if there is a God who can answer him. He writes, "And if I am compelled to be involved, where is the manager—I have something to

---

99. Ibid., 198–99.
100. Ibid., 197.
101. Ibid., 200.
102. Ibid.

say about this. Is there no manager? To whom shall I make my complaint?"[103] In any case, the "manager," even in questioning his existence, displays his desire to speak to a superior in the way that Job does. He does not mention Job explicitly in the letter and one wonders if that is because he has become Job. Many of the questions he asks could have been from the mouth of Job and he concludes that he is "still in the right."[104] His situation, he reminds us, is that he has broken off his engagement with the girl for a reason that he seems unable to explain. Nevertheless, despite the limits of language and its ability to express these inner feelings, he maintains that he is still in the right. Others may disagree with him, but they do not have the perspective that he has on the situation. In much the same way, the friends of Job cannot see how Job can be in the right. They cannot reconcile what has happened to Job with what Job claims he has done or has not done. But they do not have Job's perspective on his own life. So the young man, seeing this dilemma, can identify with Job and enters into Job, appropriating Job's stance as his own.[105]

The young man also makes a veiled reference to Job's parody of Psalm 8. Job 7:17, 18 reads, "What are human beings that you make so much of them, that you give them so much attention, that you examine them every morning and test them every moment?" The young man, who will admit later that he does not quote Job directly, asks, "Must I perhaps repent that the world plays with me as a child plays with a beetle?"[106] So the young man has appropriated Job into himself in more than just attitude.

The young man signs this letter, not as he has in the past with "*your nameless friend,*" but with "*your devoted.*" If the addressee is God, here, the relationship would be different than it would have been between the young man and Constantin or Job. If the young man is to appropriate Job's attitude, he must also place himself under God's trust by trusting in God. Despite his exasperation and confusion in the matter at hand, he recognizes that Job never lessens his devotion to God. Thus the young man devotes himself to his silent confidant, God.

---

103. Ibid., 200. The subject of the young man's agnosticism will arise again below.

104. Ibid., 201.

105. One might note a discrepancy between Job and the young man in that Job is a passive recipient of misfortune while the young man actively engages in the life of Job. By the end of the letters, the young man seems to have realized the discrepancy on his own and chooses to let go. Of course, even here, the young man cannot escape the dilemma if the key to his hermeneutic is to actively appropriate a character.

106. Ibid., 202.

15 November

Constantin Constantius seems the likeliest of addressees of the November letter. The young man discusses Job and God in the third person, but curiously, the letter ends without salutations or a signature. The nameless young man even lacks a title. One must wonder if this gives rise to a text-critical issue in the manuscripts of Kierkegaard. On the other hand, the tone and message of the letter are quite unique and so the missing finale signifies that the young man is perhaps identifying with Job in another way. The young man spends the majority of this significantly less harried letter laying out his hermeneutical method of reading Job. The young man is not interested in scientific analysis of an ancient document. Rather, he is wholly subjective in his analysis, reading Job "with the eyes of the heart, in a *clairvoyance*."[107]

What is also noteworthy in the letter is that the young man claims to refuse to speak the words of Job with anyone else present. Mackey contends that this is because "as the language of God, Job cannot be quoted."[108] But that does not stop the young man from quoting Job while he is alone. His problem does not seem to be with Job but with Constantin. He writes, "I do not even have the heart to write one single outcry from him in a letter *to you*, even though I find my joy in transcribing over and over everything he has said."[109] Later, he states, "I stand up and read in a loud voice, almost shouting, some passage by him."[110] At this point in his journey, the multitude has replaced his life as the meaningless one. The crowd cannot handle the words of Job.

The young man, on the other hand, experiences freedom in the words. They are always fresh to him. He can and does repeat the words of Job because there is freedom in the repetition. Repetition is now something that the young man believes in and desires. He still experiences anxiety when thinking of the infinite possibilities of eternity, but he can identify with Job's words in a way that he could not before. He goes back and reads through them again, beginning with the silence before Job's outburst. He senses the absurdity of them, the crowd cannot understand, but the young man has exhausted all other possibilities and one arrives at repetition when all other possibilities have been exhausted.

---

107. Ibid., 204.
108. Mackey, *Points of View*, 88.
109. Kierkegaard, *Fear and Trembling/Repetition*, 204. Emphasis added.
110. Ibid., 205.

14 December

The tone of the December letter is markedly subdued compared to the previous ones. The young man writes with confidence and reservation and, like Job, "trusts that God can" solve his problems.[111] Job is confident that he is in the right and, despite the conclusions drawn by his friends, upholds his convictions. His friends give suggestions that could relieve his suffering, but Job recognizes that pleading guilty for a lighter sentence is beyond wrong, it is demonic. The friends focus on the result and work from there. Job, however, focuses on God. He does not place him under "ethical determinants," but loves and trusts him as an independent and subjective personality.[112] For the friends, everything is established, while Job treats everything as free, with infinite possibilities.

This conclusion is absurd, of course.[113] And so the young man introduces another category to explain Job's situation. "The whole thing is an *ordeal*."[114] The young man explains later, "Job's significance is that the disputes at the boundaries of faith are fought out in him, that the colossal revolt of the wild and aggressive powers of passion is presented here."[115] Job's ordeal is transcendent—it cannot be explained by science or ethics or even dogmatics because these are too objective. The situation in which Job finds himself relates him directly to God with no mediator. These other areas cannot give birth to repetition, as Constantin found. Rather, repetition can only come by God. This puts Job in direct conflict with his friends who view Job's situation under ethical determinants.[116] However, Job's friends seem incapable of viewing Job's situation as "religious" because to them it actually looks like godlessness, isolating Job even further from his friends who, despite working from the ethical stage, do so in the guise of the religious stage.[117] The ordeal, therefore, acts as a sign of Job's intense God-relationship in that no one else participates in that particular ordeal other than Job and God.

The young man ends the letter with "*your devoted*" again, but the addressee is clearly Constantin. The frustrations that Constantin has brought upon the young man do not change their relationship. Job's friends remain his friends, despite their wrong-headedness. In fact, the young man will sign the last three letters this way before experiencing his own storm.

111. Ibid., 207.
112. Ibid. Note here again the relationship between *Repetition* and *Fear and Trembling*.
113. See ibid., 185.
114. Ibid., 209.
115. Ibid., 210.
116. Damgaard, "My Dear Reader," 99.
117. Polk, *Biblical Kierkegaard*, 181, 189.

Each Time I Come to a Word, It Is Again Made Original

Note that at this point, the young man still lacks much similarity with Job despite imitating the biblical character. Like Constantin, the young man is still interested in results.[118] He wants what Job received and so follows Job's lead. Job, on the other hand, did not know what he would receive. He bases his posture on his principles rather than on any expectation of what might happen because of his stance. He is confident that God would declare him in the right, but does not betray any knowledge that God might reward him with material goods. The young man will begin to learn this in the later letters.

13 January

The January letter is short and acts mainly as a conclusion of the young man's exegesis of Job. The thunderstorm is over in the Job narrative and the young man uses the conclusion of the biblical story to anticipate his own repetition. Job remains friends with Eliphaz, Bildad, and Zophar and God has given him everything double. Job has stood up to God and God has rebuked him. But he is blessed because of it. The young man foreshadows this in the November letter when he writes that every word of Job "is laid upon my sick heart as a God's-hand-plaster. Indeed, on whom did God lay his hand as on Job!"[119] The hand of God can hurt and heal and either is preferable to nothing. And yet it is difficult to determine the difference between punishment and praise by God in this absurd world. In January, the young man writes, "Was Job proved to be in the wrong? Yes, eternally, for there is no higher court that the one that judged him. Was Job proved to be in the right? Yes, eternally, by being proved to be in the wrong *before God*."[120] After reading the book of Job, the young man can believe in repetition, but admits that it is elusive. Repetition occurs "when every *thinkable* human certainty and probability were impossible."[121] The friends believed that repetition occurred at the submission to punishment, but Job knew that he did not deserve it so the perceived punishment was not actually punishment at all.

But the repetition for Job is not that he received everything material back. Rather, Job received himself back. He was proved to be in the right by God, just as he was in the right before the wager between God and the Satan. Thus his person was no longer split. He became present to himself again. The young man wants the girl back, but his real desire is to be present to himself. Whether the young man was ever present to himself in the past

118. Burgess, "Repetition—A Story of Suffering," 257.
119. Kierkegaard, *Fear and Trembling/Repetition*, 204.
120. Ibid., 212.
121. Ibid.

as Job might have been is beside the point. True repetition is transcendent. Job's material items are merely a symbol of the repetition if they are even that. The young man may not fully understand this at this point. It is only after his own storm that this will become evident to him.

17 February

Whereas Constantin Constantius chooses the coach horn as his symbol and desires mobility at the end of the first section, the young man chooses immobility in order to bring on repetition. This recount of the young man's position, his "standing *suspenso gradu*," acts as an *inclusio* to Constantin's announcement at the beginning of the book that the idea of repetition immobilized him.[122] The young man has decided to let go and wait for a thunderstorm like Job in chapter 31 who had nothing more to say and so stopped speaking. His friends stopped speaking as well because Job was righteous in his own eyes (32:1). The young man mimics Job, but with the benefit of hindsight. Job was not aware of what would happen to him, the young man is hoping for the same thing that happened to Job.

To be fair, the young man is open to the possibility of the impossibility of repetition, but it is repetition he desires. What he believes repetition will mean for him is that it will make him fit to be a husband. He will receive the girl again without the anxiety that kept him from following through with that relationship. But this will require him to change drastically, so much so that he will not even recognize himself.

It is clear that he is not sure that this is what he wants. However, he has exhausted all other possibilities. There is nothing else for him to do but wait and have faith that he is in the right and the thunderstorm will come. It should be noted that he does not name the thunderstorm as God or as coming from God. The young man makes a religious move, as Constantin suggests, but he comes across as an agnostic in several of his letters. Damgaard astutely notes that in the October letter, the young man asks for a "manager" [*Dirigent*] and even wonders if there is no manager, whereas in the book of Job, no one even questions the existence of God despite the inability to answer to God's seeming inactivity.[123] Even in the letter addressed to God, God is not explicitly mentioned and, if it is God, God is "silent." So the young man is still far from Job in this sense.

---

122. Ibid., 214, 131.

123. Damgaard, "My Dear Reader," 97. See Kierkegaard, *Fear and Trembling/Repetition*, 200.

However, the young man is aware of the concept of God as presented in the book of Job and his desire is for God to meet him in a thunderstorm however impossible that seems. The young man waits, and does not write Constantin again for three months.

31 May

Before the last letter arrives, Constantin Constantius interjects with some incidental observations. Constantin has no confidence in the storm for which the young man awaits. He believes the young man must be delusional to make a religious move. The objective truth, what he calls sagacity, would have been the only true option the young man would have had, according to Constantin. Constantin is confident enough in his own advice that he believes that the young man made a mistake in not taking it.

Constantin represents at least two people outside of the narrative in *Repetition*. The first is the Hegelian who believes that "the idea . . . is the most reliable in the world."[124] The Hegelian is, of course, a common foil for Kierkegaard, so this is no surprise, but Constantin also represents Elihu here. The young man places Elihu alongside the friends of Job in the December letter. Elihu, the patient observer who has heard the debate on both sides, rises up after Job has finished speaking to explain one more time that Job is receiving punishment for his sins.[125] Here, after having heard all that the young man has said, Constantin still denies the existence of repetition. However, he does not view the young man as being punished in an archaic religious system, but rather he is not capitulating to the dominant system of the day—Hegelianism. Kierkegaard seems to see Hegelianism as a new manifestation of retributive theology, a system in its own right, detaching itself from human experience in order to gain an objective perspective of it.[126] As Stephen Crites notes, Kierkegaard views Hegel as a continuation of the Greek concept of recollection versus the Christian repetition. The world-historical system that makes up Hegel's philosophy of history does not allow for the individual's decisive moment that brings the past Christ event to the present, disrupting the organic temporal. The "simple continuity" of Hegelian history is an offense to the freedom of repetition.[127] The religious stage

---

124. Ibid., 218.
125. Ibid., 208.
126. Gardiner, "Kierkegaard, Søren Aabye." See also Thulstrup, *Kierkegaard's Relation to Hegel*, 350.
127. Crites, *In the Twilight of Christendom*, 82–83.

for Kierkegaard, by contrast, works not within a fixed, deterministic order, but with and against a personality.

When the young man writes Constantin, he announces that the girl has married. And despite his desires in the previous letter, he has experienced a repetition. He thought that a repetition was that he would receive the girl back, but it is really that he receives himself back. He revises his thesis on Job's repetition after his own subjective experience counters his previous hypothesis. "I am unified again," he writes.

> Compared with such a repetition, what is a repetition of worldly possessions, which is indifferent toward the qualification of the spirit? Only his children did Job not receive double again, for a human life cannot be redoubled that way. Here only repetition of the spirit is possible, even though it is never so perfect in time as in eternity, which is the true repetition.[128]

What the young man discovers is that the epilogue to the book of Job has deceived him. When Job receives everything back double, it is only a bonus. The true repetition comes when God declares Job in the right. It comes when Job receives a "double sense of [his life's] meaning."[129] What he knows about the world had been validated. The truth comes not from a system akin to mathematics, but by virtue of the absurd. The young man becomes himself again when he finds out that the girl had married. Even acknowledging the storm does not prepare him for it.

He finishes his letter with jubilation. He praises feminine generosity, the freedom of which symbolizes the freedom of eternity and the freedom of repetition. The praise overwhelms the last lines. There is no salutation, suggesting that the praise continues on to eternity. The finale is free, the goal of repetition.

CONCLUSION

The letters of the young man present the reader with a gradual unveiling of an interpretation of the book of Job. The young man clearly knows the book of Job well before he even sends the letters since he admits to having read it repeatedly. But he does not fully understand the book until he experiences something similar to Job. The two characters' experiences do not resemble each other much physically, but spiritually. The young man reflects the character of Job a great deal, at least to himself.

128. Kierkegaard, *Fear and Trembling/Repetition*, 221.
129. Ibid.

At the conclusion of the letters, the young man claims both he and Job have experienced repetitions. On the surface, however, this would not seem to be the case. Job receives everything he lost back times two except for his children. The young man, though, does not receive any physical remuneration for the ordeal he underwent. The young man, at that point in his own narrative, claims that Job's belongings must be irrelevant to his repetition. The young man receives himself back "and in such a way that [he has] a double appreciation of what this means."[130] The worldly goods have little relevance in this spiritual repetition.

This revelation of the young man bears general hermeneutical import as well as significance in Kierkegaard's interpretation of Job in particular. Job's singular experience, where a blameless person loses everything he owns and receives it back again, can still be appropriated spiritually by someone like the young man.

The transcendence of a true repetition means that one receives oneself back, not people or things outside of oneself. Job proves himself to be in the right by God, thus his person is no longer split. The young man wants his betrothed back, but he finds that his real desire is to become present to himself.

The key to understanding Job to the young man lies in Job's bravery in the face of God. Certainly this is more effective than comforting oneself with words one knows are not true. Thus the friends do not fear God so much as they are cowards before him. Job, on the other hand, truly fears God even while complaining, for he treats God as a free agent rather than as if God is an impersonal force.

The hand of God can hurt and heal and either is preferable to nothing according to both Job and the young man. However, it is difficult to determine the difference between punishment and praise by God in this absurd world. In January, the young man writes, "Was Job proved to be in the wrong? Yes, eternally, for there is no higher court than the one that judged him. Was Job proved to be in the right? Yes, eternally, by being proved to be in the wrong *before God*."[131] The November letter presents God's touch as ambiguous. It is violent, but it is also benevolent because it comes from God.

---

130. Kierkegaard, *Repetition and Philosophical Crumbs*, 74.

131. Kierkegaard, *Fear and Trembling/Repetition*, 212. The young man's assertion that Job is in the wrong before God relates to Kierkegaard's theology, which stems from his Lutheran background. Gerhard Ebeling outlines well Luther's theological anthropology as based on what he calls "*coram*-relationship" (Ebeling, *Luther*, 192–202). Luther describes one "becoming a sinner" as "referring not merely to the falling into sin of a sinless person, but of the recognition by a sinner that he is a sinner, whereby he first becomes a sinner in the strict sense" (page 197). In Luther's thought, one becomes present to another through a face-to-face relationship. *Coram* corresponds well with the Hebrew word לפני- where the presence of one implies the presence of two people

Read Him Again and Again

Looking at Kierkegaard's two works on Job, published within a few short months from each other, one might struggle to notice any similarities. In one, Job remembers, in the other, he repeats. One is a very close reading and earnest portrayal of the Job of the prologue while the other is an artistic portrayal of the poetic sections. The Job of the discourse epitomizes the "patient Job" of the Christian tradition while the Job of *Repetition* is contentious, intransigent, and even seems to flounder about while searching for the correct response to his loss.

One might be tempted to argue that Kierkegaard has chosen to separate the two different tales of Job in the canonical book as a type of form-critical reading. The earnest and prosaic style of the discourses matches well the prose narrative of the pious Job. Likewise, the poetic young man matches the Job of the poetic section—Constantin after all does proclaim the young man a poet.[132] Perhaps Kierkegaard found the two sections of the book of Job irreconcilable for a critic and chose to interpret them separately. We cannot know for sure what his motives were, but there is some sense to this logic.

On the other hand, while Kierkegaard focuses sharply on the prosaic Job in the discourse and the young man spends the majority of his letters in the poetic Job, both narrators use both sections of the book of Job to support their points. In the discourse, Kierkegaard elaborates on all that Job lost using Job's descriptions in chapters 4 and 29.[133] In the September letter of *Repetition*, the young man briefly discusses Job 1:21.[134]

More importantly, Kierkegaard's two different works on the book of Job act as complementary readings. By focusing in the discourse on the proverb of 1:20–21, showing Job at, ostensibly, his most pious, Kierkegaard reminds his readers that Job is radically monist. The Job of the prologue refuses to give the Sabeans credit for his loss, laying all of the "blame" on God. The flip side of Job's pious belief in God's sovereignty is that when he feels he does not deserve his misfortune, he can only look to God. Not so his friends, who place the blame on Job for not participating in the system they perceive at work in the world. Job, to be sure, is a believer in a version

---

face-to-face (ibid., 193). Ebeling continues: "the essential object of Luther's thought when he considers this *coram*-relationship is presence in the strict sense, the presence which makes its object present. And the presence which makes its object present is God alone. Thus the fundamental situation of the *coram*-relationship is existence *coram Deo*, existence in the sight of God, in the presence of God, under the eyes of God, in the judgement of God, and in the word of God" (ibid., 199).

132. Kierkegaard, *Repetition and Philosophical Crumbs*, 79. Constantin describes a poet as an exception, comparing the young man to Job in this regard, while drawing attention to the poetry of Job.

133. Kierkegaard, *Discourses*, 114.

134. Kierkegaard, *Fear and Trembling/Repetition*, 197.

of this system as well during the early stages, but seems to feel it has been short-circuited in some way, hence his forensic challenge to God. The young man, like Job, has a vision of what a repetition consists in, which differs from Constantin's vision. The young man seeks his repetition by following a system akin to his interpretation of the book of Job. What he realizes at the end, however, is that he cannot control the repetition since it occurs outside of a defined system. He comes to this realization and indirectly presents his reader with an interpretation of Job that views God as a personality not beholden to rules but as a free agent who sometimes acts in what a human might perceive as absurd.

4

The Goodness of God beyond Good and Evil

Wilhelm Vischer on Job as a Witness to Jesus Christ

"Does Job fear God for nought?" The words of the Satan are the driving force behind Wilhelm Vischer's exposition of the book of Job, called, "*Hiob*, Ein Zeuge Jesu Christi."[1] Many commentators find this an important verse, but do not imbue it with the same importance as Vischer. Throughout his exposition, this "for nought" is the one line to which he returns over and over. It is the question the book intends to answer, he argues, and so he traces the idea through all forty-two chapters to see how the book does answer the question. What he discovers, or at least intends to uncover for the reader, is that the question changes. A book that begins with a question about theological anthropology turns to a question about theology proper. It becomes evident to Vischer through the discourse that Job answers the first question in the affirmative. Job remains steadfast in his insistence that he is innocent, but not only that, he also remains steadfast in his devotion to God. Despite his feelings of betrayal by God, he continues to fear God. Vischer sees chapter 19 as the turning point in the book of Job, for though Job feels abandoned by

---

1. Vischer, "*Hiob*, Ein Zeuge Jesu Christi," 4–36.

The Goodness of God beyond Good and Evil

God, he firmly believes that he will see God with his own eyes. Once Job affirms his devotion to God, Vischer argues that the question of the book changes to one on the nature of God's righteousness.

The means by which the Satan and God attempt to answer the question raises another question for Job and his friends. Vischer writes, "The original question whether God's confidence in Job's piety was justified has been changed more and more clearly in the speeches into the question whether Job's trust in God's goodness is justified."[2] Job's arguments with his friends deal mainly with the question of God's righteousness and what it entails. Can one determine the nature of God's goodness and righteousness based on the laws passed down from tradition or is God's goodness a "goodness that lies beyond good and evil?"[3]

The conclusions at which Vischer arrives show how he fits into and contributes to the moral imagination that both Kierkegaard and Barth embody as well. The ethical world that the friends describe through the book is one of give and take. The economy of retribution is a universal code that anyone can parse with keen logic. Job knows that this is not the case and that code must not be above God. Echoing both Kierkegaard and Nietzsche, the God of Job suspends the ethical, for the goodness of God is beyond good and evil. This supersession of the ethical also relates to Barth's insistence on seeing the book of Job as a discourse on the freedom of God. Vischer contends that not even the law that God lays forth can be over God himself.

What follows exposits Vischer's exposition of the book of Job paying attention to his historical and cultural context, his method of interpretation, exegetical techniques, and theological presuppositions. The first section will examine his historical context, which I argue directly contributes to his unique interpretation of Job. As a Swiss outsider in interbellum Germany, his work on Job along with his similarly styled commentary on Esther, was a subversive comment on the political situation that gave rise to the Third Reich. The second section will follow his line of argument on the book of Job from the prologue through the dialogues and to the epilogue. His general method of interpretation will be evident through this exposition, but the third section will look at details of his discourse that betray his method of exegesis and attention to historical critical matters. The question will arise as to how these details contribute to his overall argument as well as if some of his arguments require omissions of other important data. The final section will then examine his Christological interpretation and the theological and exegetical presuppositions that contribute to this typology or allow for it.

2. Vischer, "Witness of Job I," 53.
3. Ibid., 42.

Read Him Again and Again

WILHELM VISCHER, THE BOOK OF JOB, AND THE SO-CALLED *JUDENFRAGE*

An Old Testament scholar during the height of the neo-Marcionite movement in the first half of the twentieth century, Vischer spent much of the early part of his career battling the hostile preconceptions concerning the Hebrew Scriptures. In retrospect, many find his approach overshoots his goal. His most famous work, an unfinished three volume commentary of the Hebrew Scriptures titled *Das Christuszeugnis des Alten Testaments*, roughly the Witness of the Old Testament to Christ, posits a typological and, some would argue, anachronistic approach to reading the Old Testament. But criticisms of his work tend toward anachronism themselves, failing to take into account Vischer's own context and goals during this period.

Throughout his works, Vischer engages in traditional Old Testament interpretation including historical criticism as well as more rhetorical approaches. However, Vischer never stops with exegesis. He was an ordained minister and felt compelled to write most of his works in order to edify the church. Because he believed Christ to be the Word of God, he argued that the Bible, both Old and New Testaments, focus on Christ as well.[4]

Vischer delivered his lecture "*Hiob, ein Zeuge Jesu Christi*" in October of 1932,[5] just before Hitler claimed power in January of 1933 and about a year before the Nazis forced Vischer to step down from his teaching post at Bethel seminary. At that time he would move back to his home country of Switzerland. Though Hitler was not yet in control at the time Vischer presented his lecture, the political climate was ripe in Central Europe for official anti-Semitic policies. The Nazis did not transform Germany as much as they reflected the sentiments already present.

The timing of his mini-commentary on the book of Job and its subsequent republications in journals such as Karl Barth's *Zwischen den Zeiten* in late 1933 and in Bonhoeffer's *Bekennende Kirche* in 1934, 1938, and 1942 and as "The Witness of Job to Jesus Christ" in *The Evangelical Quarterly* in early 1934 and in *The Churchman* in 1934[6] suggest a timely impact among Christians concerned with the political tenor of Germany in the mid 1930s. Indeed, the *Evangelical Quarterly* piece comes attached with a note from the translator Allan Ellison on the tenuous state of Bethel Seminary during the tumultuous times of the era.

---

4. Felber, *Wilhelm Vischer Als Ausleger*, 34.

5. The text I am working with is in Vischer, "*Hiob*, Ein Zeuge Jesu Christi." The English versions are found in Vischer, "Witness of Job I," and Vischer, "Witness of Job II."

6. The last is an abbreviated version: Vischer, "God's Truth and Man's Lie," 131–46.

The Goodness of God beyond Good and Evil

After examining the general situation in the German church during this dark period in Europe, I will examine Vischer's role in the Confessing Church, specifically examining his essay on the book of Job as indicative of his prescient attitudes toward the church, the state and, perhaps, the Jews.

The General Situation in the German Church

Looking back at the relationship between the church, the Third Reich, and the Jews during the early 1930s, one tends to dichotomize the church into one of two camps—the German Christian camp and the Confessing Church. Reality, of course, points to a much more complicated situation. The Christians who criticized or opposed the Nazis did not make up a monolithic consciousness but displayed a series of complex attitudes toward the state and the Jews. Stephen Haynes discusses this in an article on "Jews and Judaism in Anti-Nazi Religious Discourse" arguing that the Confessing Church, despite its quasi-heroic status among many in retrospect, perhaps seemed so ineffective in quelling Nazi aggression toward the Jews because it actively did very little to stop it. Haynes points out that the Confessing Church "never officially protested the Nuremberg Laws[;] . . . the Barmen Declaration of 1934 avoided a direct encounter with the 'Jewish Question,' . . . Dietrich Bonhoeffer decided early on that prospects of effective resistance to Nazism did not exist in the ecclesiastical realm, and . . . after *Kristallnacht*, the confessors responded to Nazi anti-Jewish actions only when they affected church members."[7] This list, sadly, describes some of the more benign responses to the oppression of the church by the state. All too commonly, the church's defense of itself from the Nazis merely deferred persecution toward the Jews.[8]

Other attitudes did, however, emerge that expressed more tolerance for the Jews, including attempts to protect the Jewish people from further persecution, but these had their own problems. The most common of these strategies bestowed a mythical status on the Jewish people by virtue of their genetic relationship to Jesus and Christianity. The most well-known practitioner of this theory is Dietrich Bonhoeffer. Bonhoeffer, early in the Nazi takeover, described the Jews as mysterious wanderers, tossed to and fro by the course of history, and in some ways paints them as passive characters not in control of their own destiny to the point that their suffering came from divine necessity.[9]

---

7. Haynes, "Enemies," 341.

8. For examples, see ibid. Other sources include Gutteridge, *Open Thy Mouth*, Gerlach, *And the Witnesses Were Silent*. Also see Scholder, *The Churches and the Third Reich*.

9. Haynes, "Enemies," 362–65. This understanding of the Jew as mysterious

Read Him Again and Again

What hovers over these attitudes and actions of Christians and neo-Pagans between the wars is the so-called *Judenfrage* or "Jewish Question." Broadly stated, what must one do with the Jews who seem reluctant to assimilate into the European or German cultures? What began as a cultural and religious issue, though, increasingly led to questions of race. If the Jews are a cultural or religious problem, assimilation always seems possible, but if one perceives race to be at the root of the problem, the desire for assimilation increasingly leads to the necessity of extermination.

Wilhelm Vischer distinguishes himself from his contemporaries throughout this period, eventually leading to his ouster from Germany because of his views on the Jews and the Old Testament. By way of explanation, let us look briefly at some of his other works written around the same period as his Job essay. The three versions of the Bethel Confession illustrate the political and theological situation of the time well. Though many scholars contributed to the 1933 Lutheran creed, Vischer only worked on the second draft, called the August Version. Vischer specifically penned the section titled "The Church and the Jews," much of which finds its way into his interpretation of Esther several years later, perhaps because the final editors omitted much of his most pointed comments.[10] The final version, "the November Version," flattens the most pro-Jewish comments and even inserts some that one could perceive as pejorative, including a line concerning the "Judaistic enthusiasm" that distinguishes the faith of the Jewish Christian from the Gentile Christian by blood.[11] This line aside, the November Version's section on the church and the Jews mainly argues that the anti-Semitism of the state interferes with the church's job in converting and baptizing the Jews.

Both versions emphasize the importance of the church's mission to the Jews. However, Vischer's August version contains several references to the Jewish people's chosen status with God. Vischer calls them a "sacred remnant" and "the chosen people" and contends that God remains "faithful to Israel." This clearly coincides with Bonhoeffer's "mystery people" thesis and indeed Bonhoeffer preferred the August version to the subsequent final draft from November. But along with the mythic status that Vischer seems to grant to the Jews, he also writes that "it can never in any case be the

---

wanderer had prominence even among those more sympathetic to the causes of National Socialism. As a member of the NSDAP, Gerhard Kittel wrote a famous tract *Die Judenfrage*, which encourages the assimilated Jew to accept the God ordained role of a 'restless and homeless alien wandering over the earth, waiting patiently for the Promised Day of the Lord" (In Gutteridge, *Open Thy Mouth*, 113).

10. Ford, "Bonhoeffer, Luther, and the German Resistance," 18.

11. November version of Bethel Confession acquired from www.lutheranwiki.org.

The Goodness of God beyond Good and Evil

mission of any nation to take revenge on the Jews for the murder committed at Golgotha,"[12] thus anticipating and attempting to diffuse any violence committed upon the Jews in the future. Significantly, the later editors of the November version omit this line. They also omit a line that strikes an eerily foreboding note years before *Kristallnacht*. In the August Version Vischer writes, "'Gentile' Christians should be ready to expose themselves to persecution before they are ready to betray in even a single case, voluntarily or under compulsion, the church's fellowship with Jewish Christians that is instituted in the Word and sacrament."[13]

Another of Vischer's works at the time was his essay "Esther,"[14] which shares much in common with his interpretation of Job, in that it finishes a brief commentary on the book with a series of parallels between the story of Esther and the story of Jesus. Without going too deeply into his interpretation of Esther, I should point out that Vischer makes it very clear, by examining the agents of Jesus's crucifixion, that both Jews and Gentiles, that is the entire human race, share the guilt in the death of Christ. He does not excuse Pilate since Pilate was the ultimate agent of the crucifixion, a method of execution that the Jews would not allow themselves to use. More importantly, Vischer claims that God "vindicates His election and conservation of Israel, and fulfils all His promises to His chosen people" because Jesus died as the King of the Jews.[15] He even argues that the crucifixion and resurrection atones, not only for the sins between people and God but between Jew and non-Jew. In their collusion against Jesus, they "both live solely by His grace, which is proffered to them in the message that God has made One to be a curse and gloriously raised Him up again because He has mercy on all."[16]

Vischer claims God answers the Jewish Question in Christ since Christ, as the King of the Jews, dies by the hand of Jews and Gentiles alike and rises from the dead for all, precluding any need to discuss the Jewish Question. On the other hand, Vischer does not claim that the equality between Jews and Gentiles obviates discussion of Jewish peculiarity in total. The Jews and Gentiles can claim equal citizenship in the kingdom of God, but God does not revoke his promise to either.

He goes on to suggest that the delay in Christ's return results from the Jews' refusal to convert. He calls for the preservation of the Jews as opposed

---

12. "The Bethel Confession: August Version," www.lutheranwiki.org/The_Bethel_Confession:_August_Version#The_Church_and_the_Jews (accessed 20 October 2008).
13. Ibid.
14. Vischer, "Esther (German)."
15. Vischer, "Esther (English)," 15.
16. Ibid.

Read Him Again and Again

to the discrimination of them because they remain a central aspect of the Christian mission. God desires their salvation, Vischer interprets from Paul, and cannot "invalidate this possibility of salvation" since God does not break promises.[17]

Vischer's interpretation of Esther uses the entire corpus of Scripture to argue for the relenting of discrimination against the Jews in central Europe. In the end, though some may view his argumentation as archaic, one must not fail to see his purpose in writing as well as his audience. Rolf Rendtorff notes Vischer's uniqueness in his day in that he struggled with the position the Jews held in biblical studies and theology while most simply ignored the issue altogether.[18] Vischer's stance against the dominant voices of the day should be considered nothing less than brave. Just four weeks after Hitler's call for a boycott of all Jews and their businesses, to begin in April 1933,[19] Vischer presented to a conference in Lemgo an essay called "Zur Judenfrage," which consisted of three main theses:

> 1. die vom Neuen Testament gezeigte Notwendigkeit eines biblischen Kanons, der das Alte Testament enthalte, für den christlichen Glauben; 2., daß dieser doppelte Kanon dem Glauben des geistlichen Israels (= der Kirche) die Erkenntnisgrundlage für den Willen ihres Herrn ist und 3., daß derselbe für die Lebensordnung von Völkern und Staaten richtunggebend ist.[20]

What becomes clear in these three theses is how much Vischer's biblical theology contributes to his political stances. However, it may also be possible that his political circumstances contributed to his unique interpretive methods as well. They are likely in symbiosis. Note, for instance that he wrote his interpretation of Job in 1932, before the NSDAP came into power. "*Hiob*, ein Zeuge Jesu Christi" lacks not only mention of the Jews and their relationship to the Bible or the church, but also lacks the more forceful Christological interpretation that appears in the *Christuszeugnis*. Nevertheless, the Job essay of 1932 still contains a somewhat striking Christological interpretation of the book of Job that many in his cultural and historical context would have been shocked to hear. Thus, one can postulate that Vischer's theology and hermeneutical presuppositions regarding the role the Old Testament plays in the faith of the Christian leads him to his stance on the Jews and their relationship to the *Tanakh*, but that the political

---

17. Ibid., 20.
18. Rendtorff, *Canon and Theology*, 88.
19. See Scholder, *Churches and Third Reich*, 264ff..
20. Felber, *Wilhelm Vischer Als Ausleger*, 61–62.

The Goodness of God beyond Good and Evil

situation as it emerged in 1933 gave him the impetus to make more politically assertive statements.

One thing clear all along is that though the political climate of the time meant that many dismissed the Old Testament from Christian theology on account of its Jewishness even before 1933,[21] Vischer always maintained that the Old Testament was a Christian book. For Vischer, one needs the Old Testament to know about Christ, for:

> the Old Testament tells us *what* the Christ is; the New, *who* He is. . . . So the two Testaments, breathing the same spirit, point to each other, "and there is no word in the New Testament that does not look back to the Old, in which it is foretold," and all the words of the Old Testament look beyond themselves to the One in the new in whom alone they are true.[22]

The New Testament's claims about Christ sends him to the Old Testament to discover more about Christ, which points him back to the New Testament. The New Testament, though, cannot exist without the Old Testament. Wilhelm Vischer's recognition of the importance of the Old Testament to Christian theology leads him to appreciate the culture from which it arises. His essay on the book of Job shows how he depends on both testaments to interpret the text, though in a manner which is more subdued than in his work just a brief period later.

VISCHER'S INTERPRETATION OF THE BOOK OF JOB

Vischer's work begins by presupposing the general consensus of the question the book of Job intends to answer—why does God allow an innocent person to suffer? But Vischer makes some important observations early on that he expands in the body of his essay which put that question in doubt. Consider that the original controversy between God and the Satan does not concern itself with suffering. Also note that the sufferings of Job are not spelled out specifically in the dialogues. Thus, the actual question that Job intends to answer is "can someone fear God for nought?" That scholars suggest this so rarely should strike one as odd since the Satan asks the question explicitly and it spurs the suffering that Job experiences.

Vischer goes about his commentary scene by scene, highlighting and explaining the aspects of each scene that contribute to his argument. Vischer reads the whole book as if it attempts to answer the Satan's question,

21. Rendtorff, *Canon and Theology*, 78–79.
22. Vischer, *Das Christuszeugnis I*, 7.

Read Him Again and Again

"Does Job fear God *for nought*?" until a satisfactory answer can be surmised. The Satan wonders if piety can ever exist outside of self interest and doubts God's confidence in Job.

Piety, according to Vischer, means "to fear, love and trust God above all things," which Job does display after losing both his belongings and his health.[23] In the first instance, when Job loses all that he has, he only says, "The Lord gives and the Lord takes away; blessed be the Name of the Lord." In the second instance, Job responds to his wife's complaints about his integrity saying, "Shall we accept the good from God, but the evil (רע) shall we not accept?" In both of these responses, Vischer notes that Job keeps his focus on God rather than the goods that God grants. He writes with respect to Job's second saying and in a clear allusion to Nietzsche, "Er will nicht Güter, nicht das Gute, er lebt von Gottes Güte, die jenseits von gut und böse ist."[24] That is, "He wants not goods, nor the Good, he lives by God's goodness, which lies beyond good and evil."[25] One should read the rest of the book, Vischer contends, to uncover the meaning of this.

What is the nature of "God's loving-kindness, which lies beyond good and evil"? The poet of the dialogues has perhaps taken it as a challenge to elaborate on this notion that the narrator sets up in the prologue. Vischer does not use the word midrash, but the picture he draws indicates that midrash is what the poet undertakes. He writes, "But now someone takes up the challenge which is thrown down (Is it the same or another 'Poet'?), treads upon the bow as it were and stretches upon it the bowstring of the speeches with a power and tenseness such that at any moment the bow threatens to snap."[26] Thus, the dialogues of Job explore what it means to exist by God's loving-kindness, even if that loving-kindness does not manifest itself in what we generally recognize as "goods" or "good." The friends speak words and phrases with presupposed definitions of God's loving-kindness. On the other hand, Job, who has had every possession stripped away, must work out a new definition of God's loving-kindness spurred by his presuppositions being stripped away along with his possessions.

The rest of Vischer's work highlights the message of each section and relates it back to the initial issue to resolve. In most cases, he focuses on the main point, but he does wrestle with some exegetical issues, generally as they relate to the thesis of the work. Regarding chapter 3 of Job, Vischer

---

23. Vischer, "Witness of Job I," 24.

24. Vischer, "*Hiob*, Ein Zeuge Jesu Christi," 6. The Nietzschean phrase holds significance to which we will return in due course.

25. A dynamic equivalent in English might read, Job "does not desire possessions or The Good; he exists by God's loving-kindness, which lies beyond good and evil."

26. Vischer, "Witness of Job I," 42.

The Goodness of God beyond Good and Evil

notes the *Leitwort* "to hedge" סכך in verse 23, which refers back to the hedge in 1:10. Vischer notes that these are the same expressions, however, the word used in 1:10 is, in its conjugated form, the homophone—שׂוּךְ. Vischer does not discuss the technical aspects of this exegetical issue, nor does he really explain the significance of the repetition of the phrase. He merely draws attention to the phrase. What he also points out is that, despite this common phrase the prologue and chapter 3 share, Job's complaint in chapter 3 does not mention his sickness or losses.[27] Instead, he releases a "cry of a man who cannot live without God."[28] This is certainly a debatable point. Job curses the day of his birth and mimics God's speech in Genesis 1:3 but instead calls for there to be darkness instead of light. Vischer recognizes this parody but elides the next line, which calls for God not to care about it. What Vischer argues is not that Job is calling for God not to care about the day, but that God has already ceased caring for it. Job, at first glance, seems more upset by God's presence rather than his absence. In 3:20, Job asks, "Why does he give light to the one in misery?" and Vischer records this verse in his essay. However, Vischer flattens the agency in the phrase by omitting the verb.[29] The light that Job feels he lives in, Vischer implies, is not the light of God.

Before dismissing Vischer's ongoing exegesis based on this potential exegetical mishap, one must consider the complexity of Job's argument. In later chapters, Job does seem to be saying exactly what Vischer argues. Though one could criticize Vischer for betraying his prejudice despite his claim to have followed the message of the book without prejudice,[30] one must proceed through his argument to determine how accurate his claim may be.

Vischer sustains his thesis—that Job's cry "is the cry of a man who cannot live without God"[31]—throughout his work, highlighting those passages in the various speeches that argue his points. In the section on chapters 4 and 5, for instance, he accuses Eliphaz of presenting a refined temptation of the Satan by connecting piety with advantage. This, according to Vischer, actually subverts piety because the person who "does good to get good by

---

27. Though Vischer, himself, does not make this connection, it seems relevant to his argument to point out the connections between the two sections and what that means to the overall message of Job, namely, that if there exists a legitimate connection between the prologue and the dialogues and yet the dialogues do not mention the specific sufferings of Job, these sufferings play only as "the means by which the real question is brought forward for decision" (ibid., 40).

28. Ibid., 43.

29. "*Wozu dem Elenden das Licht*" (Vischer, "Hiob, Ein Zeuge Jesu Christi," 7). Cf. the MT, which reads: למה יתן לעמל אור

30. The word Vischer employs is "*unvoreingenommen*" (ibid., 4).

31. Vischer, "Witness of Job I," 43.

it does not fear God simply for God's sake—'for nought.'"[32] Vischer explains this after cleverly noticing Eliphaz attempting to do the opposite—warn Job of the cunning of the serpent in the Garden of Eden. Vischer does not equate the serpent with the Satan, but leaves his readers to connect the ironic dots. His insinuation makes the friends seem sneakier than the serpent itself. In Job 5:12, 13, Eliphaz uses the common wisdom term ערום (crafty, cunning) to discuss the futility of one's intelligence in a battle to match wits with God. Of course, one finds this same word in Genesis 3:1 describing the serpent who will claim that the eating of the fruit will bestow an intelligence near to God's for the consumer. Thus, Eliphaz, in warning Job of the serpent, becomes like the Satan, whom people will associate with the serpent by the intertestamental period.[33] Vischer notes that this early speech is "well meant . . . and . . . beautifully expressed," which heightens its duplicitous nature. Eliphaz accuses Job of falling for the serpent's temptation, but it is Eliphaz who has become the devil's advocate.

Job's responds, according to Vischer, with the "greatest prayer of his life."[34] He desires God to kill him since God has seemed to have abandoned him. However, the dynamic present in this poem is complicated, as in Eliphaz's. For instance, Job still appeals to God, as he does in all of his speeches. His friends speak to him, but Job turns from them to God. The question arises as to how Job interprets God's actions. The imagery in the book of Job presents him as feeling like a sample in a Petri dish. "What are human beings that you make so much of them?" Job asks while parodying Psalm 8. Vischer quotes this verse, but does not exposit it. Instead, Vischer discusses the meaning of righteousness. Before moving on to this discussion of righteousness, one must ask if Vischer's exegesis of this section is justifiable in light of some of what Job has to say. There certainly exist complications. One notes that Job does seem to ask God to leave him alone, but he never seems to abandon God himself. Also, note that Job will not experience any more afflictions that he could attribute to God. Rather, he experiences an inner torture throughout the dialogue that Vischer, himself, attributes to God not answering him. Job's eventual satisfaction arrives with the storm. Job complains of God's oppressive behavior because someone who dares never abandon God has no other way to explain the torture of having been abandoned. This is a difficult concept to understand for anyone, and it remains that way for Job's friends as well.

---

32. Ibid., 44.

33. Early indications that the serpent in the Garden of Eden is associated with the devil are the prologue to Job or perhaps Wisdom 2:23, 24.

34. Ibid., 45.

The Goodness of God beyond Good and Evil

When Vischer discusses God's *Gerechtigkeit* (צדקה), he has to distinguish between what, in English, can be conveyed between the two words righteousness and justice. Job concerns himself with righteousness or piety (*Frömmigkeit*) but the friends are more interested in justice (*ein juristisches Verhältnis unter dem Gesetz des Ausgleichs von Verdienst und Lohn*).[35] This distinction becomes a corollary to the main thesis of the book. The friends argue that Job receives what he deserves and, though Job does suggest elsewhere that he does not receive what he deserves, at the end of chapter 7, Job desires instead a change in focus. He asks for a pardon from God. Vischer interprets this change in focus as that of Job's interest not in deserved equivalence, but the "Goodness of God . . . from realms beyond Good and Evil."[36] God condescends to his creatures rather than seeking out justice.

The speeches continue in much the same manner, with the friends focusing on one type of *Gerechtigkeit* and Job focusing on the other. Vischer's comments mainly recount the issues, highlighting passages that move his argument forward. His comments on the friends become smaller as they repeat themselves. Job receives fuller treatment since Vischer sees Job's journey as the important theological point to exposit.

What Vischer takes care to point out is that though the friends' arguments seem to change, their main thesis remains the same. Eliphaz's generous tone in chapter 4 moves to vehemence as his frustration increases. He gives Job the benefit of the doubt, comforting Job with God's sense of justice early on. If Job acts piously then God will treat him well. By chapter 22 Eliphaz accuses Job of horrible improprieties, forgoing all pastoral comforts. However, the sentiment is the same. God acts with perfect economy, giving goods for equal value and doing nothing for nought. The speeches of Bildad and Zophar receive little treatment, Vischer mainly highlighting what they say with a few words. He implies that their thesis adds nothing to the conversation and that, despite their ignorance of the court scene in the prologue, the friends act as the Satan's advocate.

While the friends may change focus but remain on course with their thesis, Vischer contends that Job essentially develops his thesis through the course of the conversation. Eventually, the question of the book changes and one can witness this transformation through Job's speeches. The seeming betrayal of God from Job has shattered his theology. Vischer compares his theology to the potsherds that Job holds, also containing a veiled reference to his nakedness.[37] Job then listens to his friends but must dispute what

---

35. Vischer, "*Hiob*, Ein Zeuge Jesu Christi," 11.
36. Vischer, "Witness of Job I," 46.
37. Vischer does not explicitly refer to Job 1:20, 21, but could have enhanced his

they say because their opinions do not make sense with respect to his own experience. Vischer also presents Job as one in tune with a logical theology despite the transcendent God at the centre of it. The friends hold to a theology of absolute righteousness, but Job does not see how a law can stand over God. If Vischer correctly interprets Job's refutation of the friends, then the reader must reconsider what scholars generally perceive as Job's court case against God.[38] For if no law can exist above God, then a legal proceeding would not hold up. A court case assumes that the plaintiff and defendant both stand under the law.

Dhorme first mentions Job's legal action regarding chapter 13. He states, concerning 13:17–21, that Job demands a "regular lawsuit ... and he only wishes that the machinery of divine justice did not exceed his strength."[39] Dhorme's analysis reflects the typical commentator and can also be seen in more colloquial renditions of Job like Wiesel's *God on Trial*. So Vischer's interpretation, that Job's friends imagine Job putting God on trial, demands closer inspection. Whoever instigates the suit, one can feel confident of its imaginary nature. The legal proceedings work as a rich metaphor, but no actual court case occurs. However, forensic imagery appears throughout the book beginning with the Satan, whom Vischer describes as a district attorney. In the poetic dialogues, the first character to reintroduce the metaphor is actually Eliphaz in chapter 5. He argues in verse 4 that a fool's children will be crushed in court (at the gates of the village) without a defender, warning Job of taking things too far with his invective. The next mention of the metaphor comes from the mouth of Job, but he seems to resist taking God to court. In Job 9:32, Job questions the possibility of bringing a suit to God since God's transcendence renders him incapable of defeat and no arbiter exists to mediate between God and a human. In chapter 10, Job sustains the metaphor but renders the idea unfair because of the nature of God. Vischer deserves credit for noting Job's resistance to the court case. However, Job continues to broach the topic in chapter 13 despite Zophar's omission of the metaphor. Perhaps a proper understanding of the court case is that Job imagines that the friends see him as bringing a suit to God since that is the ready-to-hand metaphor for a dispute. Many translations sustain the metaphor by translating certain phrases with their legal connotations.

---

metaphor noting that when Job tears his robe he does not replace it with sackcloth; Job follows this symbolic act with a pronouncement of his nakedness in verse 21.

38. See Clines, *Job 1–20*, 305.; Newsom, "Job," 435; and Habel, *The Book of Job*, 223. Of these three, Habel seems most confident that Job is actually wanting to take God to court. However, Habel sees Job as having dismissed litigation in chapters 9–10, "but the derision of his peers seems to have spurred him to strengthen his resolve" (ibid).

39. Dhorme, *Job*, xl.

The Goodness of God beyond Good and Evil

In 13:3, Job uses the *hiphil* form of יכח which has forensic connotations. However, it can also refer to arguments outside of the courtroom. When coupled with the preposition אל, as in 13:3, it simply means to argue with someone. That Job desires a face-to-face meeting with God, rather than one mediated through an arbiter, suggests a split from the forensic metaphor. On the other hand, the word יכח in the *hiphil* is disproportionately common in the book of Job compared to other texts and appears four times in chapter 13 alone. Despite the fact that none of the uses connotes a clear forensic thrust, the common appearance of this *Leitwort* does impress upon the reader a courtroom image. However, when seen from the point of view that Vischer proposes, Job does seem to dispute the idea of a court case. Job 13:8 promotes this idea well. Job uses here the legal term ריב, but he uses it in an interrogative sentence describing the friends. Here lies a clear example of Job questioning his friends' imaginations, which see Job as bringing the suit to God. Job denounces the defenses as insubstantial—like a dream. In fact, he actually defends God to the friends in 13:9–12.

Vischer sees Job's questions as introspective as well as disputatious toward the friends. Job does seem to wonder about the true nature of his relationship to God, but Vischer argues that Job dismisses the suggestion that they share a legal relationship. Rather, Vischer sees Job in a much more intimate relationship with God. He puts it thus: "Job is concerned with a totally different kind of 'Right,' namely the question whether God's relationship to him is a legal one or a relationship of an entirely different kind. Put quite briefly, whether God is his Friend or his Enemy."[40]

So Vischer argues that, despite the appearance of a courtroom drama, Job does not take God to court. Instead, Job plays out a family dispute. He cannot take God to court but he does present his case. Vischer does not present a long argument for his interpretation but merely lays out his reading, so it remains difficult to find his reasoning behind calling the court case a figment of the friends' imagination. However, one can see that the actuality of the legal process in the dialogues is suspect and by the coming of the storm the case is all but forgotten. Because Vischer only grants this passage a small amount of space due to the scope of his essay I do not want to dwell too heavily on the passage here. However, his claim does bear a great deal of weight for the overall thesis that he shares with Barth and Kierkegaard— that of Job's disinterested devotion to God despite the events that befall him.

Note that, thus far, despite the title of his essay, Vischer has not shown Job as a witness to Jesus Christ. In the section on chapters 16 and 17, Vischer faces a passage with Christological potentialities. "But now behold

---

40. Vischer, "Witness of Job I," 50.

my Witness is in heaven," Job says, but Vischer unflinchingly attributes the Witness to the generic "God," never insinuating or raising the possibility that the Witness might be Christ. When Job says, "My 'Mediator' is my real Friend," Vischer sees this as Job's "appeal against the Enemy-God to God the Friend."[41] This leads to Vischer's discourse on chapter 19, which raises a new question that the rest of the book will attempt to answer—whether Job's trust in God is justified.

When Vischer arrives at chapter 19, his Kierkegaardian and Barthian influences shine through. He notes the importance of the intimacy between Job and God. No outsider can truly understand Job's experience or his relationship with God. He accentuates the emphatic אֲנִי in verse 25, writing, "*Und ich, ich weiß, mein Löser lebt.*"[42] One senses that he emphasizes the subjectivity of truth, but he also notes that Job's struggle is one about (*um*) God. The friends have all but disqualified themselves from the debate. Though they continue to speak, the focus is now entirely on Job and his relationship with God. Job sees this and so he looks to God to save him from God. The friends cannot save him, but Job never acted as if they could. However, Job sees God as his attacker and savior, thus everything else is stripped away.

Vischer inserts a coda after his discourse on chapter 19. He sees this as a shift in focus. Job has fulfilled his duties and proven the Satan wrong. God has won the wager. But Job cannot now be satisfied. The question of God's goodness arises. When the focus becomes that of God and Job with everything else removed, the Law of Recompense cannot remain a factor. One cannot use an outside influence to define God's goodness. Instead, we must understand God's goodness as a goodness to "me" "which transcends Good and Evil."[43] Only God can answer this.

Vischer opens himself up perhaps to a strict individualistic theology, but quickly flips that to a brief discussion on the kingdom of God. When dealing with God and the individual, one must also see the corporate nature of the individuals to whom God relates. This is no cheap safety net for Vischer, but a way for him to discuss the realm and nature of God's goodness. The friends discuss the way the world works. They concern themselves with order and cause and effect, but Job, because of his subjective experience, cannot agree. Thus, the world works differently and God must act differently than the friends suppose. God deals with each individual individually, so the systematic rule of law does not come into play. The world is not good because it is ordered to be so, but it is good "because it is the

---

41. Ibid., 51.
42. Vischer, "*Hiob*, Ein Zeuge Jesu Christi," 19.
43. Vischer, "Witness of Job I," 53.

The Goodness of God beyond Good and Evil

object of [God's] goodness which fundamentally has nothing to do with good and evil, fortune and ill-fortune, reward and punishment, advantage and disadvantage."[44]

Vischer senses this from Job's speech in chapter 21 when Job asserts that God does not seem to care about what is righteous according to humans. Humans cannot teach God knowledge, so we cannot use our understanding of righteousness to control God. The evidence lies before us: the good and evil both die; so do the wealthy and poor.

The friends, however, hold fast to their argument. Though the details change, the general tenets remain the same. Vischer argues that their skilful edifice upon which they balance their claims bears a remarkable resemblance to the Satan's skepticism in the prologue. "The kernel (*der Kern*)," says Vischer, "the very axiom of the theology of the friends is just that *not for nought*."[45] By showing how they so resemble each other Vischer further relates the prologue to the dialogues, even after the question of the book has changed. He does not argue that the same author wrote the two sections of the book and he does not seem to think that is even the case. However, by tracing the line of thought throughout the book, he argues for a linear reading of Job. This line of thinking climaxes with Bildad's last speech, which Vischer argues, sums up the friends' view of God and the world. Bildad finally says, "upon whom does not God's *Light* shine?" and "Who is *clean* in the glare of *this* Light?"[46]

When Vischer arrives at Job's final speech, he offers an alternative to the "customary view" of the passage, which he states that Job describes his earlier happiness and his current state and argues that he did not deserve this "reversal of fortune."[47] Vischer's alternative view sees God as the key to Job's state. When Job walked with God, he received honor, but since "God abandoned

---

44. Vischer, "Witness of Job II," 138.

45. Ibid., 140.

46. Ibid., 141–42. See Job 25:3, 4. Vischer does not seem to quote directly from any known German text; the second of these quotes is loosely based on 25:4—"*diesem Licht*" refers to אל in the Hebrew text.

47. Ibid., 141. Note also that Vischer moves chapter 28 just after the Elihu speeches. I discuss that move in another section. On another note, the customary view that Vischer describes is not as obviously common as he insinuates. For instance, Budde summarises chapter 29, "*Früher war ich bei Gott in Gnaden und der glückichste Mensch, jetzt in tiefster Ungnade und der unglückichste*" (Budde, *Handkommentar Zum Alten Testament*, 163). Yes, Budde discusses Job's state as happiness, but that is a result of God's grace. Dhorme displays, perhaps, a view closer to what Vischer describes. There is less of a cause/effect relationship between Job's current state and God's grace. When Dhorme quotes 29:2, he does not elaborate on God's role in his state, but lets the verse speak for itself (page lii). In a modern context, one could regard the phrase, "In the days when Eloah made me secure" as a figure of speech along the lines of "Lord-willing."

him" his honor was broken.[48] Vischer is correct in showing the importance of Job's perception of God's role in Job's honor. Job's final defense begins with an extended description of God watching over Job and his household. Not until this description is complete does Job describe his former royal role in his community.[49] One should note here that Vischer describes God as *verborgenen*. This is not Job's description, but one that Vischer likely received from his relationship with Barth and his own Lutheran background.

The most important aspect, however, is that God *is* the cause of Job's honor. The world may seem random to Job, but he remains certain that God is the cause of his fortune and misfortune. This actually differs from the friends' hypothesis which argues that *Job* causes his own fortune and misfortune because the rules exist and Job's actions, not God's, trigger God's blessing and wrath.[50] Job disputes this thesis one last time before making his mark at the base of his final plea. So Job's final stance is that he concerns himself not with the law, but with God. "The reality behind the world and Man's life is not a law but the personal *Truth* of the Creator."[51] So the question changes from "Is this man really true to God?" to "the question of faith in God's own Truth."[52] The first question has an answer—Job is the proof. To the end, Job has remained true to God despite all that opposes him. God seems to have abandoned him, but he remains true to God.

Vischer's discussion of the Elihu speeches and the hymn to Wisdom, which he places between the Elihu speeches and God's theophany, briefly summarize the sections and all but dismiss them as late interpolations that add little to the book itself. Elihu argues that God chastens his people through suffering and converts them back to him. The hymn to Wisdom presents an orthodox view of Old Testament Wisdom literature. Vischer finds no fault with either of these passages, per se. However, he argues that they do not answer Job's question and Elihu's speech, in particular, begins with the fallacious presupposition that God sent Job sufferings in order to convert him. The reader knows this not to be the case. Also, no one pays any notice of Elihu. So Vischer concludes that Elihu comes from the pen of a different author and

---

48. "*fallen lassen*" (Vischer, "*Hiob*, Ein Zeuge Jesu Christi," 24).

49. Eventually, Andre Caquot will elaborate on the royal traits in Job and dedicate his paper to Vischer in Vischer's festschrift (Caquot, "Traits Royaux").

50. Recall that Aquinas and Calvin, among others, argue that the book of Job has much to say about God's providence, which would seem to be the case with Vischer as well. The differences between the interpretations far outweigh the similarities, however. See especially Calvin, who elevates Elihu in his reading. Vischer, as noted below, essentially dismisses Elihu as inconsequential to the narrative presented in the book of Job.

51. Vischer, "Witness of Job II," 143.

52. Ibid.

The Goodness of God beyond Good and Evil

that the hymn to Wisdom, though majestic in many ways, also merely delays the gratification that comes from the storm that arrives in chapter 38.

When God does arrive at the climax of the book of Job, Vischer sees it as the definitive answer to the questions laid out in the book. Many have complained that the speeches accomplish little with regards to the message of Job, but Vischer argues that no other answer would do. The issue of *chinnam* arises again and God most definitely lands on the side of freedom. The Satan argues that Job acts according to God's gifts to him and the friends argue that God acts according to Job's actions. Job, however, shows that he serves God despite his personal state and God, in his speeches, shows his people that "not aim and not advantage, but God's free, happy goodness is the meaning and cause of the world."[53] God directs his will to the creature and "the creature toward Him."[54] It is not immediately clear what Vischer means by God's "goodness." Recall that in discussing Job's response to his wife that Vischer suggests that Job desires "not goods, not the thing which is good; he lives of God's goodness which lies beyond good and evil."[55] God's goodness is somewhat ineffable in that our human understanding of morality is intrinsically based on our understanding of good and evil. If God's goodness lies beyond a human understanding of morality, Job must trust God and not any by-product of God's activity.

Vischer's use of the clause "beyond good and evil," as mentioned earlier, certainly stems from Friedrich Nietzsche's book *Beyond Good and Evil*.[56] It is difficult to say how much Vischer had Nietzsche's ideas in mind when he used the phrase since he does not elaborate on the thought or mention him by name. On the other hand, Nietzsche "dominated the intellectual and cultural landscape in Germany" in the 1930s[57] to the point that allusions like the ones in Vischer's essay would certainly have evoked some nod in the philosopher's direction by the casual reader of Vischer.[58]

Using some caution, one should also note that Nietzsche's description of the phrase "beyond good and evil" actually goes far in helping to explain what Vischer might have meant by the phrase in this context. In fact,

---

53. Ibid., 147. Vischer quotes Calvin on Psalm 104:31, who writes "*Status mundi in Dei laetitia fundatus est.*" Vischer's reformed tradition draws him to Calvin's theology, which influences the thesis of Vischer's essay. Note again, however, that Vischer does not cite Calvin on Job in any place.

54. Ibid.

55. Vischer, "Witness of Job I," 42.

56. Nietzsche, *Beyond Good and Evil*.

57. Leiter, *Nietzsche on Morality*, 290.

58. Vischer would also allude to Nietzsche a few times in the *Christuszeugnis*, quoting him at length in one footnote. (Vischer, *Das Christuszeugnis 1*, 156 n.160).

Read Him Again and Again

much of Nietzsche's book *Beyond Good and Evil* resembles Job's complaints about his friends and their philosophy as interpreted by Vischer. Nietzsche himself writes, "To recognize untruth as a condition of life: that, to be sure, means to resist customary value-sentiments in a dangerous fashion; and a philosophy which ventures to do so places itself, by that act alone, beyond good and evil."[59] The truth is elusive and "false judgments" are a part of life, according to Nietzsche. It is not obvious to him that we can discover the truth as many philosophers insist we can.

Much of the first section of *Beyond Good and Evil* comes in the form of Nietzsche describing and disparaging the philosophers who came before him, suggesting that their quest for truth and value lacked the undergirding they claimed it had. He describes his predecessors as displaying "insufficient honesty" regarding their practice . . .

> while making a mighty and virtuous noise as soon as the problem of truthfulness is even remotely touched on. They pose as having discovered and attained their real opinions through the self-evolution of a cold, pure, divinely unperturbed dialectic . . . while what happens at bottom is that a prejudice, a notion, an "inspiration," generally a desire of the heart sifted and made abstract, is defended by them with reasons sought after the event . . .[60]

Likewise, Job's friends focus on the results of Job's life as evidence of his original actions. They are so tied to their interpretation of the system in which they perceive God to work that when Job suffers without evidence of having sinned, they work backward to determine that he must have sinned. Everything that occurs on the earth is tied to their notions of morality.

They have reduced their religion to a system or a metaphysic.[61] That is, while Job devotes himself to God, the friends seem to devote themselves to the laws that God purveys. The laws themselves, though, are seemingly corrupt. That is, the friends' perceptions of the laws of nature as set in motion by God are faulty. They are based more on tradition than anything else.[62]

---

59. Nietzsche, *Beyond Good and Evil*, 36.

60. Ibid.

61. See Tanner on section 6 of *Beyond Good and Evil*: "For although we think of Christianity as primarily a religion, it is, like all systems of religious belief, based on a set of views about the way things are, in other words a metaphysic" (Tanner, "Introduction," 14).

62. See Job 8:8, 9: "Ask the former generation and find out what their ancestors learned, for we were born only yesterday and know nothing."

The Goodness of God beyond Good and Evil

Nietzsche later in the book seems to describe the mentality of Job's friends in what he calls human herds:

> (family groups, communities, tribes, nations, states, churches), and always very many who obey compared with the very small number of those who command—considering, that is to say, that hitherto nothing has been practiced and cultivated among men better or longer than obedience, it is fair to suppose that as a rule a need for it is by now innate as a kind of *formal conscience* which commands: . . . in short "thou shalt."[63]

Job stands out from his friends in that he does not blindly follow the laws established by the generations that preceded him. He does not work backward from his suffering to what might have instigated it.

Here, however, Vischer's Job and Nietzsche part ways. They are both seeking that which is beyond good and evil, but Job seeks the "goodness of *God* which lies beyond good and evil." Job does not seem to be a part of the "herd," which relies on the law as instilled in tradition, but he does resemble Nietzsche's description of "slave morality" in that he devotes himself to the originary purveyor of the law.[64] Both the Job of the dialogues and Nietzsche agree that values are not natural, they do not exist "in the fabric of the world . . . to be discovered by us,"[65] but Nietzsche argues that value is something we have invented. Job, on the other hand, sees the values as thrust upon us by an outside force who exists above the values and is capable of overriding them by his very nature. The existence of God as purveyor of the law allows Job to differentiate himself from Nietzsche, who regarded "the great men of the nineteenth century with suspicion, with the signal exceptions of Napoleon and Goethe, the two men who emphatically didn't think of themselves as acting in obedience to laws from beyond or outside."[66] Vischer's Job differentiates himself from Napoleon and Goethe in that he acts in obedience to something from the outside—only that something lies beyond good and evil.

Beyond Good and Evil begins with Nietzsche's assumption made clear in *The Gay Science* and *Thus Sprach Zarathustra* that God is dead. Tanner describes it as "in large part an exploration of how greatness is rendered impossible if we continue in the habits of thought instilled by two millennia of Christianity while abandoning the presupposition of the whole enterprise:

---

63. Nietzsche, *Beyond Good and Evil*, 120.
64. Ibid., 197.
65. Tanner, "Introduction," 19.
66. Ibid., 24. See Nietzsche, *Beyond Good and Evil*, 138–40.

God."⁶⁷ Note also Nietzsche's more well known follow-up to *Beyond Good and Evil*, *On the Genealogy of Morality*, where he writes, "Fortunately I learned early on to distinguish theological from moral prejudice and no longer sought the origin of evil *behind* the world."⁶⁸ Here he shows that he is relatively uninterested in the idea of God as origin of morality. He takes as *a priori* the non-existence of God. Job finds the abandoning of God anathema. The friends seem to avoid God as a personal being by focusing on his laws and actions. Job's focus is on the purveyor of the laws over and sometimes against the laws themselves, which Vischer maintains is the key difference between Job and his friends.

If, then, the answer has to do not with human morality as tied to the understanding of good and evil but with the goodness of God beyond good and evil, the only satisfactory answer for Job must be a revelation of God. The friends cannot answer questions about God even if they had the right answer. Vischer takes this further, arguing that physics, metaphysics, apologetics, and even dialectic theology lack when trying to describe God. God is "*unbekannte*" and "just when He reveals Himself in Truth as *our* God, as the Friend of Job, then is His revelation of Himself the abyss which no man can fathom."⁶⁹ So the purpose of the speeches is to reveal God to Job, but in such a way as to maintain the hiddenness of God—the *Deus Absconditus*. By remaining hidden, God remains free and thus he answers the second question of the book of Job, according to Vischer. God does not act according to a code or law, but acts beyond good and evil. The friends cannot contain the righteousness with which they occupy themselves. Righteousness comes only through relationship with the hidden God and God remains hidden, even in relationship, so that the relationship can remain *for nought*.

After his analysis of God's speeches, Vischer presents a rather brief summary of the epilogue. He does not add much in the way of interpretation. Vischer forwards the uncontroversial reading of Job repenting in dust and ashes. Because of this, Job's theocentric view of the world brings more pleasure to God than the friends' apologetics, which place conditions above God. Therefore, God grants Job blessings that go beyond his pre-catastrophic state. One shortcoming of this analysis is the question concerning Job's blessing. What is the cause of that blessing? Vischer seems to suggest that God pays Job back for his devotion, but this seems to threaten the idea that Job is pious for nought. Vischer does suggest earlier that Job has proven his piety during the

---

67. Tanner, "Introduction," 26.
68. Nietzsche, *On the Genealogy of Morality*, 2. Emphasis in the original.
69. Vischer, "*Hiob*, Ein Zeuge Jesu Christi," 29. Vischer, "Witness of Job II," 148.

dialogues and now God must prove his devotion to Job. But Vischer does not say this and only leaves his readers with the dots to connect.

Finally, after the full exegesis of the book of Job, Vischer ties his reading together with his Christology—something promised in the title of the article itself. Vischer seems aware of the controversy that he may instigate with such a figural reading. This becomes evident in his introduction of a quote by Bernhard Duhm. Duhm suggests that the epilogue of Job is an addition to the poetry in order to appease the readers. Vischer highlights Duhm's comparison of the ending to that of Shakespeare's plays taken from earlier sources. What Duhm means is less important than that Vischer takes this anachronism of a Shakespearian ending to an ancient Near Eastern poem as license to make a much less anachronistic comparison between the book of Job and the Christian story. It is natural to see parallels between stories and often fruitful to make such parallels. Vischer indicates that his Christological approach begins with this parallel between two culturally related texts. The Jesus story did not arise out of a vacuum but was the product of a particular literary tradition and *Weltanschauung*. The New Testament constantly refers to the Old Testament to make its case, positing its foundation on the literary tradition of the Hebrew Bible. Vischer states that the conclusion to the book of Job "has a genuinely Israelite and biblical touch," which it also has in common the story of the empty tomb of the Gospels.[70] Because it has this close connection with the Gospel story and other biblical texts, the book of Job has ethical implications as well. He writes:

> The realistic earthly conclusion of the Book of Job points strongly to the lesson that the practical decision whether God is really God, that is to say is *our* God, falls *in this present life*. Faith lives [from] the reality of communion with God in the practical things of this earthly life; either God is here and now my god, Victor over sin and death, or He is not my God. That is, as we have seen entirely the faith of the Job speeches.[71]

Vischer's claim here echoes what he insinuates in other words earlier and what he will repeat a few paragraphs later—that the book of Job points beyond itself. The literal meaning has spiritual implications. The very format of the book illustrates this. Earlier, he says that the "conclusion, which is closely connected with the initial paragraphs of the story, has, after the spiritual turn given to the problem through the speeches, a remarkable force."[72] That is, the concreteness of the prose and the heightened style of the dia-

70. Ibid.
71. Ibid.
72. Ibid.

logues suggest a concrete-spiritual dualism. The book of Job is not just a story, but an ethical call. The book and its message refer the reader to God. When the fundamental question of the book changes from "can a human serve God for nought?" to "is Job's trust in God's goodness justified?"[73] the book refers back to God. In doing this, the natural referent becomes the ultimate answer to these questions. The Christian will certainly see Christ as a component of the affirmation of these questions. It would be naïve to think the Christian reader can bracket Christ out of the reading of Job. Vischer does not speak of influence—whether Job has any bearing on the telling of the Gospels—but implies that the framing of the stories are inherently alike because of the shared context of their cultural and literary traditions.

He does not leave it there but presents several parallel examples of the Jobian trajectory in the Gospel narratives beginning with Jesus's temptation by Satan himself. Next comes the comparison of Peter to Satan when the disciple rebukes Jesus. This is an obvious parallel to the friends of Job whom Vischer likens to the Satan of the prologue throughout his piece. The cultural and literary contexts of the two stories apply a pressure that influences such thinking. Akin to this is Vischer's next example, which shows Satan embodying Judas. In all of these examples, Jesus does not sin despite the great temptations. However, the biggest temptation comes as he suffers on the cross and the people wonder why he does not save himself. Yet Jesus, like Job, knows he is right and resembles Job again in his recitation of Psalm 22. These are remarkable parallels that make a good case for Vischer's thesis. He downplays the typology implied by the parallels and lets the parallels speak for themselves.

Recall briefly the cultural context in which Vischer presents his interpretation. The book of Job, found in the Hebrew Bible, a collection of books deemed unimportant to Christian theology at best, and harmful to European culture at worst,[74] Vischer argues is intrinsically related to Christian theology. Christ and Job react to their similar sufferings similarly, which

---

73. Vischer, "Witness of Job I," 53.

74. Richard Gutteridge provides many examples of this type of anti-Semitism, among them Friedrich Delitzsch who writes in his new edition in 1921 of *Die grosse Täuschung* ('The Great Deception'), "all the Old Testament books from Genesis to Daniel have in their religious bearing for today, and especially for us Christians, absolutely no significance" (Gutteridge, *Open Thy Mouth*, 41). One should note, however, that included among the anti-Semitic voices of the era are those who saw the Old Testament as useful as a tool *for promoting* anti-Semetism. Gutteridge presents as an example Helmut Schreiner who "insisted that there was no greater witness against modern Jewry than the whole spirit of the Bible" (ibid). Examples abound of both, but especially the former, which seemed to have dominated the *Zeitgeist*, evidenced by the dwindling provision of chairs of Old Testament studies at the universities in Germany (ibid., 55).

should come as little surprise since they are offspring of the same culture and worldview. They are also servants of the same God and are so devoted to that God that they resemble each other in their devotion.

Vischer ends his analysis with a brief homiletic flourish. He encourages those living in "the midst of the battle of Faith, it may be in darkness and perplexity, in conflict and suffering."[75] Recognizing the possible impetus for Vischer's writing on Job as argued in the opening section of this chapter, one could see his conclusion as a reference to the battle of Faith within the German context. One year later he would compose the Bethel Confession, which confronts the darkness and perplexity of interbellum Germany head on. In his interpretation of Job, he recognizes the suffering that comes from theological conflict and shows that both Job and Christ trod through it similarly.

Summary

Vischer's exegetical method shares many similarities with Karl Barth with significant differences. The differences will be spelled out more thoroughly in the evaluative chapter, but the similarities are obvious. For one, neither shies away from historical criticisms regarding the history of the text. It does not seem to be a problem for interpretation to Vischer that some passages from Job were written at different times than others. On the other hand, he does attempt to present a final form reading, albeit using a non-extant final form than those at hand. That is, he modifies sections according to his own critical hypotheses but interprets the story from beginning to end. It is imperative to his interpretation, for example, that the Job of the prologue and the Job of the speeches and the Job of the epilogue are all the same Job, but it may be necessary for reasons not fully explained to move chapter 28 to a different location. This is problematic, of course, because it leaves Vischer open to the criticism that he moves segments of the text in order for them to fit his theology. Theological presuppositions are unavoidable, whatever one's convictions regarding historical criticism, but Vischer hurts his credibility when he moves passages around in what seems like a way to endorse his position. Of course, it is difficult to say what came first, his critical conclusions or his theology. The next section will detail Vischer's method of interpretation of Job in order to place it beside his interpretation and theological claims, which come after. Following the next section will come an evaluation of his method and interpretation.

---

75. Vischer, "Witness of Job II," 150.

Read Him Again and Again

METHOD OF INTERPRETATION

As mentioned above, Vischer insists on interpreting the book of Job as a whole. The prologue of the book of Job drives his interpretation. At first glance, this would seem the appropriate way to interpret Job. The prologue sets up all we need to know before the reader moves into the dialogues which are poetically vague and universal in their descriptions of sufferings. The prologue gives us something to pin to the dialogues. Vischer is very aware of what is at stake in the prologue and this drives his interpretation of the dialogues. However, what is at stake is not Job's suffering but the freedom of God and humanity.

Despite Vischer's insistence on reading the book of Job through the message of the prologue, he generally accepts many historical critical claims on the book from scholars in his historical and geographical context. This is not widely evident in the first half of his study, which is par for the course in Job studies. The more problematic sections of the book arrive in later chapters. Vischer begins his discourse on chapters 23–27 questioning whether the words in these chapters stand in their right place.[76] He is concerned with the lack of symmetry in the speeches and suggests attempting to restore the text to its original composition. In the previous two cycles of speeches, Job speaks in between the comments offered by Eliphaz, Bildad, and Zophar, respectively, but in this section Job responds to Eliphaz and Bildad only. Zophar offers no council and Bildad's comments, in merely six verses, are much shorter than anything previous. This is a common concern in Job studies and has remained so for a long time.[77] Vischer, whether because of space, the genre of his work, his hermeneutic, or a combination, does not present his own reconstruction. What he does say is that "The symmetry of the conversation is upset; and we ought perhaps to endeavor to restore the

---

76. Vischer, *Hiob*, Ein Zeuge Jesu Christi," 23.

77. In Clines's recent commentary on Job 21–37, he moves 24:18–24 to the end of chapter 27 in order to give Zophar a last chance to speak. But Clines also reassigns 27:7–23 to Zophar, thus giving Zophar a full speech. Clines' explanation is reasonable in some respects and he makes his reader aware of some of his motivations. But to grant Zophar a full speech means that he must also reassign passages from chapters 25 and 26 and reorganize that section in order to grant Bildad a fair number of lines. Clines is aware of the difficulties in such a reconstruction and catalogues up to seven different reconstructions on chapters 25 and 26 by various commentators. Clines himself makes some important comments regarding hermeneutics and the role of the commentator. He claims that "it is necessary for the sake of the exegesis to make decisions, right or wrong, about who is speaking at any point." Clines is, by no means, the first to attempt such a reconstruction and his catalogue includes several works that would have been available to Vischer at the time of his writing, including Good, Dhorme, Strahan, and Duhm. (Clines, *Job 21–37*, 629).

The Goodness of God beyond Good and Evil

original arrangement. But any such attempt must in no case be based upon the misconception that Job maintains, in contradiction to the friends, that it ever finally goes well with the ungodly. That would be a one-sided distortion of his meaning."[78] That is, that Job's words might resemble his friends in that they all do see God as just. Job, however, argues that one might lack the perspective that would allow one to interpret it. Vischer's summary of the text omits discussion on the disputed passages, a move the relative scope of his essay allows him to undertake.

Vischer, therefore, opens up the possibility of a reconstruction of 23–27 but avoids having to make a decision because the passage as it stands does not hurt his overall thesis any more than a reconstruction would help it. On the other hand, there are cases where Vischer does not shy from radical reconstruction of the text. His readers will notice in the very next section that he skips over chapter 28 with nary a word to discuss chapters 29–31. He does not just excise the chapter from the book, but places it after the Elihu speeches. Neither of these passages, it turns out, contribute much to the story, according to Vischer, and both have questionable provenance. Note that Vischer gives little evidence of their extra-Joban milieu other than a vague description of their "Kennzeichen."[79] No one in the narrative seems to take notice of Elihu and chapter 28, he claims, is not motivated by the context. Nevertheless, he does not excise the passages from his own interpretation of Job. Rather, he gives them their due and shows that they neither add nor take away anything from the broader meaning of the book.

It is not entirely clear why Vischer moves chapter 28 to where he does. He, along with many scholars regard it as a later interpolation, but he does not explain why it fits better between Elihu's speech and God's speech. In fact, it seems to disrupt Elihu's mention of the storm in his speech that foreshadows God's arrival in a tempest. Vischer presents vague motivations and seems intent to deflect attention away from the chapter without wholly excising it from the book. Clines, likewise, wonders why it remains in the book since, in its received locale, it is generically an aberration.[80] However, most commentators seem content to keep it in its traditional place. Clines views it as the last section of Elihu's speech since it does not carry a prose introduction. He moves chapter 28, then, to a position after chapter 37 and

---

78. Vischer, "Witness of Job II," 141. "*Die Symmetrie des Gesprächs ist gestört. Man muß vielleicht versuchen, die ursprüngliche Verteilung wieder herzustellen. Nur darf ein solcher Versuch auf keinen Fall von dem Mißverständnis ausgehen, Hiob behaupte im Gegensatz zu den Freunden, daß es den Gottlosen immer gut ergehe*" (Vischer, "Hiob, Ein Zeuge Jesu Christi," 23).

79. Ibid., 27.

80. Clines, *Job 21–37*, 908.

then moves Job's final speech after chapter 28 so that Job has the last word until God arrives on the scene. Vischer takes a less radical approach, but does place chapter 28 directly after chapter 37.

Chapter 28 does not come from the mouth of Elihu, according to Vischer, but he argues that it does have a similar message. The general redundancy of the Elihu speeches and the hymn to Wisdom adds to the sense of delayed gratification one perceives while reading the book of Job. The devotion Job has to God makes all the words of those other than God like burning embers on his head. However, Vischer does not excise the superfluous texts. He places them just before God speaks from the tempest. By then Job has made his case and "it is *God* he wants," not more arguments defending God.[81]

One should also recall the importance of chapter 19 in Vischer's exegesis of Job. Recall that Vischer sees that chapter as the main turning point in the book since he feels it definitively answers the Satan's question in the prologue. The second question, which asks about the nature of God's righteousness, can only be answered by God himself. Because God does not arrive on the scene of the drama until chapter 38, Vischer can change the positions of the remaining chapters of the dialogue with little risk of disrupting the narrative since they seem merely to delay the gratification of the tempest. Chapter 28, along with raising the problems that Vischer highlights, ends by declaring that only God can answer the question raised in the dialogues. It seems strange to voice this position and then postpone following through on it for another ten chapters, thus Vischer's relocation of several of the passages between chapters 19 and 38 may be partially driven by his thesis of the book of Job as well as his genuine historical critical concerns.

Other indications of Vischer's indebtedness to general historical critical scholarship appear in his acknowledgments of other sources in the ancient Near East. For instance, he suggests that Job's final defense compares favorably with the Egyptian Book of the Dead.[82] He backs up this claim with a quote from the "Book of the Dead" to show how this may be the case but does not cite which specific text he quotes.[83] The connection may be only that, "*ein Anschluß*," he does not suggest which book is influencing which or even the obvious differences between the two. It is not really a very helpful comparison since it does not suggest the significance of the connection. When one looks more closely at the passage he cites, a closer connec-

---

81. Vischer, "Witness of Job II," 144.

82. Ibid., 142.

83. The specific text he quotes is "The Protestation of Guiltlessness" (Pritchard, ed. *ANET*, 34–36).

tion seems evident. The "Protestation of Guiltlessness," the passage Vischer cites from the Egyptian Book of the Dead, acts as a "negative confession" of guilt for a recently deceased person. After the passage that Vischer notes as parallel to Job 31:6 ("Let him weigh me on scales of righteousness; let God know my integrity"), the supplicant recites a long list of actions he did not commit, much as Job does in the remaining verses of chapter 31. Vischer's comparison between Job's final confession and the Book of the Dead actually reveals more the influences of his own work rather than the influences of the book of Job. Vischer does not offer much in the way of his secondary sources, but these nods to findings among critical scholars display his interests in historical criticism. Because his interest ultimately lies in the theology to which the book of Job points, he does not dwell much on the historical aspects of the text. The book of Job may contain parallels to extra-biblical sources, but it is not the pre-history of Job with which Vischer concerns himself.

Besides presenting a reconstructed text and recognizing extra-biblical sources, Vischer attempts to exegete the entire text of Job as a single narrative though the narrative is one of his reconstruction. One fascinating interpretive move arises among another potentially corrupt text. Job 19:27–29 has troubled interpreters for a long time because of its grammar as well as its message.[84] Pope comments on verses 28 and 29, "These lines are a jumble of verbiage and possibly the text is damaged or misplaced."[85] Dhorme, whose commentary precedes Vischer by only a few years, follows Ball in declaring the MT of verse 29 "ungrammatical and untranslatable," and so lists modern interpreters' reconstitutions of the text based on the Greek version.[86] Vischer, according to his translator Allan Ellison, is content to allow the verse to stand as it does in the MT rather than reconstruct it based on other texts. However, because of its difficult interpretation based on its overwrought grammar, he seems to interpret the phrase as incoherent babble from the mouth of the character of Job rather than a corrupt text. Vischer's interpretation of 27b is that "Hiob verliert das Bewußtsein."[87] Ellison adds an editorial note in parentheses, "The exclamation 'My reins are consumed in me!' together with the sobbing incoherence of the next two verses, suggests that Job, in the agony of his great declaration of faith,

---

84. "If you say, 'How we will persecute him!' and, 'The root of the matter is found in him'; be afraid of the sword, for wrath brings the punishment of the sword, so that you may know there is a judgment" (Job 19:28, 29 NRSV).

85. Pope, *Job*, 135.

86. Dhorme, *Job*, 288.

87. Vischer, *Hiob*, Ein Zeuge Jesu Christi," 20.

loses his sense for some time."[88] The German original of Vischer's text is not so clear. Vischer does not explain his interpretation of verse 27 and seems to ignore 28 and 29 altogether. This may result from a number of possible interpretations. He may, as Ellison indicates, view the jumbled incoherence of 28 and 29 as coming from the mouth of one who has feinted, speaking unconsciously. Secondly, he may merely not deal with the two verses just as he does not deal with much of Job, because they do not advance his argument. Thirdly, the verses in question are not only difficult grammatically, but also theologically. Vischer would not be the only critic to have a problem with the retributive message in 28 and 29 coming from the mouth of Job. Pope questions whether the verses should not be somewhere in the speeches of the friends and Vischer may agree. Moving them would certainly help Vischer's argument concerning the message of Job. Dealing with these verses in a critical manner, however, would not fit the genre of Vischer's work and so rather than argue for their proper place, he likely skips over them altogether. It will become clear in his later discussions that Vischer would not have a huge problem with a reconstructed Job that includes moving entire chapters to more apt settings for this is what he does with chapter 28. However, with two verses, he may have thought it disruptive to the larger task of interpretation.

JOB AS A WITNESS TO JESUS CHRIST

The larger task of interpretation for Vischer leads to the finale of his essay—how the book of Job bears witness to Christ. It is safe to say that whatever fame Vischer has enjoyed over the years, much of it is due to his essays and books that show how the Old Testament bears witness to Christ. His most famous book is entitled *Das Christuszeugnis des Alten Testaments* and bears a resemblance to the essay on Job and his other essay on Esther mentioned earlier. In all of these texts, Vischer exposits Old Testament passages (in the cases of Job and Esther, the entire books) and shows how they resemble either passages of the Gospels or aspects of the character of Jesus Christ. In *Das Christuszeugnis*, however, the parallels are made much more explicit.

As an example of how the book differs from Vischer's essay on Job, note how Vischer treats Cain's sign in Genesis as an idea of a covenantal sign binding people to God. He notes that in Ezekiel 9:4, an angel receives instruction from Yahweh to mark the foreheads of those that sigh and groan for the abominations done in the land. The mark (the word *taw* in Hebrew,

---

88. Vischer, "Witness of Job I," 52.

The Goodness of God beyond Good and Evil

the last letter of the alphabet spelled out), Vischer notes, would have been in the shape of an X in the Old Canaanite alphabet. Vischer then writes:

> We may thus with a fair degree of probability assume that the cross with which Cain was branded and which in Christianity received a new significance is the ancient sign of Jahweh. The fact that in Revelation 7, in almost literal dependence on Ezekiel 9, the 144,000 slaves of our God are marked on the brow with this seal . . . before destruction is let loose . . . confirms the view that the Christian seal of the living God is the same symbol as the sign found in the vision of Ezekiel and upon Cain.[89]

Vischer makes a similar point in describing Job 31:35 where Job presents his mark (*taw*). However, despite translating *taw* as cross in his essay, he merely leaves it at that.[90] Vischer does no more than call the mark a cross, which it technically would have been. He does not speculate that this cross bears any relationship to the cross of Christ other than draw the reader to its possibility on his or her own.

To be clear, Vischer points briefly to the *taw* in Job 31:35, but of course presents a more expansive Christological reading at the end of his exposition on Job. Thus, the differences between the *Christuszeugnis* and his essay on Job are not drastic, but are mainly due to emphases.

Where the passage on Cain's sign resembles the Job essay is how his understanding of influence seems almost elusive. He does not find the cross on which Christ died in the Old Testament. He is not allegorizing in the same way as many pre-critical scholars might have. Instead, he is subtly implying a cultural connection between the narrative of Cain, the prophet Ezekiel, the author of Revelation, and symbol of Christ's atoning sacrifice. To be sure, he holds to a theology of a sovereign God directing these connections, but related to that is the intrinsic relationship between the Old Testament and the New Testament.

The inherent relation between the two testaments is also one of the important, yet subtle points of his essay on Job. As I argue in the first section of this chapter, one of his reasons for this may have been his valid concern that the Old Testament had been increasingly seen as unimportant in Christian theology and in New Testament studies, based partly on rampant and established anti-Semitism in Europe at that time.

In the final chapter, I will compare the typological imagination of Vischer in his essay on Job with those of Barth and Kierkegaard in their respective works on Job. In doing so, I will examine closely Vischer's later

---

89. Vischer, *The Witness of the Old Testament to Christ*, 75.
90. Vischer, "*Hiob*, Ein Zeuge Jesu Christi," 26.

claims to oppose allegory and typology as hermeneutical tools in his exegesis.[91] In brief, he finds the use of allegory as strained and as ignorant of the meaning present in the text. When comparing Job to Christ, he uses the terms *Zeichnis* (sign), *Gleichnis* (parable), and *Vorbild* (model), resisting more spiritual connections for terms that point to resemblance or literary parallels. The conclusion to "*Hiob,* ein Zeuge Jesu Christi" seems to act merely to point at the resemblances between the story in the book of Job and the life, death, and resurrection of Christ.

The import of the resemblances is that the book of Job "points beyond itself."[92] The beginning of the book of Job asks the question of whether a human could be a disinterested devotee to God. Job answers that in the affirmative with his life and his speeches. The question Job asks is to what end does he devote himself to God. In other words, the book of Job points beyond itself and back to God. Christ embodies the movement displayed in the book of Job in his life, death, and resurrection, thus the book of Job eventually points to Christ, whose life also points to God.

In Vischer's Job, everything points to God and God remains the end point to all questions. The friends appeal to reason and tradition, imagining that Job desires to put God on trial, but that would place God under reason and tradition. For Vischer and the Job he presents, nothing can be above God. God, therefore, is a completely free entity in the book of Job, a notion on which Karl Barth will elaborate in volume four of his *Church Dogmatics*, the subject of the next chapter.

---

91. See Vischer, "La Méthode."

92. Vischer, "Witness of Job II," 148.

5

A Witness to the True Witness
Karl Barth's Unique Contribution to the Interpretation of the Book of Job

KARL BARTH'S EXPOSITION OF Job in §70 in *Church Dogmatics* IV/3.1 has garnered little attention in the years since it has been published and almost none from biblical scholars. Daniel Migliore compares Barth's reading to Ernst Bloch's, detailing the significance of Barth's adherence to the final form over and against Bloch's search for a subversive text behind the final form.[1] The value of Migliore's essay notwithstanding, the end product is more concerned with Bloch than Barth; Barth is more important as a supporting reference than a subject of examination. Harold Schulweis uses Barth's text on Job as a way to compare Barth's view on God to a Jewish understanding—the book of Job being a text that both Jews and Christians have in common.[2] Nicholas Adams compares Calvin, Barth, and Aquinas's readings of Job as a platform on which to discuss the merits of public debate.[3] Otto Bächli presents a detailed exposition of Barth's interpretation of Job in his book *Das Alte Testament in der Kirchlichen Dogmatik von Karl Barth*.[4] Though a valuable resource, Bächli mainly

---

1. Migliore, "Barth and Bloch on Job."
2. Schulweis, "Karl Barth's Job," 156–67.
3. Adams, "The Goodness of Job's Bad Arguments."
4. Bächli, *Alte Testament*, 210–24.

lets Barth speak for himself, granting an extraordinary amount of space to the words of Barth rather than his own analysis of how Barth's Job fits into his larger work on "The True Witness." Bächli's introduction contains his most astute analysis of Barth's method of exegesis in §70, stating that exegesis is for Barth not so much *Illustration*, but rather *Quellenangabe*, thus exegesis does not play the role of *Hilfsfunktion*, but rather *Grundfunktion*. Of the few scholars that discuss Barth's Job in detail, Susannah Ticciati's published dissertation is the work that most closely resembles the approach of biblical scholarship in that her purpose is to introduce Barth's interpretation of Job as a platform for her own interpretation of Job.[5] Ticciati focuses on Barth's attention to the character of Job as right and wrong and sees obedience as the main issue at stake in the book of Job. The following differs from all of these previous publications in that it is concerned with Barth's interpretive strategy in his discourse on Job and how that strategy leads to his interpretation. Ticciati sees Barth's focus on Job's free obedience as key to his reading—his already developed theology driving his exposition.[6] She discusses Barth's use of historical criticism in a brief footnote, arguing that his comments are clearly "not integral to his argument."[7] This chapter argues that, though Barth does not contribute to historical criticism in ways that advance the historical-critical agenda, he does broadly use the findings of historical criticism to advance his own theological agenda. That is, he does not dismiss historical-critical theories on Job in the way that Ticciati seems to insinuate, but incorporates them in unique, and perhaps eclectic ways. What follows is an analysis of Barth's interpretive strategy of the book of Job, including his interest in the history of the authorship of the book, showing that his integrated approach, which includes historical criticism, theology, and a proto-canonical approach, contribute to a typological reading of Job that presents to Barth's reader a picture of a freely obedient Job, a freely active God, and a group of friends who view God in such a restricted manner that they exhibit a sinfulness destructive to Christian theology.

As one reads through Barth's interpretation of Job many familiar themes in Barth's theology emerge. These topics share such an enmeshed relationship that discussion of one of his theories necessitates the knowledge of another. I will begin my discussion on Barth's Job with discussion on Barth's doctrine

---

5. Ticciati, *Disruption*. N.B.: She is not really approaching Job as a biblical scholar herself but as a theologian.

6. Ibid., 1–3.

7. Ibid., 4.

of revelation, which relates to Job in that it explains how the Old Testament fits into Barth's doctrine. Revelation also helps explain how Barth interprets the God speeches in the book of Job, and also begins to shed light on Barth's Christological exegesis and typological imagination. Following the brief discussion on Revelation comes an exploration on how historical-criticism of the book of Job aids Barth's interpretation of the book as a cross-section of the church's relationship to God. Next I discuss typology and the placement of Barth's interpretation of Job under the heading "The True Witness." Before concluding with an evaluation of Barth's method and interpretation, I will look closely at how the theme of freedom underlies Barth's discourse. Space precludes an extended exploration of this major theme in Barth's *Dogmatics* but even a cursory reading of Barth's Job will note the importance of Job's freedom in obedience to God and God's freedom in electing Job and how this freedom eventually mediates the extended discourse on suffering that Job and his friends undertake in the bulk of the book.

At one point in the large print of §70 in *Church Dogmatics* IV/3.1, Karl Barth discusses the problem with doctrine and the person of Jesus Christ as follows:

> Doctrine ... participates or does not participate in the truth to the extent and in the measure that directly or indirectly it teaches Him or fails to do so. But he cannot be enclosed or confined in any doctrine concerning Him, not even the most correct Christology.... He is not conditioned by nor bound to it, as it is conditioned by or bound to Him.[8]

This brief statement addresses many of the points that Barth will engage in the next one hundred pages of his *Dogmatics*. Most directly, it deals with the freedom of God in his relation to humanity—that no doctrine can contain God for then it will be superior to God.[9] Secondarily, this statement leads to the importance of the historicalness and personality of God's true Witness in Jesus Christ. Since doctrine is generally abstract and does not account for one-to-one contact, it is not a wholly adequate medium with which to discuss God. Thirdly, since he dedicates roughly 40 percent of the next 100 pages to his exegesis of Job, it is difficult not to notice how Barth's writings might relate to his excursuses on Job. One way this particular quote relates to Job is that it instructs the reader to resist a one-to-one correspondence between Jesus and Job. It is tempting to think of typological exegesis as one-to-one comparison, but in Barth's case it is closer to metaphor in

8. Barth, *CD* IV.3.1, 376.

9. Recall Vischer's assessment that God is not subservient to the law that God purveys.

that the type *points to* the anti-type or some *tertium quid*. If a critic were to describe a character with the common designation "modern-day Falstaff," the description would break down awfully quickly if using strict allegorical parameters. But if the one describing the character only means that Falstaff points to the modern-day figure, then a "type" of allegory seems to have been employed. This is what Barth will do with Job and Jesus to some extent and this is indicated in the line quoted above. If Barth were employing allegory à la Gregory the Great then Christ, as the anti-type to Job, would be *bound* to the description of Job just as he explains cannot happen with a free Christ. On the other hand, one could equally fall into the trap of thinking that Job is bound to Barth's Christology. Neither of these is the case, as will be shown below.

Barth discusses Jesus Christ as the true Witness in three sections, each followed by an interpretation of an element of the character of Job. After his discourse on Jesus and Job, he discusses the falsehood of humanity. He finds this analogous with Job's friends, the interpretation of whom follows.

The first section on Jesus Christ discusses his relationship with God and describes it as one based on freedom—the freedom of God to crown the man Jesus Christ and the freedom of Christ to obey God.[10] Jesus as a man is able to relate to humanity but his relationship with God gives him the ability to condemn humans as well. Barth then describes the aspects of Job that are similar to this as an illustration of a free relationship between a human and God. He admits that any number of New Testament passages could suffice when illustrating what he has described in the large print thus far. However, the story of Job seems to draw him more and he even suggests that it is the story of Job that is the basis for the large print rather than vice versa. What follows is a general introduction to Job which leads to a description of the man Job. This is based on the prose description in the book, which Barth suggests is the pure form of Job. He sees him as pious and unique to the point that, despite his fallibility, he will not fail in the wager placed on him. God in his infallibility can guarantee that Job will succeed. Nevertheless, Barth's main point about Job and his relationship to God is that this is a relationship based on freedom—God's freedom to elect and Job's freedom to obey.[11] When God blesses Job at the beginning and end of the story, it is a free act, not one based on reward and punishment. Taking his cue from Vischer, Barth sees the key phrase in the book to be Satan's wager questioning Job's decision to follow God "for nought" (*chinnam*) in the same way

---

10. Ibid., 383.
11. Ibid., 386.

that God blesses Job freely.[12] After introducing this hermeneutical key to his interpretation of the story of Job, Barth moves back to his description of the true Witness. Job acts as a type of the true Witness because, like Christ, he is a "free servant of the free God," but Barth is very careful to point out that Job's similarities with Jesus Christ should not be exaggerated.[13] Job, instead, "belongs to the context of the witness of the history of Israel which is only moving towards the history of Jesus Christ."[14] Barth leaves his essay on Job behind for a while to continue his exposition of Jesus as true Witness, noting that Job should remain in one's mind as a "type of Jesus Christ, a witness to the true Witness."[15]

The image of the suffering Christ dominates the large print of this section of §70. When explaining the depths to which Christ will plunge himself in order to relate to humanity's suffering, Barth commonly uses the phrase "Gethsemane and Golgotha." Christ becomes hidden and unrecognizable to us but does not leave his pure form of Victor behind.[16] This idea is Barth's basis for exegeting the sufferings of Job, putting into question the traditional position of Job as theodicy. "God Himself suffers with us as [Christ] suffers," Barth writes.[17] Thus, Barth continues to focus on free obedience as the main problem in Job, complicated by an unknown form of God. Just as Christ takes on a different form in his suffering, so does Job. The transformation of Job from chapter 2 to chapter 3 is as striking as the transformation of Christ in Philippians 2. Barth continues, "It is not that he does not remain the same. As the same both in God's relationship to him and his to God, he will later reappear in the pure form which for the moment is concealed."[18] However, Christ's person complicates the analogy by acting not only as the anti-type to Job but also to God. God also appears in an alien, transformed image and this mysterious persona of God—a veiled revelation—is the source of Job's suffering. Job cannot reconcile the God whom he worshipped in the prologue with the God whom he worships in the dialogues. Thus the suffering comes from the worship itself—though he is ignorant of this God, he remains faithful. Barth's attraction toward paradox comes to the fore here—human and divine, hidden and revealed, right and wrong—however,

---

12. Vischer, "*Hiob*, Ein Zeuge Jesu Christi," 4.
13. Barth, *CD* IV.3.1, 388.
14. Ibid.
15. Ibid.
16. Ibid., 395.
17. Ibid., 397.
18. Ibid., 398.

Job's relationship with God remains intact and the tension between these opposites creates tension in Job.

The Word and words of God as a response to God's alienation to humanity is Barth's third topic. Through the power of the Holy Spirit, God speaks the word only he can speak through all of history. This is emulated in the activity of Christ on the Cross. The event that Barth uses to describe this effective word is the sigh that Christ breathed when he died. "It is at once the death-cry of the man who dies in Him and the birth-cry of the man who comes to life in Him."[19] The reconciling power of God reveals itself through a suffering person. Humanity's response is to "be ready to be told by Him that we shall find Him precisely where we do not think we should look for Him, namely, in direct confrontation with and at the very heart of our own reality. . . . The lonely man of Gethsemane and Golgotha, the lonely God, then comes together with lonely man isolated in his deepest need."[20] Barth illustrates this in God's speeches to Job—a fascinating interpretation of God's confusing response in the Old Testament book. When God speaks to Job out of the whirlwind, Job's response suggests that he is not confused. Barth reasons that this is because God reveals himself to Job as the God Job has not ceased to worship. The tension that Job feels between the God who has blessed him and the one who attacks him is released when it is revealed that they are one and the same and that God makes a movement toward Job. The election of God by Job is shown to have been reciprocated. Thus Barth finds in the book of Job, not an unsolvable quagmire but a profound illustration of the free God and free human in dynamic relationship.

Barth follows this last section of "The True Witness" with a discourse on "The Falsehood of Man." This particular type of sin, Barth explains, is "possible and powerful only in this age. It takes place as man desires and attempts to avoid Jesus Christ as the true Witness encountering him. Man would rather escape this encounter."[21] The reason for this is that "man in this era is exposed to a relatively much stronger unsettlement and constriction by the painful truth of God than in any other sphere"—that being the truth of God present in the suffering and death of Christ.[22] Despite this being a distinctively Christian sin, Barth finds his most adequate illustration of this falsehood in the pre-Christian Old Testament, presumably because Job has so far done an excellent job of emulating the true Witness in his suffering and communicating with God. The friends are so confident of their doc-

---

19. Ibid., 413.
20. Ibid., 416.
21. Ibid., 435.
22. Ibid., 452.

trines that they refuse to see the true Word of God revealed in the suffering normally reserved for the sinful and cursed human.

The above, then, is the context in which one finds Barth's Job, which seems unusual in the modern era. It is uncommon for commentators to discuss Job Christologically, but Barth cannot deny the context in which he, himself, finds the book of Job. Its placement in the canon focuses the interpretation on what Barth sees as the centre of the canon—Jesus Christ. Because of this, he is able to see a different side of the speeches of God—a side where God is not merely (and to many, inadequately) responding to Job in the whirlwind, but where God is speaking to Job through the suffering Job is experiencing. Thus, Barth presents a reading of Job that bypasses theodicy by virtue of a canonical approach and a theology of address that stems from his doctrine of revelation.

REVELATION AND THE BOOK OF JOB

As noted in the brief analysis of John Calvin's sermons on Job, Calvin interested himself greatly in the hiddenness of God in the book. God's veiled state leads to the suffering of Job more than his physical ailments. As a Reformed theologian himself with Lutheran influence, Barth's interest in God's veiling should not surprise. One may recall Calvin's interpretation of the book of Job as meditation on the hiddenness of God's providential activity. However, Barth's interpretation of Job shares little in common with Calvin's in most other ways. In fact, the hiddenness of God in the book of Job is less overt in Barth's reading, perhaps because it is a presumed feature of God based on Barth's aversion to natural theology. The dialectical theology that he espouses takes the veiling of God as an *a priori* fact about God that only God can overcome. The dialectical method of theology that Barth helped to establish early in his career has undergone many explanations by many theologians over the years.[23] Rather than retread this well-worn path, I will merely highlight the features of it that benefit this present study.

Dialectical theology relates to Barth's Job in that the tension that the dialectical theologians attempted to hold between the *via positiva* of the scholastic method and the *via negativa* of mysticism mimics the tension between Job and his friends during their dialogue.[24] Job's friends' attempts to describe God definitively frustrate Job and his personal experience which seems to negate the friends' objective reasoning. In the end, Barth shows

---

23. For recent discussions on dialectical theology and Karl Barth, see McCormack, *Barth's Critically Realistic*; Dorrien, *Barthian Revolt*; and Chalamet, *Dialectical Theologians*.

24. Richardson, "Rise," 319.

that Job's friends, like the established theologians of previous generations, are both right and wrong and that Job is both wrong and right. God alone can intervene in the discussion and even then does not directly answer the question, remaining veiled even in his revelation.

The Bible witnesses to God's revelation in Jesus, whom Barth calls "The True Witness" in the section of *Dogmatics* where one finds his interpretation of Job. The Word of God, thus, comes to us in three forms: God reveals the Word in Christ, but the Word is proclaimed in preaching and it is written in the Bible.[25] As Colin Gunton explains, however, God remains veiled in this act because even though the hidden God finally reveals himself in the person of Jesus Christ, "it is not obviously God . . . , it [is] just a man wandering around teaching."[26] However hidden God remains in Jesus, one cannot separate God from Jesus. God, in some ways, must be revealed in Jesus Christ because God is not God without Jesus Christ.[27] So when Barth discusses the book of Job and what it says about God's relationship to humanity, he must also discuss Jesus Christ since Jesus, the "God with man," is the true revelation of God.[28] Though Christ does not appear in Scripture until the New Testament, his intrinsic relationship with God the Father necessitates discussion of him in the Old Testament.

If Jesus is God revealed and the Bible acts as that revelation written down, Barth does draw a distinction between the two Testaments. The Old Testament documents the expectation of God's revelation and the New Testament recollects God's revelation. This is not to say that the time for expecting the revelation of God in Jesus Christ is not revelation itself, for Barth says that "because it is the time for expecting it, it is itself revelation-time."[29] The Bible's authority comes in its witness to revelation of the highest order even though it bears the words of humans.[30]

Barth finds reason to hold to this doctrine of the Old Testament in the writings of the New Testament. Because the New Testament treats the Old Testament as an authoritative witness to the revelation the New Testament

---

25. Ibid., 321. Mark Gignilliat describes it as "general human history and time operat[ing] as the veil hiding revelation from us" (Gignilliat, *Fifth Gospel*, 31).

26. Gunton, *The Barth Lectures*, 80.

27. Ibid., 112.

28. Keller, "Expectation," 167.

29. *CD* I/2, 86. Roger Keller may explain this better than Barth himself when he writes, "revelation in the OT is actually the expectation of revelation, or most properly, *expected* revelation. . . . Because the OT community awaited and expected God's revelation of himself in the future, they already had and participated in that revelation" (ibid., 168).

30. Kraeling, *Old Testament*, 168. See also Richardson, "Rise," 322.

A Witness to the True Witness

recollects,[31] one should not shy from the position that the Old Testament participates in the revelation of Christ, however hidden Christ is in the words of the Old Testament. This does not mean that Barth holds the New Testament in a more dignified place, only that both Testaments witness to Christ, one before the Incarnation and one after it.[32]

Barth's doctrine of revelation explains in part Barth's readiness to find Christ in the book of Job, since Christ is present in the Old Testament in this unique way. However, before we look more closely into the intricacies of his typology it is necessary to explore his use of historical criticism. Barth's aversion to natural revelation means that God does not work through human agents (other than Jesus). Thus, the words of the Bible are not God's words but bear witness to God as Word.[33] The words of the Bible, therefore, may contain histories independent of the canonical text. The book of Job is certainly not immune to these histories.

HISTORICAL CRITICISM IN BARTH'S TREATMENT OF JOB

Barth's use of historical criticism is not a major aspect of his exegetical method.[34] In some passages, he deals theologically with what seems like a source-critical issue. Ticciati insinuates that this is the case throughout Barth's Job discourse, writing that "he proceeds with his argument in a way that bypasses [the results of historical criticism], not allowing them to get in

---

31. Keller, "Expectation," 169. Barth writes, "But the New Testament writers are utterly unanimous in seeing, not in Judaism—not one of them was concerned with that—but in the history of Israel attested in the Old Testament canon the connecting point for their proclamation, doctrine and narrative of Christ; and *vice versa*, in seeing in their proclamation, doctrine and narrative of Christ the truth of the history of Israel, the fulfillment of the Holy Scripture read in the synagogue" (CD I/2, 72).

32. Kraeling, *Old Testament*, 169.

33. Richardson, "Rise," 322.

34. Barth's use of the historical-critical method is quite complex and it seems that he uses it in different ways throughout the *Church Dogmatics*. Greene-McCreight, *Ad Litteram* lays out a bibliography of several works regarding Barth and historical-criticism on note 84 of page 233 to which I would add discussions by McGlasson, *Jesus and Judas*; Cunningham, *What is Theological Exegesis?* Gignilliat, *Fifth Gospel*, and Davis, "Typology in Barth's Doctrine of Scripture," 33–49. For a useful work describing Barth and historical criticism in his commentary on Romans, see Burnett, *Karl Barth's Theological Exegesis*. For Barth in his Philippians commentary, see McCormack, "Significance," and Francis Watson, "Barth's *Philippians* as Theological Exegesis."

Read Him Again and Again

the way of his theological insights."[35] This may be the case in a few passages. For instance, in discussing the divine names in Job, he writes:

> it cannot be an accident, that this proper name of God in the Old Testament [Yahweh] ... is predominant in the explanatory opening chapters (1–2), being always used except in a few more general references, but that in the whole of the central section ... it is replaced by the generic names Elohim and Shaddai, only to recur quite suddenly in the introductory verses to the divine speeches ... and to become predominant again in [chapter] 2. Thus Yahweh, the Lord of Israel and its history ... is the God whose servant is Job the Edomite.[36]

If this were to come earlier in Barth's discourse, it would perhaps seem a little naïve. One can easily attribute the change in divine names to the multitude of authors writing in various settings which utilize different names for God. However, Barth *is* aware of the finer points in the history behind the text and even seems to have a strategy in dealing with these sources, though it does not fall into the conventional usage of his day.[37]

In *CD* IV/2, Barth explicitly discusses how he incorporates biblical criticism into his exegesis. In introducing his interpretation of the Numbers 13–14 narrative concerning the spies of Moses in the Promised Land, he discusses the transmission of the text into its final kerygmatic form from chronicle, saga, and "that which has been consciously fashioned, or invented, in a later and synthetic review."[38] It is clear that the history behind the text has some importance in providing information regarding purpose. In the case of Numbers, Barth recognizes a typological relationship between the initial failings in the conquest of the Promised Land presented in the Num-

---

35. Ticciati, *Disruption*, 4.

36. Barth, *CD* IV.3.1, 427.

37. That being said, his source-critical assumptions are not widely attested today. He largely follows the conclusions of the day. He mentions Oettli, Lamparter, Hölscher, and R. de Pury in addition to Vischer and Kierkegaard. Often though, he criticizes their conclusions to make his point. Hölscher, his contemporary, he chides for trying to identify Job's illness in 7:4 as elephantiasis (399). On the other hand, Hölscher seems to provide Barth with theory that Job 28:28 is not original to chapter 28 (Hölscher, *Das Buch Hiob*, 68). With Oettli, a scholar from the previous generation, Barth accepts a new translation and a summation of Job's last speech. One assumes that he consulted other sources and accepted the consensus opinions, but we cannot be sure.

38 Barth, *CD* IV.2, 478–79. Though he does not say so, it is possible he has in mind the three constituent parts—J, P, and E—that make up this narrative according to historical critics. (See Noth, *Numbers*, 101–3, as well as Knierim and Coats, *Numbers*, 7, 183–93. The original German version of Noth's commentary is from 1966, so would have succeeded *CD* IV.3 but typifies the consensus of the era nonetheless.)

bers narrative and anxieties in Israel's return from exile—when part of the narrative was presumably written. This background is only one part of the interpretation of the text and once distinctions have been made concerning the makeup of the text, "they can be pushed again into the background that the whole can be read . . . as the totality it professes to be."[39] Thus, the background of the text is merely that—background. The text as Barth receives it is the important element to him, no matter how historically accurate the narrative or the findings of historical critics purport to be. By pushing the history into the background Barth promotes an interpretive stance that he calls a "tested and critical naivety."[40]

The tested and critical naivety relates to his doctrine of revelation. Gunton explains that Barth viewed the Bible as imposed on humanity. That is, the readers of the Bible are in some ways passive agents who receive the Bible, thus Barth accepts the Bible as correct in its proclamations. God reveals himself in the Scriptures and we trust God more than ourselves. Therefore we must take historical criticism as useful but not entirely trustworthy. It can benefit us as long as we are aware of our prejudices in encountering its conclusions.[41] Most importantly, the results of historical criticism should not act as ends in and of themselves. In the case of his commentary on Philippians, Barth concerns himself less with Paul as subject of his study than Paul as witness to revelation.[42] His approach changes somewhat between the publication of his Romans commentary and his Philippians commentary and this is evident in his exegesis in the *Church Dogmatics*. Historical criticism is no longer anathema but a tool.[43] When the tool, however, proves inappropriate for the job at hand, Barth sets it aside, as seems evident in his work on Numbers and also Job. Barth's acknowledgement and use of historical criticism contributes to his typological reading of Job by taking the focus away from authorial intent or the original *Sitz im Leben*. He instead reads every text of Scripture in the light of the Bible as a whole. Problems do arise, however, when he interprets according to some of his theological presuppositions and in other cases does not follow his own post-critical theories.

---

39. Barth, *CD* IV.2, 479. See also Gignilliat, who writes of Barth's Old Testament exegesis following Greene-McCreight, "It is the text which governs the interpretive process rather than historical-critical reconstruction" (Gignilliat, *Fifth Gospel*, 4).

40. Barth, *CD* IV.2, 479.

41. Gunton, *Lectures*, 73–74.

42. McCormack, "The Significance of Karl Barth's Theological Exegesis of Philippians," xviii.

43. Watson, "Barth's *Philippians* as Theological Exegesis," xxx.

Read Him Again and Again

When Barth recognizes the history behind the text, particularly in Job, it is not always clear that he does much more than acknowledge this history. One might surmise that he is merely attempting to gain credibility with the biblical scholars of his era who are preoccupied with historical criticism. Thus he agrees with their assessments with little or no protest. However, Barth's hermeneutic does not allow him to dwell on what the text used to be. Instead, he focuses on the writings that would be canonized as Holy Scripture later in their existence.[44] In his reading concerning God's speeches to Job, Barth muses, "we have here two different compositions which have been brought together from obviously different sources. (The question suggests itself whether there did not once exist a whole corpus of Job literature of which a selection has now been assembled in the present Book)."[45] This parenthetical statement brings to light Barth's confidence in the existence of multiple sources of the book of Job—sources that are unavailable to us but whose hypothetical existence still affects one's interpretation in subtle and nuanced ways. The "existence" of words that are unavailable have no definable meaning; for a dogmatician, these hypothetical words do nothing but bring one's focus to the seams of the text. At these seams, two seemingly disparate texts rub against each other and the friction creates some of the energy that Barth draws from to make theological claims. He begins this interpretive technique early in his work on Job.

Early in his discourse, Barth acknowledges the likelihood of seven authors of the book of Job composing the following sections: the prose chapters 1–2 and 42; the dialogues with the friends at 3–24, 27, and 29–31; problematic dialogues in 25–26; the Elihu speeches at 32–37; God's first response at 38–39; God's second response at 40–41; and the hymn on wisdom at 28. Although he does not say it, Barth presumably would acknowledge an eighth author who writes connecting verses at the seams such as some of the verses at the beginning of 42 that would make little sense without the dialogues but are written in the style of 1–2 (unless these could be answered by the missing sections of the folktale). A ninth author would likely have

---

44. Early in his discourse on Job, Barth expresses the importance he places on the received text in a parenthetical note on C. G. Jung's *Antwort auf Hiob*. He writes, "From the human standpoint this is a very penetrating study, and incidentally it throws a good deal of light on the psychology of the professional psychologist. As an attempt to explain Job and the Bible, however, it suffers quite hopelessly from the fact that according to his own declaration on p. 15 the author is quite 'unashamedly and ruthlessly' giving expression to his very remarkable impressions. Hence he cannot possibly read and consider what is actually there, and his work is quite useless in this regard" (Barth, *CD* IV.3.1, 384).

45. Ibid., 428.

A Witness to the True Witness

written 28:28.[46] Barth then states that "at some time and by some person all this came to be seen and understood as the unity which it now constitutes in the Canon. We remember these problems and hypotheses as we now turn to consider the whole."[47] It might occur to Barth's addressee that "remember these problems" is all that he does. He is, in actuality, rarely explicit concerning the purpose of remembering these problems. However, the acknowledgement of the history behind the text does seem intimately related to the overall interpretation of the text, especially with regard to the one who will eventually arrange these disparate texts.

The real author to Barth is the redactor[48] who lends meaning to the speeches by placing them aside the other speeches and then places that unit of speeches in the text as a response to Job and his friends and as the climax to the "folktale."[49] This body of work, the book of Job, is then placed by another editor (perhaps the community of believers) in the context of the canon, lending it more meaning. In a way, the book of Job acts as a microcosm of the canon as a whole. The smaller pieces contain some meaning, but the meaning is focused or generated as the context changes.

As in the canon itself, the independent documents in Job are difficult to reconcile with each other. But the tension should not merely be reconciled. Another explanation could be sought after. In Barth's own words:

> It might ... be suggested that in chapters 3–31 we have an independent text which really intends to leave matters like this, both as between Job and God and also as between Job and his friends, thus indicating the indissolubly problematic existential situation of man at peace and yet also at odds with God. But we cannot be satisfied with this if we consider the whole span of the Book. The overriding purpose of the whole is to show that this situation is intolerable and that it is in fact resolved.[50]

A source-critical analysis that finds several different stories and can reconstruct the plots would not be an invalid scholarly project. One story would

---

46. Ibid., 426.

47. Ibid., 384.

48. Cf. Franz Rosenzweig (1886–1929), who argued that even if the Torah was a composite of several different sources writing in different periods, the redactor was the true "Rabbenu" (Our Teacher). "The Torah which speaks to the Jewish soul is the Torah which is now in our hands" (Jacobs, *The Jewish Religion*, 429).

49. Note, however, that occasionally he suggests that the text itself has its own motivation. For instance, when discussing the various histories present in the final form of Numbers 13–14, he states, "It is only then that they can say what they are trying to say." This is likely only a literary device and should not be understood in a mystical way.

50. Barth, *CD* IV.3.1, 422.

be of a man who loses everything and gains it back two fold and the other would be of a man with unidentified loss carrying on a debate over existential matters with a group of people with no resolution—like an ANE *Waiting for Godot*. But these independent narratives are non-extant and instead we have a single plot that is filled with tension.

Barth has two strategies for dealing with this tension.[51] The first is in the level of the final form of the book of Job and the second is based on his theological presuppositions. On page 398 of *CD* IV/3.1, Barth intimates the importance of the redactor to the interpretation of the book of Job. The contrast between the character of Job in the folktale and the dialogues is so surprising that one could hardly expect a single author to produce such a work, so Barth implies. In fact, the redactor, or so it seems to Barth, sees a problem in Job's initial responses to his injury in 1:21 and 2:10. Hypothetically,[52] the redactor has in hand two texts. One is the folktale and the other is the poetic dialogues. The dialogues need an introduction to set the stage of Job's complaint. The problem is that the folktale seems to raise a problem and solve it in a relatively short manner lacking much drama. Thus, by attaching the dialogues to the folktale, he suggests that Job's comments in 1:21 and 2:10, which imply that God has won the wager versus the *Satan*, do not tell the whole story. As Barth writes, "with the fine sayings in 1:21 and 2:10 he has merely plotted the way, according to the obvious view of the redactor and apparently of the incomplete folk-saga reproduced [*sic*] in the Book. He has now to tread it."[53] Thus, to Barth, Job's suffering is not in his loss of possessions or in his illness but in what comes later, in the treading. For later, in the dialogues, he comes to the realization that his piety must not have mediated to him the knowledge of God since he cannot reconcile the God that he worshipped on behalf of his sons with the one that has caused his suffering. This is what Barth calls the "knowledge and ignorance of God in headlong collision and unbearable tension."[54]

From a literary standpoint, the above explanation is unusual but certainly not unacceptable. It is common in narratives to present an ostensibly resolved conflict only to have it uprooted by previously overlooked psychological issues or unexpected outside influences. In the ancient world, the Oedipus trilogy comes to mind. Cosmic influences are also not rare in narrative and drama throughout the ages. Thus, in Barth's explanation, the

---

51. Resolving is not the right word since tension is an important element of his exegesis.

52. The irony of the following reconstruction is noted at both the level of the attention to the history behind the book of Job and the authorial intent of Karl Barth himself.

53. Ibid., 398.

54. Ibid., 401.

history (*Geschichte*) at play in the Job story is subject to the true history of God. As Barth himself explains:

> If there is no doubt that the poem is related to the saga, that it is inspired by it and links up with it, there is also no doubt that the picture which is given of Job cannot be harmonized with that of the saga nor the words put in Job's mouth literally interpreted in the light of it in the sense of pragmatic history.⁵⁵

Rather, one needs to interpret them in the sense of true history. Thus, the story of Job, in its final form, is to be interpreted in light of the cosmic reality behind the history that humanity experiences on a day-to-day basis.⁵⁶ This is the basis for Barth's typology in his Job discourse. He is not merely exegeting Job for the sake of understanding the text itself. He is interested in the true history, the object of the text. How Barth does this is the topic for the next section below.

TYPOLOGY IN BARTH'S JOB

Theoretically, Barth's reading of Job would not need as much attention to the background of the text as he gives. One could explain the drastic change in Job's character from the prologue to the dialogues and back through a variety of means. One can easily imagine a psychoanalytic reading of the character of Job that argues that Job is experiencing the effects of posttraumatic stress disorder, for instance.⁵⁷ In a more rhetorical-critical reading, Job's confidence in God might be shaken through his waiting on the ash heap. The reader questions Job's integrity because of the discrepancy between Job's initial reaction to his suffering and how he expresses himself in the dialogues. In the end, the reader's definition of integrity and his understanding of Job's suffering change because of the effect the text has on its audience. At first, it seems plausible that Barth's attention to historical-critical matters is merely a product of his own cultural and historical context. The culture in biblical scholarship and theology in the middle of the last century necessitated such discourse since opponents could question one's credibility for not

---

55. Ibid.

56. This is not a perceived cosmic reality, of course, without God revealing it.

57. Of course, it should surprise no one to find out these studies exist. See Haughn and Gonsiorek, "The Book of Job: Implications for Construct Validity of Posttraumatic Stress Disorder Diagnostic Criteria," 833–45. Another article that hints that Job might suffer from PTSD is Johnson, "A Phonological Existential Analysis to the Book of Job," 391–401. Jung's previously mentioned *Antwort auf Hiob* acts more as a psychoanalytic reading of God than of Job (Jung, *Answer to Job*).

taking seriously such minutiae. But perhaps Barth has a different strategy in mind altogether. His interest does not seem at all to be to bolster his image among the broader academic community. His stature at the time of writing *CD* IV/3 was massive and, after all, he was writing a *church* dogmatics. His attention to critical matters could very well have come from his culture or his interest in the truth of history. However, it could also be an intrinsic part of his typological reading of the Bible.

In the juxtaposition of the multitudinous texts of Job that Barth hypothesizes, a single Job narrative emerges. Barth does not deny that the various sources of Job have their own integrity, but to reconstruct these stories is to lead one astray from the story before the reader. As mentioned above, the book of Job has much in common with the Bible as a whole. Multiple texts with various authors placed into a particular context create a single unit with a particular focus in the Bible as well.

By drawing attention to the multitude of texts that make up the final form of Job, Barth does not merely "provide a starting point" for exegesis or "help to prevent subjective excess" as Bruce McCormack argues.[58] Barth also shows the futility of searching too hard for authorial intent or meaning behind the text.[59] And yet he still is able to use the text for his theology because it is not the author that generates the meaning. Rather than the text as the source for meaning alone, Barth sees the text as pointing to the object of the text. Thus, one could argue that the book of Job is no different than any of the other books of the Bible, since they all point to Jesus Christ. However, it is clear that Barth sees the book of Job as unique in the way that it points to the true Witness and also to what aspects of Christ that it points.

In its context, Barth's interpretation of Job is used to illustrate his doctrine of reconciliation and Jesus's role in it as the true Witness. Thus, Barth treats Job as "an analogy in relation to Jesus Christ, and with suitable qualifications Job may thus be called a type of Jesus Christ, a witness to the true Witness."[60] To call Job merely analogous to Jesus, however, would not have the same force that Barth employs. There is clearly more significance to the book of Job than its ability to illustrate the object of faith. Nevertheless,

---

58. McCormack, "Historical-Criticism," 221.

59. McCormack faults Mark Wallace for anachronism when Wallace argues that Barth interprets under the assumption of the intentional fallacy. Of course Wallace could contest McCormack's claim by citing the intentional fallacy with regard to Barth himself. Barth's actual intent with his use of historical criticism can only be hypothesized. Furthermore, as Cunningham and McGlasson have both suggested in their analysis of Barth's exegesis, what he says he will do and what he does do not always match up, so trying to determine Barth's hermeneutic based on his explicit intentions is flawed. See Wallace, "Karl Barth's Hermeneutic," esp. 400–402.

60. Barth, *CD* IV.3.1, 401.

Job as analogy of Christ is clearly important and he shows how it works on a number of levels. Primarily, however, Job is analogous to Christ in his relationship to God in the face of adversity.[61]

There is little controversy in Barth's explication as to the potential meanings of difficult passages in Job. Since it is not a proper commentary, it is possible that Barth wrestled over ambiguous passages before settling on a particular meaning. Perhaps his proto-canonical approach confirmed one meaning over another because of the context in which Job finds itself. Whatever the case, Barth writes with confidence that the advocate (16:19) and redeemer (19:25) to whom Job appeals in his ostensible court case against God is God himself. This reading is certainly plausible, but it is not definite. However, it is very important for Barth's particular interpretation.[62] In Barth's own words, Job . . .

> looks to the one and only God who "even now" (16:19), even in the hostility of His attitude, is the same as He will be, who will set that limit in His own time and manner, who is thus his Witness, Advocate and Guarantor, who even now is for him as He is against him. In this way, and this way alone, Job is a real Israel, a witness of the truth, and as such also a witness of Jesus Christ.[63]

Even in the worst of his suffering, Job does not cease to cling to God. He worships his enemy even as he accuses him. Barth sees in this a parallel with Christ who obeys the God who sends him to suffer. He is worshiping and obeying the one who forsakes him. In the case of Job, God appears alien and foreign, in opposition to Job's previous understanding of him and

---

61. In the earlier example of a modern literary character described as a "modern-day Falstaff," the signifier is Falstaff and the signified is, say, Ignatius J. Reilly of *A Confederacy of Dunces* by John Kennedy Toole. The goal is to describe Reilly as a fat blowhard and an effective way to supplant that image in someone's mind is to conjure up an already existing, well-known character. This seems to be Barth's main goal in describing Job as a witness to Christ—Job is the signifier and Christ is the signified. However, there are elements in Barth's interpretation that turn the signifier-signified relationship around. The signifier-signified relationship in this type of description is not limited to chronology, not just in Barth's reading of the Bible, but also with the history of literature. A later text may gain notoriety beyond the text that precedes it as Shakespeare's plays have done with regard to his influences such as Ovid. See Higton, "The Fulfilment of History," for a related phenomenon with regard to Dante, Virgil, and Barth himself.

62. The reading popularized by Handel that the redeemer in 19:25 is the person of Christ is significantly not the reading that Barth presents. The scope of this project does not allow for a full evaluation of Barth's Trinitarian theology; it should be enough at this point to refer to the primary way in which Barth's typology works—Job is a witness to the true Witness. Thus Christ is seen as pointing to God in this case more than he is one with God and that Job is identified with Christ more than appealing to him.

63. Barth, *CD* IV.3.1, 425.

Job's friends' current understanding of him. And yet Job does not stray for a better God—one who fits into his paradigm. His understanding of God changes, but it is the same God. This clinging as Christ clings leads to his witnessing to Christ in other ways.

In all four of his sections on Job, Barth discusses the unmasking effect both Job and Christ have on sin. Barth describes this particular sin as that which is pious and even sincere.[64] The friends of Job seem so theologically astute and even pastorally attentive that one must remind oneself that God will ultimately condemn their talk and uphold Job's borderline blasphemy.[65] Their theological acumen, however, is why their sin, in the end, is so insidious. "We should not be dealing with the falsehood of man if it openly betrayed itself in the speeches of these men," Barth writes.[66] They are right when they argue with Job that God is always "holy, righteous and wise, and therefore is always to be glorified."[67] However, in the case that appears in the text, the situation is that Job is in the right despite his words and that the friends are in the wrong despite theirs. Barth attributes this primarily to the posture towards God of each friend. The friends speak as though they are speaking for God and standing alongside God. Job, however, "simply stands before and under God."[68] Job is not interested in helping God, but in confronting God. "The real truth of God and man," Barth writes, "is valid when God and man are engaged in eye-to-eye and mouth-to-ear encounter."[69] It seems as though Barth, though he never gives a linguistic or philological explanation, is not convinced by the German translations of Job 42:7, 8. Most English translations render God's rebuke of Job's friends as "You have not spoken right *of* me/*about* me as my servant Job has." See KJV, NRSV, RSV, NIV, ESV. The Unrevidierte Elberfelder (1905), Luther Bibel (1912), and German Schlachter Version (1951), German versions available to Barth at his writing, all render the prepositional phrase in question „von mir." While these are justified readings, the MT contains the phrase /לֹא דִבַּרְתֶּם אֵלַי *lo' dibbartem 'elay*, which would be more naturally translated "you have not spoken *to* me." The implication with the more literal rendering is that Job's speaking *to* God is more important than his friends speaking *about* God.

While it is generally dangerous to base a reading on a preposition, it is important to note how this changes the focus of how Job is right and his

---

64. Ibid., 454.
65. Ibid., 455.
66. Ibid., 454.
67. Ibid.
68. Ibid., 457.
69. Ibid., 458.

friends are wrong and how it benefits Barth's reading in particular. Barth did not use the Hebrew in his exegesis and so likely did not dwell on the phrase despite it benefiting his reading. On the other hand, he may have been influenced by the Vulgate, which translates the phrase in question "*non estis locuti* coram *me rectum*" ("you did not speak rightly to my face") in 42:7 and "*locuti estis* ad *me recta*" ("you did not speak rightly to me") in 42:8. Both of these are closer to the "literal" Hebrew while the LXX has the more vague "ου γαρ ελαλησατε ενωπιον μου αληθες ουδεν" ("you have not spoken the truth of me . . ." but which could also read "you have not spoken the truth in my presence") in 42:7 and the erroneous "ου γαρ ελαλησατε αληθες κατα του θεραποντος μου Ιωβ" ("you have not spoken the truth against my servant Job") in 42:8.

With this in mind, Barth also notes that the friends are "strikingly unhistorical" in their speech. God is "active merely as [the] Architect, Guarantor and Executor" of a system, but does not act as a true personality.[70] The friends' platitudes do not relate to Job's situation as one that is dynamic—a point that Barth sees as critical in understanding Job's relationship to God. Thus, Job's words, despite their harshness, are original and fresh and relate to a living God.

It is this falsehood that both Job and Christ reveal through their active relationship with God. In the case of Job, this revelation has less to do with Job's actions as unmasking the falsehood of the friends and more with God's reaction to Job and his friends. God announces that the friends did not speak right with respect to God while Job did. This points back to the dialogue and declares Job's friends as unhistorical and their posture with God as inappropriate. Job, however, has had the correct posture and God declares him correct. To be sure, this is not obvious as the dialogue unfolds. Even knowing how the scene in heaven has transpired, that Job's friends are wrong and Job is right still comes as a bit of a surprise by chapter 42. This may help explain why Barth chooses to write a fourth section where he exposits the falsehood of the friends. Still, the declaration is unmistakable and thus somehow Job is right in what he said or how he said it.

The specific sin that Barth discusses in this fourth section is one that "takes place as man desires and attempts to avoid Jesus Christ as the true Witness encountering him."[71] Thus, the personality of Jesus Christ is the key aspect here just as the personal, encountering God is the key concept lacking in Job's friends' theology. What relates to this thesis is that Christ reveals the free personality of God through his suffering, not merely that an in-

---

70. Ibid., 459.
71. Ibid., 435.

nocent and just person suffers because of a wrongheaded understanding of justice. Note also the revelation of the God who confronts sinners through Jesus Christ. The sinner has difficulty grasping a God who confronts his people through a suffering Messiah because the sinner does not want to accept a God that reveals himself in this way.[72] Thus, to Barth, Job as one who suffers at the hand of God is an adequate illustration of this unmasked sin. God confronts sinners in both cases in a way that is difficult to accept and only the ones who choose to confront God are seen as just. However, the story does not end here.

In the book of Job, the friends are brought back into communion with God, significantly, through the activity of Job, the witness to the true Witness. That both Job and Christ intercede marks another way in which Job is seen as analogous to Christ. "We must not forget," writes Barth, "that the true Witness does not merely unmask them but also effectually intercedes for them, and in so doing comes to share in a new, visible, divine blessing."[73]

Barth couches Job's intercessory activity not only in the two instances of sacrifice and prayer in the prologue and epilogue, but he also sees Job as intercessor in his final speech in the dialogues. In chapters 29 and 31 of the book of Job, Job gives his final defense and it is one based not on what he has *not* done but what he has done, namely what he has done for other people. Thus, Job is shown as a type of priest, doing the work of God for the common person. However, the cultic activity is primarily seen as in Job as typical of Christ.[74] It is clear that Barth sees Job as type of Christ not only in his sacrificing a burnt offering for his sons and his friends but in his sacrificing of himself for the poor, widow, and fatherless. In the large print, when discussing the true Witness, Barth describes Christ's self-sacrifice as a free act. Job, like Christ, not only gives a burnt offering at the behest of God, but also gives of himself as an act of free obedience. Here, Barth shows again the importance of seeing the entire book of Job as a unit, for the meaning is created by the juxtaposition of those three scenes—Job as priestly intercessor and Job as human sacrifice. In doing this, the example of Christ is also presented in a practical way.

As Barth states quite often, Job is not Jesus Christ. This seems obvious, but in doing so he seems to be protecting himself from anyone claiming he is allegorizing.[75] Job, rather, "belongs to the context of the witness of the

72. Ibid., 452.

73. Ibid., 386. That "new, visible, divine blessing" is Job's restored fortunes, which typify God exalting Christ "to the highest place" to be given "the name that is above every name" (Philippians 2:9).

74. Ibid., 384.

75. As shown in chapter one, Barth has a concern over his exegesis being perceived

A Witness to the True Witness

history of Israel which is only moving towards the history of Jesus Christ."[76] So despite the similarities between Job and Jesus Christ, Barth also presents differences. One obvious difference between Job and Christ that Barth repeats throughout his discourse is the sinfulness of Job. Using the Lutheran phrase *simul iustus et peccator*, Barth describes Job as "right in all his sayings as the servant of Yahweh, and in none of them as fallible man."[77] Lest anyone think that Barth sees Job as a pre-Christian Christ, the fact that he dwells on Job's sinfulness is not even a necessary reading of the character of Job from a strictly exegetical level. Clines argues that Job being described as "blameless" should be taken literally in 1:1 because in the dialogues, "the issue is never whether his sins are serious or slight but simply whether he is a sinner or not."[78] Barth does not argue for such a reading perhaps because of his belief that no one other than Christ is sinless.[79] It is more likely that Barth sees God's rebuke of Job in 38:2 and 40:2 as well as Job's response to God in 40:4 as indicative of Job's sinfulness. Whether this is a necessary exegetical move is debatable.[80] What is important for this section is that Barth does not see Job as like Christ in his blamelessness.

More specifically, the metaphysical aspects of Christ's being are a factor in their differences. Job's finite existence makes him fallible while "Jesus is already Victor even as he goes to the defeat of Golgotha."[81] Clearly, Job cannot compare to Christ in this aspect of his being. In Barth's world, Christ is a totally unique person in that he exists on a different plane. Job is not unified with God in the way that Christ is but must wait for God to confront him. The pure history, in which Christ reigns as Victor for all time, where Christ can be the focus of all history, allows Barth to distinguish between Job and Christ while also giving him the ability to present Job as a type of Christ in a way more significant than mere analogy. Though Job is analogous to Christ, Christ's eternal state, however theologically credible or dubious Barth presents it, allows Job to point to Christ in all time. So Barth

---

as allegory. However, his exegesis is "reminiscent in many ways of the exegesis of the early Fathers" despite his "vehement rejection of the ancient word 'allegory'" (de Lubac, *Scripture in the Tradition*, 77).

76. Barth, *CD* IV.3.1, 388.

77. Ibid., 386.

78. Clines, *Job 1–20*, 12.

79. Though he does not argue for the historicity of the character of Job.

80. On page 407 Barth disagrees with Kierkegaard's assessment that "in spite of everything [Job] is right." This is a point to be discussed in the beginning of the next chapter in which Barth and Kierkegaard's readings are compared.

81. Barth, *CD* IV.3.1, 388.

finding limited parallels between Job and Jesus Christ betrays not only a literary phenomenon but also a theological one.

Job is not like Christ, as Barth also explains, in that there "can be no question of any work of salvation being accomplished in the drama of his history."[82] Yes, Job intercedes in two ways, but God effects the salvation of his friends. Even so, Job's intercessions are not necessary for their salvation in the way that Christ's are. In the case of Christ, his activity at Gethsemane and Golgotha is effective in a way that Job's sufferings cannot be.

Thus, Barth's case for Job as a type of Christ is a sophisticated and complex reading of the two biblical characters. Besides exegesis, theology and metaphysics also take part in his analysis of the sufferings of Job. His explication of Job in light of his dogmatic analysis of the true Witness has many twists and turns, but they are all interconnected, mainly held together by a lengthy theology exposited in the previous three and a half volumes of the *Church Dogmatics*.[83] One related doctrine that deserves special attention is that of freedom since Barth refers to both Job and God regularly as free agents in the drama.

FREEDOM IN BARTH AND BARTH'S JOB

Before discussing freedom in Barth we should take care to note something that Barth himself does not do, which is to define what he means by freedom. Barth invokes the term *Freiheit* often and in different ways in his work, not seeming to bear in mind that many people speak of the importance of freedom in many different ways.

George Hendry lists five different types of freedom in Barth's thought, noting that Barth uses them all interchangeably and only explicitly eliminates caprice or arbitrariness from his theology.[84] The types of freedom that Barth discusses are freedom as gratuity, freedom as option or choice, freedom as self-determination, freedom as initiative, and freedom as energy, by which he means that God exists in freedom.[85] Hendry's distinctions help us in our interpretation of Barth's Job since one can see how these concepts arise in Barth's thought regarding both how God acts toward Job and how Job acts toward God. Certainly we can also eliminate caprice from his interpretation, but elements of the other distinct definitions of freedom bear out in Barth's reading.

82. Ibid.
83. Ticciati, *Disruption*, 13.
84. Hendry, "The Freedom of God," 236.
85. Ibid., 233–35.

A Witness to the True Witness

Before discussing freedom in Job, however, some background on Barth's use of freedom generally bears mentioning. In the creation of the world, God expresses freedom in all of the categories Hendry outlines.[86] God shows initiative in choosing to create the world, a wholly unnecessary act. This first act establishes God's freedom, but also arises because God exists in freedom—one cannot understand God without understanding that God is free. Even in the act of creation God sustains his freedom by remaining transcendent. God is not tied to the world and so can love the world freely.[87] This being said, God has the freedom to enter the world and becomes immanent in the revelation of Jesus Christ.[88] Thus God's whole being reflects on the freedom so intrinsic to the Trinity.

In God's freedom in the creation of the world, God bestows freedom on his creatures as well. God "does not want to rule over puppets and slaves but rather in the triumph of the free decision of faithful servants and friends."[89] God's creatures receive the freedom to choose to obey. In this act, one notes Barth's interest in Job's freedom to obey God. Job's own self determination gives him the opportunity to obey God, an aspect of the book of Job with which many interpreters do not concern themselves.

In this granting of God's creatures' freedom, humans also have the ability to disobey and, thus, live outside God's covenant. In this loss of freedom at humanity's own hands, one sees the necessity to discuss this concept in the doctrine of reconciliation, where one finds Barth's interpretation of Job. God's choice to become immanent in the person of Jesus Christ instigates the restoration of freedom in humanity. God's cooperation with humanity in the Incarnation and sacrifice of Christ brings humans back into the covenant, restoring the freedom to obey.

God's freedom, then, emanates throughout his being and activity in the world. As a consequence of God's freedom in the gospel, one cannot turn theology into a system.[90] God's freedom in his transcendence and his freedom in his immanence does not allow for rules to govern God's behavior. Likewise, humanity's call to obedience does not relate to the obedience of a series of rules or laws but a personal God—and not only a personal God, but a God who lives with us as one of us.[91]

---

86. Ibid., 230.
87. Gunton, *Lectures*, 102.
88. Gunton, "Barth, the Trinity, and Human Freedom," 317.
89. CD II/2, 195f.
90. Gunton, *Lectures*, 92.
91. Gunton, "Barth, the Trinity, and Human Freedom," 320.

Read Him Again and Again

All of this, one sees in Barth's interpretation of Job. Job chooses to obey God, not a system or a series of rules in the way that Job's friends are wont to do. Job also elects God as God is, not as he is supposed to be. Most importantly, Job serves, obeys, and elects God in his gratuitous and free choice. In Job, Barth is able to illustrate much of his theology of freedom. Job's decision to obey God reflects the divine purpose of Christ's reconciling act, but Job also anticipates Christ's reconciliation in his own cultic activity on behalf of others. At the end of the book, Job sacrifices for his friends in order to bring them back into the covenant with God so that they may have the freedom to obey God as well.

EVALUATION OF BARTH'S JOB

At the beginning of Barth's discourse on the book of Job, Barth explains that he had already had before him the character of Job as analogy for his previous discussion on "the True Witness."[92] One marvels at how much of the book of Job he engages with in order to complement his large print work on the reconciliation of Christ. The book of Job fits in very well to his program. However, like all interpretations of books so difficult as Job, Barth's discourse does warrant criticism. One need be careful to review Barth's reading in context of his apparent intentions, but even then he appears to fall short of a watertight essay.

The most egregious example of Barth's inconsistencies is in his dealing with chapter 28, the so-called "Hymn to Wisdom." Barth begins his exegesis of this passage by discussing a problem that many critics have noted—that of the poem's placement in the book. Barth is quite sure himself that "it certainly does not belong to the original body of the central poetic section of the Book, but has been inserted from another source."[93] Barth even questions the intention of the final redactor who places it in the final speech of Job since "it has no obvious connexion with what precedes or follows."[94] Nevertheless, Barth notes that "the reason for its inclusion is not difficult to see." All of this is in keeping with the rest of Barth's work in biblical criticism—that the poem is a later addition to the text is not a problem since the final form is really what should concern theology. But two red flags arise in the next paragraph that could undermine Barth's attention to the text itself,

---

92. Barth, *CD* IV.3.1, 383.

93. This is still an unresolved issue among many scholars, the most recent emendation coming from Clines who places the poem in the mouth of Elihu, but still entertains the possibility that it finds its inception in a separate source altogether (*Job 21–37*, 425).

94. Ibid.

A Witness to the True Witness

suggesting that his theological presuppositions may hold too much sway over his interpretation—perhaps he uses the canonical form of the text only when it suits his theological argument. The first issue comes at the end of his exposition of chapter 28. After working through the chapter verse by verse, he eventually reaches what he calls "the message of the poem." This is found in verse 27: "Then did he see it, and declare it; he prepared it, yea, and searched it out." The action is therefore God's—"from above downwards."[95] This leads to Barth's exposition of God's speeches which show the initiative and freedom of God. The problem is that Barth must somehow excise verse 28, which states that "the fear of the Lord, that is wisdom . . ."—a conclusion to the poem that suggests that human activity could be the key to unlocking wisdom. Barth claims that "in the original form it does not seem even to contain [this] well-known saying . . . having probably been added as v. 28 by an apprehensive scribe."[96] This is not an uncommon conclusion by any means.[97] However, it seems inconsistent with the rest of Barth's interpretive strategy. Perhaps if there were manuscript evidence to suggest that the story of Job was told without verse 28, then Barth's argument would carry more weight since there would be *an* extant final form that could conceivably be in the canon. But only scant evidence exists that more than one word in verse 28 could justifiably be excised.[98] This is, perhaps, a minor problem, but it is certainly due to his vehement opposition to natural theology and not just the text of Job.[99] It is also not the only issue that arises upon closer inspection of Barth's exegesis.

In the same paragraph as the above issue, Barth questions the inclusion of the Elihu passages in the book of Job. Earlier in the section he suggests that the Elihu speeches accomplish very little in their inclusion by stating: "In a way which is dramatically disruptive, or dramatically most effective, [the Elihu speeches] merely prolong the existing stalemate [between Job and God]."[100] This perception, in and of itself, may not create too many dif-

---

95. Ibid., 426.

96. Ibid.

97. Of the scholars that Barth sites, Hölscher omits it from the original with little discussion. (Hölscher, *Das Buch Hiob*, 68). Dhorme, whose important commentary first appeared in French in 1927, gives a much longer explanation of 28:28's likely late inclusion which reflects Barth's. Dhorme writes, "The whole poem on Wisdom was intended to show that it is inaccessible to man and that God alone can discover it . . . V[erse] 28 . . . is added in order to draw a practical conclusion" (Dhorme, *Job*, 413–14).

98. The words are either הֵן, לָאָדָם אֲדֹנָי with none in LXX.

99. Vischer sees the verse as a good summary of the chapter but that the chapter only delays the gratification of the Tempest.

100. Barth, *CD* IV.3.1, 422.

ficulties. Barth certainly is not alone in his assessment of Elihu—recall that Kierkegaard omits him entirely from his interpretation. It is unreasonable to see Elihu as the hero of the story like Calvin does.[101] Nevertheless, Elihu's speeches are quite substantial, if in nothing but length, and should probably be granted more attention than the wave of the hand Barth gives them. The problem seems to be that Elihu does very little to advance the message that Barth wants to promote. Because Barth focuses on the "true history," that object to which the text points rather than the text itself, he seems to neglect the characters and events that neglect his message. Elihu does not point to the eschatological reality that Barth wants him to, thus he does not find his way in Barth's reading.

These problems regarding the historical-critical method are certainly not many.[102] However, they do hinder Barth's overall message, throwing into question his conclusions. If his method accepts the final form of the book of Job as authoritative, regardless of its history of transmission, presenting a particular message on the sovereignty of God, then perhaps Barth's reading needs some modification, for his preferred reading is not really the final form. On the other hand, it is remarkable that he is able to do what he does at the mercy of his already developed theology.[103] Other problems persist in his typology, however.

Ticciati's complaint that Barth's reading is reductionistic is not entirely fair. Though the literature is minimal, a surprising number of writers label Barth's exposition of Job with the moniker "mini commentary," which leads to the assumption that Karl Barth is saying all that need be said concerning Job, but in a condensed manner.[104] Despite the importance of the small print texts in the *Church Dogmatics*, the context of §70 is a theology of Jesus Christ as the true Witness. Thus, a full exposition of Job would lack the focus that Barth requires at this point. It is impossible to say what a full exposition of Job would look like—if he would treat the characters (especially Elihu) more fully or not. Where Ticciati's complaint becomes more valid is in Barth's use of language. She notes that in discussing the themes of Job, Barth uses the "Barthian categories of freedom, knowledge, truth, etc." rather than terms more closely associated with Hebrew Wisdom literature.[105] This complaint has some validity perhaps, but Barth's error is, again, certainly attributable

---

101. See Schreiner, *Where Shall Wisdom*; and chapter 2 of this book.

102. One could likely find many other problems related to the accuracy of Barth's comments regarding historical criticism but they are beside the point of this chapter.

103. Ticciati, *Disruption*, 30.

104. See Migliore, "Barth and Bloch." and Schulweis, "Barth's Job."

105. Ticciati, *Disruption*, 6.

A Witness to the True Witness

to the context of his exposition—that of his broader *Church Dogmatics*. Also consider that he is expositing the book in the context of the canon. Neutral terms mitigate the differences between the various genres in the biblical text. One should recall, also, that Barth embeds his interpretation of Job within the larger context of the reconciliation of Christ. These categories that Ticciati calls Barthian are also New Testament and biblical categories.[106] Even so, this is problematic as well. Yes, Job's meaning becomes more focused in the context of the canon, but it still retains its generic particularities that help to generate meaning. The generic particularities need not be flattened because of the unity of the biblical text. Even Barth would probably agree that the diverse witnesses of the canon are more rhetorically powerful as truly diverse witnesses rather than a monolithic text. This is consistent with his recognition of the diverse witnesses of Job. Those authors, despite writing in different styles of poetry and prose, were still writing within the confines of Wisdom literature. Thus, Barthian terms may seem somewhat unnecessary throughout discussion on the text, but they also enliven Job to exist outside the confines of his own literary context.

On a more theological level, Barth's typology is unnecessarily complex and intertwined. Barth's radical version of trinitarianism raises too many problems with regard to our concept of time and Job's typological relationship to Christ. At times, Barth seems to imply that Job's relationship with God is so tied to Christ that Job loses all particularity. Job's every action is in some way treated as if he pointed to Christ. By focusing on this aspect of Job so much, it puts into question even the significance of the Incarnation itself. If Job is seen as an extension of Christ, would Job need Christ in the way the church has understood the incarnation traditionally? The metaphysical gymnastics that Barth undertakes is too speculative and thus less convincing than the mere fact that Job and Jesus are both characters in the same anthology. This raises its own problems of course, but it is much easier to argue that the church has in hand a Bible with the book of Job, four Gospels, and the Pauline corpus than to argue for the existence of a metaphysically complex "true history," even with evidence from said books in the Bible. The Bible, of course, does point to God. The individual books present a view of a God who exists independently of the Bible. The text, that is, is not all there is but preaches a true God. However, Barth's insistence of the freedom of God outside of a system starts to deconstruct itself in the realization that a system starts to emerge in Barth's theology.

---

106. The Greek words ελευθερία, αλήθεια and their cognates are used numerous times in the New Testament. The Hebrew word for knowledge, דעת, on the other hand, is a very common word in Wisdom literature, used in the book of Job ten times.

Read Him Again and Again

Barth's interpretation is heavily tied to his theology. In this way, it may betray his own maxims on the freedom of God and how God cannot be tied to a system. Does he grant enough freedom to the book of Job to let it speak on its own? Of course, much of what Barth does is unavoidable. Others may reach different conclusions regarding the book of Job, but if one enters into the book of Job with some conclusions as to who God is or what the Bible teaches, much of what emerges from the close reading of the text will be predetermined. No interpretation of the book of Job could truly withstand such criticism; if one were to read the book of Job and a radically different vision of God were to emerge from the presupposed God of the reader, the resulting theology may look different but undergirding the new vision would lie a theology that allowed for such a transformation.

6

Evaluation and Conclusion

IN SOME WAYS, THIS book is an attempt to show how the ideas of others have been disseminated into Barth's interpretation of Job. Barth has received Job, yes, but he has also received others' receptions of Job. Recall in the first chapter's discussion on hermeneutics and the defense of reception history as filtered by Bakhtin's theories of dialogue and utterance that we do not stand on the shoulders of giants as much as we stand on the shoulders of those standing on the shoulders of others, with only a few giants between us. Obviously, we can consider Gregory, Calvin, Aquinas, Luther, Kant, Kierkegaard, and Barth as giants or no giants exist, but even these giants are dependent on their predecessors to a greater extent than is often acknowledged.

The different interpretations also benefit from different approaches and the various and, at times, vivid imaginations that inspire new discoveries of the book of Job. The three interpretations focused on in the three previous chapters have much in common; the main differences might arise primarily from the different approaches warranted by the different fields in which the scholars find themselves. One writes as a philosopher, one as a biblical scholar, and the last as a theologian and the results are commensurate with their disciplines.

The results of the different approaches, however, are striking in their similarities if it is not evident at first. In comparison to the various interpretations of Job throughout history, these three are of a piece. Where they coincide the most is in their allegorical imaginations and their focuses on the themes of divine and human freedom. This concluding chapter will primarily lay bare these particular similarities in the three interpretations before looking at the direct dialogue between the different works.

BARTH'S RECEPTION OF KIERKEGAARD'S JOB

The section in which Barth depends the most on Kierkegaard is his second discourse on Job. The section supports the large print of his *Church Dogmatics* in which he argues that to understand Jesus Christ, we must examine Christ in his "pure form" of eternity, as well as "what He has concretely been and done in His history on earth."[1]

The section on Job, which is set off from the section on Christ by the size of its font, continues his interpretation of the book by showing that Job, too, has both a "pure form" in the prose prologue, which represents Job's relationship to God in eternity, in addition to his historical form in the "main central section," which shows him as more contentious.[2] But Job, himself, encounters a God who seems different to him than the pure God of his previous knowledge. God, therefore, reveals himself in two forms as well. Barth eventually shows how this affects our understanding of Job, arguing that Job's "true grief . . . and the real subject of his complaint" is his relationship with this God who presents himself in a form familiar to Job at times but who has revealed himself in a form that Job has trouble recognizing in the plot of the book.[3]

The seeming contradiction of forms signals to Barth a dynamic relationship between Job and God. God, in revealing himself to Job in an alien form, has required of Job a "step forward" to meet him.[4] To explain Job's subsequent step, Barth invokes Kierkegaard's category of repetition and continues to refer to Kierkegaard's interpretation of Job until the end of the section, sometimes supporting his interpretation with Kierkegaard's work and occasionally disagreeing with Kierkegaard. His first allusion to Kierkegaard comes when Barth suggests that Job needs to express his free faithfulness with a "repetition of his existence."[5]

It will strike careful readers of Kierkegaard's *Repetition* that Barth may be taking some liberties with the meaning of repetition. In fact, it seems that when Barth does disagree with Kierkegaard, he may really be disagreeing

1. Barth, *CD* IV.3.1, 389.
2. Ibid., 398.
3. Ibid., 404.
4. Ibid., 405.
5. Ibid.

Evaluation and Conclusion

with Constantin or the young man in *Repetition*.[6] Earlier receptions of Kierkegaard's work tended to underestimate the importance of the pseudonyms, not fully appreciating the Dane's ironic rhetoric. Barth, himself seems to have been tripped up by the significance of the pseudonyms, which should not be a huge surprise. As noted in chapter 3, the meaning of repetition has eluded many readers and some have even questioned whether repetition has any meaning at all.[7]

Barth's reception of *Repetition* is of interest because he seems dependent on Kierkegaard's theory while at the same time protesting claims by Kierkegaard or his pseudonyms that do not seem to warrant dismissal, but actually support Barth's own interpretation. Barth's understanding of the category of repetition, on the other hand, betrays a muddled interpretation of the book *Repetition* that is typical of earlier receptions of Kierkegaard. The maieutic rhetoric of Kierkegaard, which utilizes unreliable pseudonyms to draw the reader to a position or belief beyond that of the narrator, does not seem to receive the attention of Barth. That is, Barth does not appear to take into account the significance of the unreliability of the two unreliable narrators in *Repetition* when referring to Kierkegaard's work.

Barth is right that Job needs a repetition to reach a deeper understanding of God—to recognize God in the second form. On the other hand, he seems to take from Constantin's understanding that repetition is something that one can control. As Kierkegaard's book infers through Constantin's failures at repetition, one cannot bring upon a repetition through one's own will. When all avenues lead to dead ends, then repetition is possible.

Barth defines repetition as "an expression of the free faithfulness with which [Job] has turned to God."[8] Job needs, according to Barth, to express his free faithfulness with a "'repetition' of his existence with the same free faithfulness in the divinely established covenant."[9]

---

6. Nicholas Adams notes this problem as well but seems to have a different interpretation of *Repetition* than I (Adams, "The Goodness of Job's Bad Arguments"). I agree with Adams that "it is rather difficult to say boldly, as Barth does, that the remarks on Job [in *Repetition*] are whole-heartedly endorsed by Kierkegaard," but Adams seems to think that Constantin is a more trustworthy source than the young man. As chapter 3 of this book should make clear, I believe the young man, despite his changing mind throughout his letters, presents the more sympathetic understanding of repetition in the book. Consider that the young man shares much in common with Kierkegaard himself, but also that he embodies the hermeneutical principles of Kierkegaard much better than Constantin, who tends to contradict himself throughout. The young man, by contrast, displays a developing conscience.

7. See Poole, *Communication*, 79–81.

8. Barth, *CD* IV.3.1, 405.

9. Ibid.

The nuance is indeed subtle and does not underscore a major impasse between the two thinkers. The passive nature of a Kierkegaardian repetition does not preclude any action by the participant. The young man experiences a repetition because he decides to wait for his storm. The waiting, as Job indicates he does at the end of chapter 36 and which is accentuated by the subsequent arrival of and speech by Elihu, marks a decision by Job. The decision to wait may be the "free human decision" that Barth argues is required of Job. Barth suggests as much when he notes that "the first thing to be seen and said is that in it he accomplished the repetition required of him."[10] Nevertheless, Barth surprisingly seems to think that one can engender a repetition on one's own. Kierkegaard, through the experience of the young man, shows that repetition needs a transcendent action by a transcendent agent.

The end product of the analysis of this particular aspect of Barth's interaction with Kierkegaard does not derail Barth's interpretation of Kierkegaard on its own. It does, however, show that Barth's reception of Kierkegaard may lack the necessary nuance to understand Kierkegaard, due to his placement in the history of Kierkegaard studies. Full appreciation of Kierkegaard's use of pseudonyms does not emerge for several years, so Barth's understanding is expected.

What also bears mentioning, though, is where Barth openly disagrees with Kierkegaard. He obviously appreciates the path Kierkegaard takes him on the way to understanding Job, but shows an ambivalence toward some conclusions he makes. For instance, Barth quotes the young man's December 14 letter, which declares that the "vital force" in Job is that, "despite everything, [Job] is in the right." The young man declares Job an exception to the rule, proving so by his perseverance. Barth claims this goes too far, but does not deal with the January letter where the young man claims that Job was proved to be in the wrong. Thus both Barth and Kierkegaard claim that Job was both right and wrong, and their claims regarding this suggest that Kierkegaard may have influenced Barth more than Barth realizes.

Barth argues that Job, in expressing his free faithfulness, puts himself in the right and the wrong. God's initial words to Job and Job's response show God's displeasure with some part of Job's actions after his fall. God challenges Job in 38:2, asking, "Who is this that darkeneth counsel by words without knowledge?" Barth argues that Job accepts this judgment in his confession in 42:3, saying, "I have uttered that I understood not; things too wonderful for me, which I knew not," leading to his recantation and repentance in 42:6. Barth takes this passage at the face value of the German

10. Ibid., 406.

Evaluation and Conclusion

translation of the Hebrew. Many scholars have mulled over the meaning of this troubling phrase. The version in the MT is very difficult to translate since the first verb lacks an object. The LXX witness indicates that the translator may have read the unpointed verb as a *niphal* as opposed to the MT's *qal*, thus "I disparage myself" or "I am rejected." The second verb, likewise, causes translation problems. Possible translations include the traditional "I repent in dust and ashes," "I repent, being dust and ashes," "I am sorry because of dust and ashes," and "I console myself with dust and ashes."

Barth does not question the traditional meaning of Job's words in 42:6, but does note that the wrath of God, "is not really kindled against him, but against the three friends" as seen in the very next verse. This is how one knows that Job is both right and wrong to Barth. He is wrong in his complaint, shown by his recognition of his overstepping his knowledge, but he is right with regard to the limits of his knowledge. He does not recognize the God that confronts him during his trials and so is wrong in his pronouncements. However, these same pronouncements prove that he is right since he makes them as "the servant of Yahweh."[11]

Kierkegaard also claims Job is both right and wrong, and does so in relation to the eternal and the temporal as well. From the young man's January 13 letter, to which Barth does not allude, the young man writes:

> Was Job proved to be in the wrong? Yes, eternally, for there is no higher court than the one that judged him. Was Job proved to be in the right? Yes, eternally, by being proved to be in the wrong *before God*.[12]

Kierkegaard discusses this theme in several of his works, most significantly in *Either/Or*. The concluding discourse of *Either/Or* comes in the form of a sermon by a friend of the pseudonymous Judge.[13] The preacher quotes Job 40:2, where God says that "Thou shalt not contend with God." The preacher interprets the Joban passage as meaning that "you shall not wish to prove yourself in the right before Him."[14] He then argues that "there is only one way of supporting the claim that you are in the right before God—by learn-

---

11. Ibid.
12. Kierkegaard, *Fear and Trembling/Repetition*, 212. Emphasis in original.
13. It seems possible that this passage is from the point of view of the ethical stage, since the Judge indicates that it is universally beautiful. However much in the passage indicates that it is a window into the religious. I personally believe that it leans toward the religious since the book ends with this sermon and because the idea of one being justified by God by finding himself eternally in the wrong before God litters Kierkegaard's work, including his journals and his autonym works.
14. Kierkegaard, *Either/Or II*, 346.

ing that you are in the wrong," clearly anticipating the young man's arguments in *Repetition*, published later in the year. When the lily and sparrow fall, they are in the right before God, but "only man is in the wrong, for to him alone is reserved that which to all other creatures was denied . . . to be in the wrong before God."[15]

The preacher deals with the contradictions inherent in the idea that being in the wrong before God edifies the one who is wrong, which should result in being in the wrong less and less, but that not being in the wrong would deny the righteous person the edification that comes with being in the wrong. He attempts to rectify the contradiction in *Either/Or* by distinguishing between finite and infinite relationships, consistent with the young man's claims on Job. "To wish to be in the wrong," the preacher writes, "is the expression for an infinite relationship; to wish to be in the right . . . is the expression for a finite relationship. So, then, it is edifying always to be in the wrong, for only the infinite edifies, not the finite."[16]

Later in the sermon, the preacher shows how this theme relates to the Kierkegaardian notion that truth is subjectivity when he gives the following advice to his audience:

> you do not say, "God is always in the right," for in that there is no joy; you say, "Against God I am always in the wrong." Though that which was your wish were what others . . . might call your duty, though you must not only forego your wish but in a way be unfaithful to your duty, though you were to lose not only your joy but even your honor, you are joyful nevertheless.[17]

Here, the preacher focuses on the particular nature of the person speaking and not the universal nature of God. The sermon, and the book *Either/Or*, ends with the preacher expounding on the importance of subjectivity and truth in a way that sheds more light on Kierkegaard's interpretation of Job:

> only by the indescribable emotions of the heart, that for the first time you are convinced that what you have known belongs to you that no power can take it from you; for only the truth which edifies is truth for you.[18]

We determined that Kierkegaard's Job was right because he held to his convictions and reacted according to what he knew to be true. Job embodies Kierkegaard's claim that truth is subjectivity. Despite this, Job is proved to

15. Kierkegaard, *Either/Or II*, 346.
16. Ibid., 350.
17. Ibid., 355.
18. Ibid., 356.

Evaluation and Conclusion

be in the wrong before God. Actually, not despite, but because of his being proved to be in the right before God he is proved to be in the wrong before him. For Kierkegaard and the preacher in *Either/Or*, one's acceptance by God depends on being in the wrong before God.

God censures Job from the thunderstorm according to the young man.[19] The rebuke from God results in the reconciliation between Job and God—reconciliation being the broader theme under which Barth places his interpretation of Job. One would hate to think that Barth did not read beyond the December letter of *Repetition* even if it is fair to concede that Barth did not grasp the full nuances of Kierkegaard's maieutic rhetoric, but the January letter in particular seems to conform to much of what Barth proposes.

Just before invoking Kierkegaard, Barth claims that Job "would not have been obedient if he had not raised this complaint and carried it through to the bitter end in spite of all objections."[20] Job's complaint, in other words, is honorable because it is appropriate in relation to his own history with God. He takes his subjective understanding of God to its logical conclusions and is right in that case. Barth here seems to intuit Kierkegaard's maxim that truth is subjectivity and thus Job is right in his subjectivity.

Barth and Kierkegaard, therefore, both see Job as both right and wrong and his rightness relates to his subjectivity according to both thinkers. Their similarities do not end there, as we see with their similar typological imaginations, something they also share with Wilhelm Vischer, as well as all three of the scholars' focuses on freedom in the book of Job.

FREEDOM AS THE MAJOR THEME OF JOB IN KIERKEGAARD, VISCHER, AND BARTH

In all three scholars' views, the book of Job instructs its readers on the notion of freedom in the life of the person of faith and especially in the freedom of God. This is clearest in the interpretation set forth by Barth, who filters his work through the wager between the Satan and God. "Does Job fear God for naught?" the Satan asks in 1:9. That is, does Job worship God freely? Barth imports directly from Vischer's essay the idea that the hermeneutical key to the book of Job lies in the wager summed up in the question in 1:9.

Vischer and Barth share much in common regarding how freedom plays in the book of Job. Their confluence of theology does not begin in their interpretations of Job, of course. Their careers paralleled each others' in important ways, often doing so because of their similar theologies. They were both Swiss

19. Kierkegaard, *Fear and Trembling/Repetition*, 212.
20. Barth, *CD* IV.3.1, 406.

theologians who worked in Germany in the 1930s and left for Basel during the run up to the Second World War. They each drafted confessions declaring the church's independence from the state and were both reformed pastors, also influenced by Martin Luther. It should surprise no one that Vischer's interpretation of Job would contain Barthian elements and that Barth would refer to Vischer's interpretation to supplement his own study.

Though Vischer does not refer explicitly to divine and human freedom much in his essay, interpreting the entire book of Job through a wager that questions the possibility of disinterested piety shows that human freedom remains an important aspect of his interpretation. Also, though he may have been compelled to write a long essay entirely on the book of Job partly for political reasons, as explained in chapter four, the pure theology that he mines from the book of Job dominates his essay.

Barth's own work on Job might not have existed in such a fashion had he not read Vischer's essay. Vischer's work is the first source to which Barth refers in his own. When Barth eventually arrives at 1:9, he credits Vischer for giving the "for nought" the proper emphasis and writes that it was "to the best of [his] knowledge something quite new in explanation of the book, but it is something which we cannot now dismiss."[21] Barth is clearly dependent on Vischer for pointing out the most important part of the book of Job. It may even be the case that Vischer drew Barth to the book of Job as a witness of Jesus Christ even though Barth claims that "it would be difficult to read the book of Job attentively without being aware of the fact that the figure of Jesus Christ as the true Witness unmasking the falsehood of man is delineated in it in distant, faint, fragmentary and even strange yet unmistakeable outline."[22] He certainly knows Vischer's work well and expands on its basic premise to fit his own thesis.

Though Vischer does not meditate on the idea of freedom to the extent that Barth does, it is Vischer in part that allows Barth to do so. In this way then Vischer shares with Kierkegaard, for they both lay important groundwork for Barth's thesis regarding the freedom of God and humanity in the book of Job.

Preceding Vischer and Barth by around a century, Kierkegaard also views freedom as a major aspect of the book of Job. In his Upbuilding Discourse based on 1:20–21, though freedom does not emerge explicitly as a theme, he zeroes in on Job's worshipful attitude after losing his family and possessions. Kierkegaard notes the decision that Job must make on whether to worship God or not. Implicit in the discourse is the idea that Job acts

21. Ibid., 387.
22. Ibid., 384.

Evaluation and Conclusion

freely, though it is not the major focus in this work as it is in the works of Barth and Vischer.

Divine freedom, on the other hand, does figure in to *Repetition* in a much more explicit way that relates well to the image of divine freedom that Barth would draw much later. The progressing narrative of *Repetition* allows Kierkegaard to show the perils of constricting God (or a replacement for God in the life of an aesthete like Constantin) to the selfish desires of the human. Constantin seeks to control the outcome of his actions by driving for a repetition in his life. His "venture in experimenting psychology" requires the placement of God into human parameters. Constantin needs to control God for his experiment to work. For various reasons, his experiment fails, but none more important than the mere fact that he depersonalizes God, treating God like a force similar to gravity or centrifugality.

When the young man starts sending Constantin his letters telling of his own story, he displays a similar sentiment regarding the controllability of God. However, the young man eventually changes his position on God's freedom or lack of it as he grafts his life onto the narrative of Job. Once he starts to see how Job's repetition is dependent on God's freedom rather than a scientific formula, he lets go of his formulaic quest and awaits his own storm. The young man's repetition looks physically different than does Job's, but the spiritual nature of the two repetitions bear important resemblances.

The final action of the young man, where he recognizes the freedom of the deity (or what stands for God in his worldview), is also a recognition of his own freedom. Rather than constrain himself in a formula, he is able to let go of his quest. The letting go induces the repetition he desires and the letting go stems from a recognition of freedom.

Ironically, the recognition of his freedom also stems partly from appropriating the narrative of Job into his life. In seeing how God has administered a repetition in the life of a parallel character, the young man recognizes the nature of repetition as emerging by virtue of the absurd. In this recognition lies the confluence of divine freedom and typology in *Repetition*. God does not work within an impersonal system, but nor is God capricious. The God who worked in the life of Job is the same God who worked in the life of Abraham and Jesus and now the young man. *Repetition*, because of its pseudonymous, and therefore, limited nature, cannot explicitly refer to the freedom of God in such a way as Barth and Vischer can in their more conventional theological discourses, but the principle of divine freedom in the typological paradigm that the two later scholars endorse has precedence in this earlier interpretation of Job.

CONCLUSION

As argued in the introductory chapter of this book, one of the reasons for beginning this project was the belief that great literary books exist in great time and that any interpretation of that book should take into account its afterlife as readers throughout history encounter it. The chapters that follow the introduction attempt to do that with the book of Job. The three interpreters I focus on, ironically, do not seem to feel it necessary to look at their predecessors with the same verve my introductory chapter calls for. Of course their seeming lack of respect for the reception history of Job does not place them out of the great time of the book of Job. Though they seem to bypass the scholarship that comes before them, they still remain in a dialogue with their predecessors whether they recognize it or not.

More importantly, however, is that they do recognize the afterlife of Job in other important ways. Though they seemingly try to ignore the work of Gregory, Aquinas, and Calvin, they still fall in the same linear projection of Job in great time. Also, great time indicates that a great text points beyond itself. Implied in the recognition of a great literary text's placement in great time is a recognition of the texts it inspires. The text in great time points to those texts that point back to it. Recollection and repetition dwell together in that dialogue.

Though Barth, Vischer, and Kierkegaard seem suspicious sometimes of some of their forbears in Job interpretation, it is clear that they are, up to a point, dependent on them. More importantly, though, they do of course recognize that the text of Job does point beyond itself. For Barth and Vischer especially, Job dwells in the gospel story of Jesus Christ. Though they bypass their immediate predecessors to some degree, their recognition of Job's enduring value in the gospel itself suggests that they see Job as continuing to live and develop as long as humanity lives and develops.

To see Job exist in great time requires the recognition that these utterances do not end the dialogue. Dialogue is unfinalizable and any utterance anticipates response. This book is an explicit attempt to participate in this dialogue by bringing to the fore these utterances and how they relate to their focus. I have attempted to show how they act as a thread. These three participants in the dialogue are like a small grouping of MPs from a political party at a parliamentary meeting. They are arguing for a particular cause, but with different styles and, perhaps, for different constituents. In their cases, the constituents belong to different epochs. When they are done speaking, the dialogue does not cease and neither do their causes. The unfinalizability of the dialogue means that it would be somewhat irresponsible to suggest

Evaluation and Conclusion

that what they say about Job is the end of what can be said about Job. It also means that more can be said about what they say about Job.

It would go beyond the scope of this particular book to attempt to say much more about how they contribute to the larger dialogue of Job in great time. What I can show is where their contribution to the dialogue might lead. What does the exploration of these particular utterances unlock about Job that requires further exploration and future utterances? These last few pages are meant to show how Kierkegaard, Vischer, and Barth might direct the reader to think about Job for future participation in this dialogue. Specifically, I will look at the first speech by Bildad the Shuhite.

Kierkegaard, Vischer, and Barth have very little to say about Job's friends individually. They tend to consider them as a group rather than individual characters. Vischer does deal with their speeches individually, but each of the friends acts more as a synecdoche for the trio. Barth deals with all of the friends as a group, noting that "they are only secondary characters with no particular individuality."[23] Kierkegaard also treats them synecdochically, collecting them within the person of Constantin. Nevertheless, their brief works do inspire further research on the individual poems.

Though each contributor highlighted in this book has a place in each of these potential directions for further Job research, I want to begin with areas that the individual actors inspire in particular. The chapter above on Kierkegaard's interpretation of Job in his Upbuilding Discourse and *Repetition* explores in depth his particular hermeneutic in approaching the book. It looks at his use of different genres to explore the generic differences between the prologue and dialogues in the biblical book. It also looks at the maieutic rhetoric in the second half of *Repetition*, where the scholar narrator, Constantin Constantius, proves to be a less convincing guide toward a proper understanding of the philosophical category of repetition than the young man he councils. The result of discovering this irony inspires the reader to recognize the similar irony in the book of Job. Job's friends, like Constantin, are able to spout off generally acceptable theological theories and yet Job is proven right in the end.

Because Kierkegaard leaves Constantin generally silent throughout the young man's letters, *Repetition* does not have much to say explicitly on the words of the friends. The friends remain relatively silent in general scholarship as well. God does not hold their words up in the final chapter, as he does with Job, and so they remain relatively unexplored outside of the requisite space warranted in the commentary genre. Kierkegaard's unusual hermeneutical method lends importance to them despite bypassing them himself.

23. Barth, *CD* IV.3.1, 461.

Read Him Again and Again

Consider, in particular, the words of Bildad in chapter 8. Recall Calvin's general reluctance to judge the friends since so much of what they say fits orthodox theology. General assessments of the friends, however, recognize that God condemns their speeches as not speaking right of God. Bildad's first speech has much in common with Constantin's narration in *Repetition* despite sharing little thematically. Bildad's speech begins with several points of irony that serve to draw attention to his faulty theology.

The speech begins with Bildad criticizing Job's words as a "mighty wind" (רוח כביר),[24] which leads him to discuss Job's children's sins and their punishment for them. Of course, Job's children died from a "great wind" (רוח גדולה), which may have been Bildad's insensitive way of arguing that Job's words are destructive.[25] However, a strong wind can also be creative in the Hebrew Bible and Bildad does not seem to account for this. Genesis 1:2 describes the "spirit of God/mighty wind" (רוח אלהים) as the initiator of creation in the Priestly narrative. More importantly for this story, God answers Job from a tempest (סערה) in 38:1. Elihu prepares the reader for this mighty wind throughout chapter 37, describing God's voice as thunderous and windy, a voice that God will use to describe his creation. With that stormy voice, God will also vindicate Job and condemn the words of Bildad and his companions. Job's tempestuous talk, then, is much closer to God's than is Bildad's.

The irony continues in verses five to seven when Bildad recommends that Job look to and plead with God and be pure (זך) and upright (ישר). If he does those things, God will restore him to his rightful place. Of course we learn in the very first verse that Job was blameless (תם) and upright (ישר). We also learn throughout the dialogues, as stressed in the analyses above on Kierkegaard, Vischer, and Barth, that Job differentiates himself from his friends by consistently turning to God in the second half of his speeches. Bildad, therefore, may arguably and ironically be right in his prediction, but he does not seem to be aware that Job fits his description. However, his lack of awareness of the wager in the heavenly court makes his words, as Barth might put it, right and wrong at the same time.

To be sure, Constantin does not reproduce the words or sentiments of Bildad. On the other hand, the irony is remarkably similar. Constantin regularly gives advice to the young man, never seeming to realize that the young man's path fits the profile of Job, who experiences the type of repetition the young man seeks. Also, recall that Constantin's comments on

---

24. Clines describes the words as "tempestuous and devastating" in Bildad's eyes; "they make an assault upon heaven" (Clines, *Job 1–20*, 202).

25. Newsom, "Job," 400.

Evaluation and Conclusion

repetition seem to deconstruct themselves. Constantin seeks a repetition, but not the repetition that he experiences. He wants to repeat his journey to Berlin but makes several adjustments along the way to insure he does not actually repeat the journey in full (i.e., by sitting in the wrong part of the coach, by visiting Berlin during a different part of the year, etc.). The irony of Constantin's statements draws the reader to contemplate an alternative to what Constantin is proposing. That they blatantly contradict themselves in the first half of the story invites the reader to consider the young man as that alternative.

When Bildad speaks, much of what he says seems orthodox. Eliphaz explains in 4:8 that "those who sow trouble reap the same," upon which Bildad avers. Bildad speaks with authority since he speaks from within his own tradition (8:8–10). Yet, his words deconstruct themselves by reminding the reader of the prologue. Job loses his children from a great wind through no fault of their own or Job's. The book opens with the narrator declaring Job blameless and upright and describing his habitual sanctification of his children so that they would be blameless before God themselves. Bildad's words seem orthodox on the surface, but their place in the narrative draw the reader to contemplate an alternative. At the same time Bildad points forward, predicting what happens to Job in the epilogue, but ironically. Bildad surely does not believe that Job is looking to God or is pure and upright or his words would likely be more sensitive. There is also irony in God's condemnation of Bildad's words at the end. Job must sacrifice for Bildad much like he did for his children. Yet his children died from a great wind. Bildad's words work more to condemn himself than they do to judge Job.

The result is that the narrator argues maieutically, much like Kierkegaard in *Repetition*. The friends as a group argue one way and are not only wrong, but their words contribute to our understanding of who God is and how God acts. One does not need *Repetition* to come to this conclusion. The utterances lie in the ancient book of Job. However, Kierkegaard's book lends another model with which to compare Bildad's words. Kierkegaard does not offer the model explicitly, either, but leaves it like fruit for the reader of Job to pick.

Barth dedicates one of his four sections of his Job interpretation to the friends collectively under the heading "The Falsehood of Man." He does not deal with the characters individually and rarely mentions individual passages by the friends. His general comments about them, however, can help illumine individual passages such as Bildad's first speech. "If they are wrong," Barth writes, "as they are, it is in such a way that they are also right."[26] Barth's

---

26. Barth, *CD* IV.3.1, 454.

phrasing sheds a different light on the speech while the speech sheds a different light on Barth's essay. Barth writes mainly about the orthodoxy the friends pronounce and how its impersonal nature hinders the friends from having the right posture towards God. When applied to Bildad's first speech, a different vision arises of his wrongness and rightness. Bildad's opening remarks contain a remarkable number of both right and wrong statements, but said in such a way that in hindsight, the rightness and wrongness are difficult to pry loose from each other.

Even in retrospect Bildad's words seem as if they must be right. If Job is pure (זך) and upright (ישר), God will restore him to his rightful place (נות צדקך) (8:6). At the end of the speech, Bildad reassures Job that God does not reject the blameless (לא ימאס-תם) (8:20). He uses the same words with which the narrator describes Job in the first verse of the first chapter of the book of Job. Bildad is, of course, right, but in a way that he is also wrong. Job does experience these blessings from God, and he is the kind of person Bildad suggests is the kind of person to experience these blessings, but the rest of the narrative of Job puts into doubt the cause and effect relationship of Job's character and his final blessings, not the least of which being God's condemnation of Bildad's words in 42:7, 8. Of course, other words of Bildad seem, if not blatantly wrong, then ill-qualified for the context.

In 8:8–13, Bildad suggests that Job should look at the tradition for knowledge rather than their own generation. Those who do not pay attention to their heritage, he insinuates, will be like a papyrus with no marsh. These, people, he also argues, are akin to the godless. "Such are the paths of all who forget God," he says in 8:13. Bildad may be right in this passage, but it is irrelevant. Job clearly has not forgotten God. After he loses all his belongings, he praises Yahweh (1:21). After he is struck down with sores all over his body, he maintains his integrity with God at the bewilderment of his wife (2:9–10). Even after he comes close to cursing God in chapter 3, he never ceases to remember God. The passage Bildad follows is Job directly addressing God. Perhaps Bildad questions Job's attitude in Job's parody of Psalm 8, where Job seems to want to be invisible to God, but the passage does not really fit the situation. Thus, Bildad may actually be right, but in a way that is wrong; the context does not fit the wisdom he ostensibly purveys.

Finally, let us look at Vischer, who actually addresses Bildad's speech, though briefly and generally. Nevertheless, Vischer's theme of Job seeking the goodness of God which lies beyond good and evil is useful in extracting meaning from Bildad which might otherwise lay buried. In fact, just before he reaches chapter 8, Vischer reiterates the theme, writing, "And that is the great question of the Book of Job, whether righteousness is the deserved

Evaluation and Conclusion

equivalence of being good and having good things, or is the Goodness of God, which, from realms beyond Good and Evil, condescends to His creatures to whom He wills to be good for His own sake."[27] Bildad's speech, of course, says otherwise. Justice is a set phenomenon to which God must conform his actions. "Does God bend (יְעַוֵּת) justice?" he asks. Job's children paid a penalty commensurate to their sins, but Job can reap the benefits of upright living. Looking at the plotlines of the book of Job, the logic of Bildad's claims falls apart. Job's children die *because Job* was upright and blameless and yet God will still restore Job to his right state in the end, though for what reason we are left to speculate. Though Bildad's statements seem logical in the way they define an economy of justice, they deconstruct themselves when viewed through the lens of the narrative itself. Bildad is not just wrong, but inapplicable. When comparing Bildad's speech with Vischer's major thematic determinations (the Goodness of God which lies beyond Good and Evil, does Job serve God for nought? and is Job's trust in God justified?), the themes seem that much starker. The cold logic of Bildad is set in contrast to a divine logic that seems almost colder in its arbitrariness. The only certain thing we can determine is Bildad's wrongness in his speech on right and wrong.

Altogether, Kierkegaard, Barth, and Vischer expand and illumine this single passage in a way neglected in the traditional literature. The friends garner little attention by themselves from most scholars, including from the three we have chosen to examine. However, the scholars' unique perspectives, individually and collectively, help us see this speech by Bildad in new light. What looking at this passage in light of the writings of Kierkegaard, Barth, and Vischer also shows is how complementary they are to each other. The irony in Bildad's speech relates to Kierkegaard's maieutic rhetoric, Barth's paradoxical claims that the friends are wrong in a way that they are also right, and Vischer's claim that God's Goodness is a goodness beyond Good and Evil. Kierkegaard, Vischer, and Barth do not merely repeat each other but bring the discussion of Job forward. Their own readers can bring Job further.

Kierkegaard, Barth, and Vischer plot the way. Those who receive their plotting must tread it.[28] Of course every utterance in a dialogue inspires another. There are no last words. Because the book of Job exists in great time, it will never cease to inspire more utterances. Job's friends speak as if their words could be the final ones. The economy of answerability is closed.

---

27. Vischer, "Witness of Job I," 46.

28. See Barth, *CD* IV.3.1, 398, who writes, "with the fine sayings in 1:21 and 2:10 he has merely plotted the way, according to the obvious view of the redactor and apparently of the incomplete folk-saga reproduced [sic] in the Book. He has now to tread it.

177

Read Him Again and Again

They become frustrated when their repetition of the doctrine of retribution fails to satisfy Job. Job, however, continues to speak until he receives a response from God. The narrator of Job then finalizes his own utterance, but the dialogue continues.

Bibliography

Adams, Nicholas. "The Goodness of Job's Bad Arguments." *Journal of Scriptural Reasoning* 4.1 (2004) No Pages. Cited 21 January 2008. Online: http://etext.lib.virginia.edu/journals/ssr/issues/volume4/number1/ssr04-1-f01.html.

Alonso-Schoekel, Luis. "Toward a Dramatic Reading of the Book of Job." *Semeia* 7 (1977) 45–61.

Alsop, John E. "Typology." In *The Anchor Bible Dictionary*, edited by David Noel Freedman, 682–85. New York: Doubleday, 1992.

Amsler, Samuel. "Texte et Événement." In *Maqqél Shâqédh: La Branche d'Amandier: Hommage à Wilhelm Vischer*, edited by Daniel Lys, 12–19. Montpellier: Causse, Graille, Castelnau, 1960.

Aquinas, Thomas. *Expositio Super Iob Ad Litteram*. Rome: Sanctae Sabinae, 1965.

———. *The Literal Exposition on Job: A Scriptural Commentary concerning Providence*. Translated by Anthony Damico. Edited by Carl A. Raschke. Vol. 7. The American Academy of Religion Classics in Religious Studies. Atlanta: Scholars, 1989.

———. *On Evil*. Translated by Richard Regan. Oxford: Oxford University Press, 2003.

———. *Quaestiones Disputatae de Malo*. Rome: Commissio Leonina, 1982.

Arbaugh, George E. and George B. *Kierkegaard's Authorship: A Guide to the Writings of Kierkegaard*. Rock Island, IL: Augustana College Library, 1967.

Astell, Ann W. "Job's Wife, Walter's Wife, and the Wife of Bath." In *Old Testament Women in Western Literature*, 92–107. Conway, AR: UCA Press, 1991.

———. "Translating Job as Female." In *Translation Theory and Practice in the Middle Ages*, 59–69. Kalamazoo, MI: Western Michigan University Press, 1997.

Aubin, Paul. "Intériorité et Extériorité dans les Moralia in Job de Saint Grégoire le Grand." *Recherches de science religieuse* (1974) 117–66.

Auerbach, Erich. "Figura." In *Scenes from the Drama of European Literature*, 11–76. Gloucester, MA: Smith, 1973.

Baasten, Matthew. *Pride according to Gregory the Great: A Study of the Moralia*. Studies in the Bible and Early Christianity, Vol. 7. Lewiston, NY: Mellen, 1986.

Bächli, Otto. *Das Alte Testament in der Kirchlichen Dogmatik von Karl Barth*. Neukirchen-Vluyn: Neukirchener, 1987.

Bachmann, E. Theodore, and Helmut T. Lehmann, editors. *Luther's Works*, Vol. 35. *Word and Sacrament I*. Philadelphia: Fortress, 1960.

Baglow, Christopher T. *"Modus Et Forma": A New Approach to the Exegesis of Saint Thomas Aquinas with an Application to the "Lectura Super Epistolam Ad Ephesios."* Vol. 149, Anbib. Rome: Editrice Pontificio Istituto Biblico, 2002.

Bibliography

Baker, D. L. *Two Testaments, One Bible: A Study of Some Modern Solutions to the Theological Problem of the Relationship Between the Old and New Testaments.* Leicester, UK: InterVarsity, 1976.

Bakhtin, Mikhail M. "Author and Hero in Aesthetic Activity." In *Art and Answerability: Early Philosophical Essays*, edited by Michael Holquist and Vadim Liapunov, 4–256. Austin, TX: University of Texas Press, 1990.

———. "The *Bildungsroman* and Its Significance in the History of Realism (Toward a Dhistorical Typology of the Novel)." In *Speech Genres and Other Late Essays*, edited by Caryl Emerson and Michael Holquist, 10–59. Austin, TX: University of Texas Press, 1986.

———. *The Dialogic Imagination: Four Essays.* Translated by Caryl Emerson and Michael Holquist. Edited by Michael Holquist. University of Texas Press Slavic Series. Austin, TX: University of Texas Press, 1981.

———. "Discourse in the Novel." In *The Dialogic Imagination: Four Essays*, edited by Michael Holquist, 259–422. Austin, TX: University of Texas Press, 1981.

———. "Forms of Time and of the Chronotope in the Novel: Notes toward a Historical Poetics." In *The Dialogic Imagination: Four Essays*, edited by Michael Holquist, 84–258. Austin, TX: University of Texas Press, 1981.

———. "The Problem of Speech Genres." In *Speech Genres and Other Late Essays*, edited by Caryl Emerson and Michael Holquist, 60–102. Austin, TX: University of Texas Press, 1986.

———. "The Problem of the Text in Linguistics, Philology, and the Human Sciences." In *Speech Genres and Other Late Essays*, edited by Caryl Emerson and Michael Holquist, 102–31. Austin, TX: University of Texas Press, 1986.

———. *Rabelais and His World.* Translated by Helene Iswolsky. Bloomington, IN: Indiana University Press, 1984.

———. "Response to a Question From the *Novyi Mir* Editorial Staff." In *Speech Genres and Other Late Essays*, edited by Caryl Emerson and Michael Holquist, 1–9. Austin, TX: University of Texas Press, 1986.

———. *Speech Genres & Other Late Essays.* Translated by Vern W. McGee. Edited by Michael Holquist and Caryl Emerson. University of Texas Press Slavic Series. Austin, TX: University of Texas Press, 1986.

———. "Toward a Methodology for the Human Sciences." In *Speech Genres and Other Late Essays*, edited by Caryl Emerson and Michael Holquist, 159–72. Austin, TX: University of Texas Press, 1986.

———. *Toward a Philosophy of the Act.* Translated by Vadim Liapunov. Edited by Vadim Liapunov and Michael Holquist. Austin, TX: University of Texas Press, 1993.

Barr, James. "Allegory and Historicism." *JSOT* 69 (1996) 105–20.

———. *The Bible in the Modern World.* London: SCM, 1990.

———. *Biblical Faith and Natural Theology. Gifford Lectures 1991.* Oxford: Clarendon, 1993.

———. "The Literal, the Allegorical, and Modern Biblical Scholarship." *JSOT* 44 (1989) 3–17.

———. "Wilhelm Vischer and Allegory." In *Understanding Poets and Prophets*, edited by A. G. Auld, 38–60. Sheffield, UK: Sheffield Academic Press, 1993.

Barrett, Lee C., and Jon Stewart, editors. *Kierkegaard and the Bible: Tome I: The Old Testament.* Aldershot, UK: Ashgate, 2010.

Bibliography

———, editors. *Kierkegaard and the Bible: Tome II: The New Testament*. Aldershot, UK: Ashgate, 2010.

Barth, Karl. "An Prof. Dr. Wilhelm Vischer, Montpellier, 1955." In *Offene Briefe 1945–1968*, edited by Diether Kock, 356–61. Zürich: Theologischer Verlag Zürich, 1955.

———. *Church Dogmatics*. Vol. III.2. Translated by G. W. Bromiley and T. F. Torrance. Edited by G. W. Bromiley and T. F. Torrance. Edinburgh: T. & T. Clark, 1960.

———. *Church Dogmatics*. Vol. IV.2. Translated by G. W. Bromiley and T. F. Torrance. Edited by G. W. Bromiley and T. F. Torrance. Edinburgh: T. & T. Clark, 1960.

———. *Church Dogmatics*. Vol. IV.3.1. Translated by G. W. Bromiley and T. F. Torrance. Edited by G. W. Bromiley and T. F. Torrance. Edinburgh: T. & T. Clark, 1956.

Baskin, Judith R. "Job as Moral Exemplar in Ambrose." *Vigiliae christianae* 35.3 (1981) 222–31.

———. *Pharaoh's Counsellors: Job, Jethro, and Balaam in Rabbinic and Patristic Tradition*. Brown Judaic Studies ; 47. Chico, CA: Scholars, 1983.

Beuken, W. A. M., editor. *The Book of Job*. BETL, Vol. 114. Leuven: Leuven University Press, 1994.

Bigelow, Pat. *Kierkegaard and the Problem of Writing*. Edited by Mark C. Taylor. Kierkegaard and Postmodernism. Tallahassee, FL: University of Florida Press, 1987.

Biggar, Nigel, editor. *Reckoning with Barth: Essays in Commemoration of the Centenary of Karl Barth's Birth*. London: Mowbray, 1988.

Boer, Roland, editor. *Bakhtin and Genre Theory in Biblical Studies*. Semeia Studies, Vol. 63. Atlanta: Society of Biblical Literature, 2007.

Boersma, Hans. *Nouvelle Théologie and Sacramental Ontology: A Return to Mystery*. Oxford: Oxford University Press, 2009.

Bonhoeffer, Dietrich. *No Rusty Swords: Letters, Lectures and Notes 1928–1936 From the Collected Works*. Translated by Edwin H. Robertson. Vol. I, London: Collins, 1970.

Brandt, Lori Unger. "Kierkegaard's Use of the Old Testament: From Literary Resource to the Word of God." In *Kierkegaard and the Bible: Tome I: The Old Testament*, edited by Lee C. Barrett and Jon Stewart, 231–51. Aldershot, UK: Ashgate, 2010.

Brekelmans, C., Menahem Haran, and Magne Saebø, editors. *Hebrew Bible/Old Testament: The History of Its Interpretation*. Vol. 1, Göttingen: Vandenhoeck & Ruprecht, 2000.

Bromiley, Geoffrey William. *Introduction to the Theology of Karl Barth*. Grand Rapids: Eerdmans, 1979.

Brunner, Emil. *Revelation and Reason: The Christian Doctrine of Faith and Knowledge*. Translated by Olive Wyon. London: SCM, 1947.

Bruns, Gerald L. *Hermeneutics Ancient & Modern*. Yale Studies in Hermeneutics. New Haven: Yale University Press, 1992.

Budde, Karl. *Handkommentar Zum Alten Testament: In Verbindung Mit Anderen Fachgelehrten. Abt.5, 2, Die Poetischen Bücher. Band 1, Das Buch Hiob*. Göttingen: Vandenhoeck & Ruprecht, 1896.

Burgess, Andrew J. "Repetition—A Story of Suffering." In *Fear and Trembling and Repetition*, edited by Robert L. Perkins, 247–62. Macon, GA: Mercer University Press, 1993.

Burnett, Richard E. *Karl Barth's Theological Exegesis: The Hermeneutical Principles of the Römerbrief Period*. WUNT. Tübingen: Mohr Siebeck, 2001.

Busch, Eberhard. *Barth*. Abingdon Pillars of Theology. Nashville: Abingdon, 2008.

Caesar, Lael O. "Job: Another New Thesis." *VT* 49.4 (1999) 435–47.

Bibliography

Calvin, John. *Ioannis Calvini Opera Quae Supersunt Omnia*. Edited by Guilelmus Baum et. al. Vol. 33–35, *Corpus Reformatorum*. Brunsvigae: Apud C. A. Schwetschke et Filium, 1887.

———. *Sermons on Job*. Translated by Arthur Golding. Edinburgh: Banner of Truth Trust, 1993.

Caputo, John D. *How to Read Kierkegaard*. London: Granta, 2007.

Caquot, André. "Traits Royaux Dans Le Personnage De Job." In *Maqqél Shâqédh: La Branche D'Amandier: Hommage À Wilhelm Vischer*, 32–45. Montpellier: Causse, Graille, Castelnau, 1960.

Chalamet, Christophe. *Dialectical Theologians: Wilhelm Herrmann, Karl Barth, and Rudolf Bultmann*. Zürich: Theologischer Verlag Zürich, 2005.

Chardonnens, Denis. "L'Espérance De La Résurrection Selon Thomas D'Aquin, Commentateur Du Livre De Job: "Dans Ma Chair, Je Verrai Dieu" (Jb 19,26)." In *Ordo Sapientiae Et Amoris*, 65–83. Fribourg, Switzerland: Universitätsverlag Freiburg Schweiz, 1993.

———. *L'Homme Sous Le Regard De La Providence: Providence De Dieu Et Condition Humaine Selon L'Exposition Littérale Sur Le Livre De Job De Thomas D'Aquin*. Vol. 50, *Bibliothèque Thomiste*. Paris: Vrin, 1997.

Childs, Brevard S. "Critical Reflections on James Barr's Understanding of the Literal and the Allegorical." *JSOT* 46 (1990) 3–9.

———. "Karl Barth: The Preacher's Exegete." Paper presented at The Lyman Beecher Lectureship on Preaching, Yale University, New Haven, 1989.

———. "Old Testament in Germany 1920–1940: The Search for a New Paradigm." In *Altes Testament, Forschung Und Wirkung: Festschrift Für Henning Graf Reventlow*, edited by Peter Mommer and Winfried Thiel, 233–46. Frankfurt am Main: Lang, 1994.

Christman, Angela Russell. "The Spirit and the Wheels: Gregory the Great on Reading Scripture." In *In Dominico Eloquio*, 395–407. Grand Rapids: Eerdmans, 2002.

Clark, Maudemarie. "Nietzsche, Friedrich." In *Routledge Encyclopedia of Philosophy*, No Pages. Edited by E. Craig, London: Routledge, 1998. Online: http://www.rep.routledge.com/article/DC057

Clines, David J. A. *Job 1–20*. WBC Vol. 17. Waco, TX: Word, 1989.

———. *Job 21–37*. WBC Vol. 18a. Nashville: Thomas Nelson, 2006.

———. "Job and the Spirituality of the Reformation." In *The Bible, the Reformation and the Church*, edited by W. P. Stephens, 145–71. Sheffield, UK: Sheffield Academic Press, 1995.

Connell, George, and C. Stephen Evans, editors. *Foundations of Kierkegaard's Vision of Community: Religion, Ethics, and Politics in Kierkegaard*. Atlantic Highlands, NJ: Humanities, 1992.

Crites, Stephen. "'The Blissful Security of the Moment' Recollection, Repetition, and Eternal Recurrence." In *International Kierkegaard Commentary: Fear and Trembling and Repetition*, edited by Robert L. Perkins, 225–46. Macon, GA: Mercer University Press, 1993.

———. *In the Twilight of Christendom: Hegel Vs. Keirkegaard on Faith and History*. Aar Studies in Religion, Vol. 2. Chambersburg, PA: AAR, 1972.

Crowell, Steven. "Existentialism." *The Stanford Encyclopedia of Philosophy*, No Pages. Cited 6 May 2010. Online: http://plato.stanford.edu/archives/spr2006/entries/existentialism/.

Bibliography

Croxall, T. H. *Kierkegaard Commentary.* London: Nisbet, 1956.
Cunningham, Mary Kathleen. *What is Theological Exegesis? Interpretation and Use of Scripture in Barth's Doctrine of Election.* Valley Forge, PA: TPI, 1995.
Dailey, Thomas F. "And Yet He Repents—on Job 42,6." *ZAW* 105.2 (1993) 205–9.
Damgaard, Iben. "Kierkegaard's Rewriting of Biblical Narratives: The Mirror of the Text." In *Kierkegaard and the Bible: Tome I: The Old Testament*, edited by Lee C. Barrett and Jon Stewart, 207–29. Aldershot, UK: Ashgate, 2010.
———. "'My Dear Reader': Kierkegaard's Reader and Kierkegaard as a Reader of the Book of Job." In *Receptions and Transformations of the Bible*, edited by Kirsten Nielsen, 93–105. Aarhus, Denmark: Aarhus University Press, 2009.
Davis, Leroy A. "Typology in Barth's Doctrine of Scripture." *AThR* 47.1 (1965) 33–49.
Dawson, David. *Allegorical Readers and Cultural Revision in Ancient Alexandria.* Berkeley: University of California Press, 1992.
Dawson, John David. "Figural Reading and the Fashioning of Christian Identity in Boyarin, Auerbach and Frei." *Modern Theology* 14 (1998) 181–96.
de Greef, Wulfert. "Calvin as Commentator on the Psalms." In *Calvin and the Bible*, edited by Donald K. McKim, 85–106. Cambridge: Cambridge University Press, 2006.
Delecroix, Vincent. "Quelques Traits d'une Hermémeutique Kierkegaardienne." *RSPT* 86.2 (2002) 243–57.
Delitzsch, F. *The Book of Job.* Vol. I. Translated by Francis Bolton. Clarks Foreign Theological Library. Edinburgh: T. & T. Clark, 1866.
———. *The Book of Job.* Vol. II. Translated by Francis Bolton. Clarks Foreign Theological Library. Edinburgh: T. & T. Clark, 1866.
Dell, Katherine Julia. *The Book of Job as Sceptical Literature.* Berlin: de Gruyter, 1991.
Despland, Michel. *Kant on History and Religion.* Montreal: McGill-Queen's University Press, 1973.
Dhorme, Édouard. *A Commentary on the Book of Job.* Translated by Harold Knight. London: Nelson, 1967.
Dobbs-Weinstein, Idit. "Medieval Biblical Commentary and Philosophical Inquiry as Exemplified in the Thought of Moses Maimonides and St. Thomas Aquinas." In *Moses Maimonides and His Time*, 101–20. Washington, DC: Catholic University of America Press, 1989.
Dorrien, Gary J. *The Barthian Revolt in Modern Theology: Theology without Weapons.* Louisville: Westminster John Knox, 2000.
Dru, Alexander, editor. *The Journals of Søren Kierkegaard.* London: Oxford University Press, 1938.
Dubois, Marcel. "Mystical and Realistic Elements in the Exegesis and Hermeneutics of Thomas Aquinas." In *Creative Biblical Exegesis*, edited by Benjamin Uffenheimer and Henning Graf Reventlow, 39–54. Sheffield, UK: JSOT, 1988.
Ebeling, Gerhard. *Luther: An Introduction to His Thought.* Translated by R. A. Wilson. London: Collins, 1972.
Eliot, T. S. *The Sacred Wood: Essays on Poetry and Criticism.* 7th ed. London: Methuen, 1950.
Ellis, E. Earle. *The Old Testament in Early Christianity: Canon and Interpretation in the Light of Modern Research.* Edited by Martin Hengel and Otfried Hofius. WUNT, Vol. 54. Tübingen: Mohr (Siebeck), 1991.
Evans, C. Stephen. *Kierkegaard: An Introduction.* Cambridge: Cambridge University Press, 2009.

Bibliography

―――. *Kierkegaard's Fragments and Postscript: The Religious Philosophy of Johannes Climacus.* Atlantic Highlands, NJ: Humanities, 1983.

Evans, Gillian R. *The Thought of Gregory the Great.* Cambridge Studies in Medieval Life and Thought Vol. 4.2. Cambridge: Cambridge University Press, 1986.

Felber, Stefan. *Wilhelm Vischer als Ausleger der Heiligen Schrift: Eine Untersuchung zum Christuszeugnis des Alten Testaments.* Edited by Reinhard Slenczka and Gunther Wenz. Forschungen zur Systematischen und Ökumenischen Theologie. Göttingen: Vandenhoeck und Ruprecht, 1999.

Ferreira, M. Jamie. "Faith and the Kierkegaardian Leap." In *The Cambridge Companion to Kierkegaard*, edited by Alastair Hannay and Gordon D. Marino, 207–34. Cambridge: Cambridge University Press, 1998.

Fishburn, Janet Forsythe. "Soeren Kierkegaard, Exegete." *Int* 39 (1985) 229–45.

Ford, Charles. "Bonhoeffer, Luther, and the German Resistance." Paper presented at the Dietrich Bonhoeffer Conference, Fort Wayne, IN, January 4, 2006.

Ford, David F. *Barth and God's Story: Biblical Narrative and the Theological Method of Karl Barth in the Church Dogmatics.* Frankfurt: Lang, 1981.

―――. "Barth's Interpretation of the Bible." In *Karl Barth*, edited by Stephen Sykes, 55–87. Oxford: Clarendon, 1979.

Frei, Hans W. *The Eclipse of Biblical Narrative: A Study in Eighteenth- and Nineteenth-Century Hermeneutics.* New Haven: Yale University Press, 1974.

Froehlich, Karlfried. "Christian Interpretation of the Old Testament in the High Middle Ages." In *Hebrew Bible/Old Testament*, edited by Magne Saebo, 496–558. Gottingen: Vandenhoeck & Ruprecht, 2000.

Frye, Northrop. *The Great Code: The Bible and Literature.* San Diego: Harcourt Brace, 1982.

Gardiner, Michael. *The Dialogics of Critique: M. M. Bakhtin and the Theory of Ideology.* London: Routledge, 1992.

Gardiner, Patrick. "Kierkegaard, Søren Aabye (1813–55)." In *Routledge Encyclopedia of Philosophy*, No Pages. Edited by E. Craig, London: Routledge. Cited on 11 May 2010. Online: http://www.rep.routledge.com/article/DC044.

Garrett, Susan R. "The Patience of Job and the Patience of Jesus." *Int* 53.3 (1999) 254–64.

Gerlach, Wolfgang. *And the Witnesses Were Silent: The Confessing Church and the Persecution of the Jews.* Translated by Victoria J. Barnett. Lincoln, NE: University of Nebraska Press, 2000.

Gignilliat, Mark S. *Karl Barth and the Fifth Gospel: Barth's Theological Exegesis of Isaiah.* Barth Studies. Aldershot, UK: Ashgate, 2009.

Glatzer, Nahum Norbert. *The Dimensions of Job: A Study and Selected Readings.* New York: Schocken, 1969.

Good, Edwin M. *Irony in the Old Testament.* London: SPCK, 1965.

Gordis, Robert. *The Book of God and Man: A Study of Job.* Chicago: The University of Chicago Press, 1965.

Gradl, F. *Das Buch Ijob.* NSKAT, Vol. 12. Stuttgart: Verlag Katholisches Bibelwerk, 2001.

Green, Barbara. *Mikhail Bakhtin and Biblical Scholarship: An Introduction.* Semeia Studies, Vol. 38. Atlanta: Society of Biblical Literature, 2000.

Green, Joel B. "Scripture and Theology: Failed Experiments, Fresh Perspectives." *Int* 56.1 (2002) 5–20.

Green, Ronald Michael. *Kierkegaard and Kant: The Hidden Debt.* SUNY Series in Philosophy. Albany, NY: SUNY, 1992.

Bibliography

Greene-McCreight, Kathryn. *Ad Litteram: How Augustine, Calvin, and Barth Read the Plain Sense of Genesis 1–3*. Issues in Systematic Theology Vol. 5. New York: Lang, 1999.
Greenslade, S. L., editor. *The Cambridge History of the Bible*, Vol. 3. Cambridge: Cambridge University Press, 1963.
Gregory I, Pope. *Morals on the Book of Job*. Translated by Anonymous. 3 vols. A Library of the Fathers of the Holy Catholic Church. Oxford: Parker, 1844.
Greschat, Katharina. *Die Moralia in Job Gregors des Großen: Ein Christologisch-Ekklesiologischer Komentar*. Edited by Christoph Markschies. Studien und Texte zu Antike und Christentum, Vol. 31. Tübingen: Mohr Siebeck, 2005.
Grimsley, Ronald. "'Dread' as a Philosophical Concept." *The Philosophical Quarterly* 6.24 (1956) 245–55.
Gunton, Colin. *The Barth Lectures*. Edited by P. H. Brazier. London: T. & T. Clark, 2007.
———. "Barth, the Trinity, and Human Freedom." *ThTo* 43.3 (1986) 316–30.
Gutteridge, Richard. *Open Thy Mouth for the Dumb! The German Evangelical Church and the Jews, 1879–1950*. Oxford: Blackwell, 1976.
Haar, Murray J. "Job After Auschwitz." *Int* 53.3 (1999) 265–75.
Habel, Norman C. *The Book of Job*. OTL. London: SCM, 1985.
Hall, G. B. "Karl Barth and Historicism." In *In Divers Manner: A St. Mary's Miscellany*, edited by D. W. D. Shaw, 228–45. St. Andrews, UK: St. Mary's College Press, 1990.
Harrison, William Pope. "Christ in the Book of Job." *Methodist Quarterly Review* 27.3 (1888) 390–400.
Haughn, Clifford and John C. Gonsiorek. "The Book of Job: Implications for Construct Validity of Posttraumatic Stress Disorder Diagnostic Criteria." *Mental Health, Religion & Culture* 12.8 (2009) 833–45.
Hayashi, Tadayoshi. "Kierkegaard über Hiob." *Kwansei Gakuin University Humanities Review* 1 (1996) 71–81.
Haynes, Stephen R. "Who Needs Enemies? Jews and Judaism in Anti-Nazi Religious Discourse." *Church History* 71.2 (2002) 341–67.
Hays, Richard B. "Can the Gospels Teach Us How to Read the Old Testament?" *ProEccl* 11.4 (2002) 402–18.
Healy, Nicholas M. "Introduction." In *Aquinas on Scripture: An Introduction to His Biblical Commentaries*, edited by Daniel A. Keating, John P. Yocum, and Thomas G. Weinandy, 1–20. London: T. & T. Clark, 2005.
Helm, Paul. *John Calvin's Ideas*. Oxford: Oxford University Press, 2004.
Hendrix, Scott H. "Luther against the Background of the History of Biblical Interpretation." *Int* 37.3 (1983) 229–39.
Hendry, George S. "The Freedom of God in the Theology of Karl Barth." *SJT* 31 (1978) 229–44.
Hesse, Franz. *Hiob*. ZB. Zürich: Theologischer, 1978.
Higton, Mike. "The Fulfillment of History in Barth, Frei, Auerbach and Dante." In *Conversing with Barth*, edited by M. A. Higton and J. C. McDowell, 120–41. Aldershot, UK: Ashgate, 2004.
Hoffman, Yair. *A Blemished Perfection: The Book of Job in Context*. JSOTsup, Vol. 213. Sheffield, UK: Sheffield Academic Press, 1996.
Holm, Isak Winkel. "Kierkegaard's Repetitions: A Rhetorical Reading of Søren Kierkegaard's Concept of Repetition." *Kierkegaardiana* 15 (1991) 15–28.

Bibliography

Hölscher, Gustav. *Das Buch Hiob*. Edited by Otto Eissfeldt. HAT, Vol. 17. Tübingen: Mohr Siebeck, 1937.

Jackson, Timothy P. "Must Job Live Forever: A Reply to Aquinas on Providence and Freedom, Evil and Immortality." In *Human and Divine Agency*, 217–52. Lanham, MD: University Press of America, 1999.

Jacob, Edmond. "Deux Lectures de l'Ancien Testament—Une Même Fidélité en Souvenir D'André Néher et de Wilhem Vischer." *FoiVie* 89.1 (1990) 1–6.

———. "L'Œuvre de Wilhelm Vischer." *ÉTR* 50 (1975) 231–35.

Jacobs, Louis. *The Jewish Religion: A Companion*. Oxford: Oxford University Press, 2003.

Jauss, Hans Robert. "Literary History as a Challenge to Literary Theory." *New Literary History* 2.1 (1970) 7–37.

Johnson, Fred. "A Phonological Existential Analysis to the Book of Job." *Journal of Religion and Health* 44.4 (2005) 391–401.

Jordan, Mark D., and Kent Emery Jr, editors. *Ad Litteram: Authoritative Texts and Their Medieval Readers*. Notre Dame Conferences in Medieval Studies, Vol. 3. Notre Dame, IN: University of Notre Dame Press, 1992.

Jung, C. G. *Answer to Job*. Translated by R. F. C. Hull. London: Routledge & Kegan Paul, 1954.

Jüngel, Eberhard. *Karl Barth, A Theological Legacy*. Translated by Garrett E. Paul. Philadelphia: Westminster, 1986.

Kallas, Endel. "Kierkegaard's Understanding of the Bible with Respect to His 'Age.'" *Di* 26.1 (1987) 30–34.

Kant, Immanuel. *The Moral Law: Groundwork of the Metaphysic of Morals*. Translated by H. J. Paton. London: Routledge, 1991.

———. "On the Failure of All Attempted Philosophical Theodicies (1791)." In *Kant on History and Religion*, edited by Michel Despland, 283–97. Montreal: McGill-Queen's University Press, 1973.

———. *Religion within the Limits of Reason Alone*. Translated by Theodore M. Greene and Hoyt H. Hudson. New York: Harper Torchbooks, 1960.

Kaplan, L. J. "Maimonides, Dale Patrick, and Job xlii 6." *VT* 28.3 (1978) 356–58.

Keller, Roger R. "Karl Barth's Treatment of the Old Testament as Expectation." *AUSS* 35.2 (1997) 165–79.

Kelsey, David H. "Appeals to Scripture in Theology." *JR* 48.1 (1968) 1–21.

———. *The Uses of Scripture in Recent Theology*. London: SCM, 1975.

Kessler, Stephan C. "Gregory the Great: A Figure of Tradition and Transition in Church Exegesis." In *Hebrew Bible/Old Testament*, edited by Magne Saebø, 135–47. Göttingen: Vandenhoeck & Ruprecht, 2000.

———. "Gregory the Great (c. 540–604)." In *Handbook of Patristic Exegesis: The Bible in Ancient Christianity*, edited by Charles Kannengiesser, 1336–68. Leiden: Brill, 2004.

Kierkegaard, Søren. *Christian Discourses and the Lilies of the Field and the Birds of the Air and Three Discourses At the Communion on Fridays*. Translated by Walter Lowrie. London: Oxford University Press, 1939.

———. *Concluding Unscientific Postscript to Philosophical Fragments I*. Edited and translated by Howard V. Hong and Edna H. Hong. Kierkegaard's Writings, Vol. XII.1. Princeton: Princeton University Press, 1992.

———. *Eighteen Upbuilding Discourses*. Edited and translated by Howard V. Hong and Edna H. Hong. Princeton: Princeton University Press, 1990.

Bibliography

———. *Either/Or, Part I*. Edited and translated by Howard V. and Edna H. Hong. Kierkegaard's Writings, Vol. III. Princeton: Princeton University Press, 1987.
———. *Either/Or, Part II*. Edited and translated by Howard V. and Edna H. Hong. Kierkegaard's Writings, Vol. III. Princeton: Princeton University Press, 1987.
———. *Fear and Trembling/Repetition*. Edited and translated by Howard V. Hong and Edna H. Hong. Princeton: Princeton University Press, 1983.
———. *Papers and Journals: A Selection*. Translated by Alastair Hannay. Edited by Alastair Hannay. London: Penguin, 1996.
———. *Repetition and Philosophical Crumbs*. Translated by M. G. Piety. Oxford: Oxford University Press, 2009.
———. *Repetition: An Essay in Experimental Psychology*. Translated by Walter Lowrie. Oxford: Oxford University Press, 1942.
———. *Samlede Værker*. Vol. 3. Edited by J. L. Heiberg A. B. Drachman, and H. O. Lange. Copenhagen: Gyldendal, 1921.
———. *Samlede Værker*. Vol. 4. Edited by J. L. Heiberg, A. B. Drachman, and H. O. Lange. Copenhagen: Gyldendal, 1923.
———. *Works of Love*. Edited and translated by Howard V. Hong and Edna H. Hong. Kierkegaard's Writings, Vol. XVI. Princeton: Princeton University Press, 1995.
Knierim, Rolf P., and George W. Coats. *Numbers*. FOTL, Vol. IV. Grand Rapids: Eerdmans, 2005.
Köhlmoos, M. *Das Auge Gottes: Textstrategie im Hiobbuch*. FAT, Vol. 25. Tübingen: Mohr Siebeck, 1999.
Kraeling, Emil G. *The Old Testament Since the Reformation*. London: Lutterworth, 1955.
Krell, Marc A. "Repositioning the 'Holy Remnant' of Israel: German Jewish Negotiations with Christian Culture on the Eve of the Holocaust." *Studies in Christian-Jewish Relations* 2.1 (2007) 21–35.
Kretzmann, Norman. "Introduction." In *The Cambridge Companion to Aquinas*, edited by Norman Kretzmann and Eleonore Stump, 1–11. Cambridge: Cambridge University Press, 1993.
Kuske, Martin. *The Old Testament as the Book of Christ: An Appraisal of Bonhoeffer's Interpretation*. Translated by S. T. Kimbrough. Philadelphia: Westminster, 1976.
Lamb, Jonathan. *The Rhetoric of Suffering: Reading the Book of Job in the Eighteenth Century*. Oxford: Clarendon, 1995.
Langleben, Maria. "M. Bachtin's Notions of Time and Textanalysis." *Russian Literature* 26 (1989) 167–90.
Laporte, Jean B. "Gregory the Great as a Theologian of Suffering." *Patristic and Byzantine Review* 1.1 (1982) 22–31.
Lawrie, Douglas. "How Critical is it to be Historically Critical? The Case of the Composition of the Book of Job." *JNSL* 21.1 (2001) 121–46.
Lebowitz, Naomi. *Kierkegaard: A Life of Allegory*. Baton Rouge, LA: Louisiana State University Press, 1985.
Leiter, Brian. *Nietzsche on Morality*. Routledge Philosophy Guidebook. London: Routledge, 2002.
Levinger, Jacob. "Maimonides' Exegesis of the Book of Job." In *Creative Biblical Exegesis*, 81–88. Sheffield, UK: JSOT, 1988.
Lindsey, William D. "The Problem of Great Time." *JR* 73.3 (1993) 311–28.
Lippitt, John. *Humour and Irony in Kierkegaard's Thought*. Houdmills, UK: MacMillan, 2000.

Bibliography

Loades, A. L. *Kant and Job's Comforters*. Newcastle upon Tyne, UK: Avero, 1985.
Longenbach, James. "Mature Poets Steal." In *The Cambridge Companion to T. S. Eliot*, edited by A. David Moody, 176–88. Cambridge Collections Online. Cambridge University Press, 1994.
Louth, Andrew. "Allegorical Interpretation." In *A Dictionary of Biblical Interpretation*, edited by Coggins and Houlden, 12–14. London: SCM, 1990.
Lubac, Henri de. *Medieval Exegesis. Vol. 1, The Four Senses of Scripture*. Translated by Mark Sebanc. Ressourcement. Grand Rapids: Eerdmans, 1998.
———. *Medieval Exegesis: The Four Senses of Scripture. Vol. 2*. Translated by E. M. Macierowski. Ressourcement. Grand Rapids: Eerdmans, 2000.
———. *Scripture in the Tradition. Milestones in Catholic Theology*. New York: Crossroad, 2000.
———. *Typologie, Allegorie, Geistiger Sinn: Studien Zur Geschichte Der Christlichen Schriftauslegung*. Translated by R. Voderholzer. Theologia Romanica, Vol. 23. Freiburg: Einsiedeln, 1999.
Luther, Martin. *Word and Sacrament I*. Translated by Charles M. Jacobs. Edited by Helmut T. Lehmann and E. Theodore Bachmann. Luther's Works, Vol. 35. Philadelphia: Fortress, 1960.
Lys, Daniel, editor. *Maqqél Shâqédih: La Branche d'Amandier: Hommage à Wilhelm Vischer*. Montpellier: Causse, Graille, Castelnau, 1960.
Maag, Victor. *Hiob: Wandlung und Verarbeitung des Problems in Novelle, Dialogdichtung Und Spätfassungen*. Göttingen: Vandenhoeck & Ruprecht, 1982.
Mackey, Louis. *Points of View: Readings of Kierkegaard*. Edited by Mark C. Taylor. Kierkegaard and Postmodernism. Tallahassee, FL: University of Florida Press, 1986.
Markus, Robert Austin. *Gregory the Great and His World*. Cambridge: Cambridge University Press, 1997.
Materer, Timothy. "T. S. Eliot's Critical Program." In *The Cambridge Companion to T. S. Eliot*, edited by A. David Moody, 48–59. Cambridge: Cambridge University Press, 1994.
Matzov, Anna. "The Idea of Time in the Works of Bachtin." *Russian Literature* 26 (1989) 209–17.
McAuliffe, Jane Dammen, Barry D. Walfish, and Joseph W. Goering, editors. *With Reverence for the Word: Medieval Scriptural Exegesis in Judaism, Christianity, and Islam*. New York: Oxford University Press, 2003.
McCarthy, Vincent A. "'Repetitions' Repetitions." In *International Kierkegaard Commentary: Fear and Trembling and Repetition*, edited by Robert L. Perkins, 263–82. Macon, GA: Mercer University Press, 1993.
McCormack, Bruce. "Historical-Criticism and Dogmatic Interest in Karl Barth's Theological Exegesis of the New Testament." *LQ* 5 (1991) 211–25.
———. *Karl Barth's Critically Realistic Dialectical Theology: It's Genesis and Development 1909–1936*. Oxford: Oxford University Press, 1997.
———. "The Significance of Karl Barth's Theological Exegesis of Philippians." In *The Epistle to the Philippians By Karl Barth: 40th Anniversary Edition*, v–xxvi. Louisville: Westminster John Knox, 2002.
McCracken, David. "Character in the Boundary: Bakhtin's Interdividuality in Biblical Narratives." *Semeia* 63 (1993) 29–42.

Bibliography

McDonald, William. "Soren Kierkegaard." In *The Stanford Encyclopedia of Philosophy*, No Pages. Edited by Edward N. Zalta. Cited 20 July 2009. Online: plato.stanford. edu/archives/sum2009/entries/kierkegaard/.

McGlasson, Paul. *Jesus and Judas: Biblical Exegesis in Barth*. Atlanta: Scholars, 1991.

McKane, William. "The Theology of the Book of Job and Chapter 28 in Particular." In *Gott und Mensch im Dialog*, 711–22. Berlin: de Gruyter, 2004.

McKenzie, David. "A Kantian Theodicy." *Faith and Philosophy* 1.2 (1984) 237–46.

McKinnon, Alastair. "Kierkegaard's Perception of the Bible." *Kierkegaardiana* (1980) 132–47.

McNeil, Brian. "Typology." In *A Dictionary of Biblical Interpretation*, edited by R. J. Coggins and J. L. Houlden, 713–14. London: SCM, 1990.

Meier, Samuel A. "Job and the Unanswered Question." *Proof* 19 (1999) 265–76.

Mertin, Jörg. "Hiob-Religionsphilosophisch Gelesen: Rezeptionsgeschichtliche Untersuchungen zur Hioblektüre Herders, Kants, Hegels, Kierkegaards und zu ihrer Bedeutung für die Hiobexegese Des 18. Und 19. Jahrhunderts." PhD diss., Universität-Gesamthochschule Paderborn, 1991.

Michaud-Quantin, Pierre. "L'Édition Critique de l'Expositio Super Iob de Saint Thomas D'Aquin." *RSPT* 50.3 (1966) 407–10.

Migliore, Daniel L. "Barth and Bloch on Job: A Conflict of Interpretations." In *Understanding the Word*, 265–80. Sheffield, UK: JSOT, 1985.

Mihailovic, Alexandar. *Corporeal Words: Mikhail Bakhtin's Theology of Discourse*. Edited by Caryl Emerson. Studies in Russian Literature and Theory. Evanston, IL: Northwestern University Press, 1997.

Minear, Paul Sevier, and Paul S. Morimoto. *Kierkegaard and the Bible: An Index*. Princeton, NJ: Princeton University Press, 1953.

Mittleman, Alan. "The Job of Judaism and the Job of Kant." *HTR* 102.1 (2009) 25–50.

Mooney, Edward F. "Introduction." In *Repetition and Philosophical Crumbs*, vii–xxix. Oxford: Oxford University Press, 2009.

———. "Kierkegaard's Job Discourse: Getting Back the World." *International Journal for Philosophy of Religion* (1993) 151–69.

———. *Selves in Discord and Resolve: Kierkegaard's Moral-Religious Psychology From Either/Or to Sickness unto Death*. Routledge, 1996.

Morris, James C. "The Book of Job and the Revelation of the Messiah." *Methodist Quarterly Review* 52.3 (1903) 498–506.

Morrow, William. "Consolation, Rejection, and Repentance in Job 42:6." *JBL* 105.2 (1986) 211–25.

Morson, Gary Saul, and Caryl Emerson. *Mikhail Bakhtin: Creation of a Prosaics*. Stanford: Stanford University Press, 1990.

Müller, Hans-Peter. *Das Hiobproblem: Seine Stellung und Entsehung im Alten Orient und im Alten Testement*. Darmstadt: Wissenschaftliche Buchgesellschaft, 1995.

———. "Welt als 'Wiederholung': Sören Kierkegaards Novelle als Beitrag Zur Hiob-Interpretation." In *Werden und Wirken des Alten Testaments: Festchrift für Claus Westermann zum 70. Geburtstag*, edited by Rainer Albertz et. al., 355–72. Göttingen: Vandenhoeck & Ruprecht, 1980.

Müller, Mogens. "Kierkegaard and Eighteenth- and Nineteenth-Century Biblical Scholarship: A Case of Incongruity." In *Kierkegaard and the Bible: Tome II: The New Testament*, edited by Lee C. Barrett and Jon Stewart, 285–328. Aldershot, UK: Ashgate, 2010.

Bibliography

Murphy, Roland E. "Patristic and Medieval Exegesis—Help Or Hindrance?" *CBQ* (1981) 505–16.
Newkirk, Terry. "Via Negativa and the Little Way: The Hidden God of *The Moviegoer*." *Renaiscence* 44.3 (1992) 183–202.
Newsom, Carol A. "The Book of Job: Introduction, Commentary, and Reflections." In *NIB Vol. 4*, 317–637. Nashville: Abingdon, 1996.
———. *The Book of Job: A Contest of Moral Imaginations*. New York: Oxford University Press, 2003.
———. "Reconsidering Job." *Currents in Biblical Research* 5.2 (2007) 155–82.
Nietzsche, Friedrich. *Beyond Good and Evil: Prelude to a Philosophy of the Future*. Translated by R.J. Hollingdale. London: Penguin, 1990.
———. *On the Genealogy of Morality*. Translated by Maudemarie Clark and Alan J. Swensen. Indianapolis: Hackett, 1998.
Noth, Martin. *Numbers: A Commentary*. Translated by James D. Martin. Edited by Peter Ackroyd et. al. OTL, Vol. 7. London: SCM, 1968.
O'Hara, Mary L. "Truth in Spirit and Letter: Gregory the Great, Thomas Aquinas, and Maimonides on the Book of Job." In *From Cloister to Classroom*, 47–79. Kalamazoo, MI: Cistercian, 1986.
Oberhänsli-Widmer, Gabrielle. *Hiob in Jüdischer Antike und Moderne: Die Wirkungsgeschichte Hiobs in der Jüdischen Literatur*. Neukirchener Vluyn: Neukirchener, 2003.
Oden, Thomas C., editor. *The Humor of Kierkegaard: An Anthology*. Princeton: Princeton University Press, 2004.
Oeming, M., and K. Schmid. *Hiobs Weg: Stationen von Menschen im Leid*. Neukirchen-Vluyn: Neukirchener, 2001.
Oettli, Samuel and Wilhelm Volck. *Die Poetischen Hagiographen: Buch Hiob, Prediger Salomo, Hohelied und Klagelieder*. Edited by Hermann Strack und Otto Böckler. Kurzgefakter Kommentar zu den Heiligen Schriften. Nördlingen, Germany: Beck'schen, 1889.
Opitz, Peter. "Calvin's Exegesis of the Old Testament." In *Hebrew Bible / Old Testament: The History of Its Interpretation*, edited by Magne Saebø, 438–51. Gottingen: Vandenhoeck & Ruprecht, 2008.
Parris, David Paul. *Reception Theory and Biblical Hermeneutics*. Princeton Theological Monograph Series. Eugene, OR: Pickwick, 2009.
Percy, Walker. *The Moviegoer*. London: Methuen, 2004.
Perdue, Leo G., and Clark W. Gilpin, editor. *The Voice from the Whirlwind: Interpreting the Book of Job*. Nashville: Abingdon, 1992.
Pereboom, Derk. "Kant on God, Evil, and Teleology." *Faith and Philosophy* 13.4 (1996) 509–32.
Perkins, Robert L., editor. *Fear and Trembling and Repetition*. International Kierkegaard Commentary, Vol. 6. Macon, GA: Mercer University Press, 1993.
———. "For Sanity's Sake: Kant, Kierkegaard, and Father Abraham." In *Kierkegaard's Fear and Trembling: Critical Appraisals*, edited by Robert L. Perkins, 43–61. Tuscaloosa, AL: The University of Alabama Press, 1981.
Perry, Edmund. "Was Kierkegaard a *Biblical* Existentialist?" *JR* 36 (1956) 17–23.
Petersen, Joan M. "The Biblical and Monastic Roots of the Spirituality of Pope Gregory the Great." In *Monastic Studies*, 31–41. Bangor, UK: Headstart History, 1991.

———. "The Influence of Origen upon Gregory the Great's Exegesis on the Song of Songs." *StPatr* 18 (1985) 343–47.
Plato. *The Last Days of Socrates*. Translated by Hugh Tredennick. London: Penguin, 1954.
Polk, Timothy H. *The Biblical Kierkegaard: Reading by the Rule of Faith*. Macon, GA: Mercer University Press, 1997.
———. "Kierkegaard's Use of the New Testament: Intratextuality, Indirect Communication, and Appropriation." In *Kierkegaard and the Bible: Tome II: The New Testament*, edited by Lee C. Barrett and Jon Stewart, 237–48. Aldershot, UK: Ashgate, 2010.
Pons, Jolita. *Stealing a Gift: Kierkegaard's Pseudonyms and the Bible. Perspectives in Continental Philosophy*. New York: Fordham University Press, 2004.
Poole, Roger. *Kierkegaard: The Indirect Communication*. Charlottesville, VA: University of Virginia Press, 1993.
———. "The Unknown Kierkegaard: Twentieth-Century Receptions." In *The Cambridge Companion to Kierkegaard*, edited by Alastair Hannay and Gordon D. Marino, 48–75. Cambridge: Cambridge University Press, 1998.
Pope, Marvin H. *Job: Introduction, Translation, and Notes*. AB, Vol. 15. Garden City, NY: Doubleday, 1965.
Porteus, N. W. "Old Testament Theology." In *The Old Testament and Modern Study: A Generation of Discovery and Research*, edited by H. H. Rowley, 311–45. Oxford: Clarendon, 1951.
Pritchard, James B., editor. *Ancient Near Eastern Texts Relating to the Old Testament*. 3rd ed. Princeton: Princeton University Press, 1969.
Quinn, Phillip L. "Kierkegaard's Christian Ethics." In *The Cambridge Companion to Kierkegaard*, edited by Alastair Hannay and Gordon D. Marino, 349–75. Cambridge: Cambridge University Press, 1998.
Rabate, Jean-Michel. "'Tradition and T. S. Eliot." In *The Cambridge Companion to T. S. Eliot*, edited by A. David Moody, 210–22. Cambridge University Press, 1994.
Rasmussen, Joel D. S. "Kierkegaard's Biblical Hermeneutics: Imitation, Imaginative Freedom, and Paradoxical Fixation." In *Kierkegaard and the Bible: Tome II: The New Testament*, edited by Lee C. Barrett and Jon Stewart, 249–84. Aldershot, UK: Ashgate, 2010.
Reed, Walter L. *Dialogues of the Word: The Bible as Literature according to Bakhtin*. New York: Oxford University Press, 1993.
Rendtorff, Rolf. *Canon and Theology*. Translated by Margaret Kohl. OBT. Minneapolis: Fortress, 1993.
———. "Christologische Auslegung als >>Rettung<< des Alten Testaments? Wilhelm Vischer und Gerhard Von Rad." In *Schöpfung und Befreiung: Für Claus Westermann zum 80. Geburtstag*, edited by Rainer Albertz, Friedemann W. Golka, Jürgen Kegler, 191–203. Stuttgart: Calwer, 1989.
Reventlow, Henning. *Problems of Old Testament Theology in the Twentieth Century*. Translated by John Bowden. London: SCM, 1985.
———. "Towards the End of the 'Century of Enlightenment': Established Shift from *Sacra Scriptura* to Literary Documents and Religion of the People of Israel." In *Hebrew Bible / Old Testament: The History of Its Interpretation*, edited by Magne Saebø, 1034–40. Gottingen: Vandenhoeck & Ruprecht, 2008.

Bibliography

Richardson, Alan. "The Rise of Modern Biblical Scholarship." In *The Cambridge History of the Bible, Vol. 4: The West From the Reformation to the Present Day*, edited by S. L. Greenslade, 319–38. Cambridge: Cambridge University Press, 1963.

Ricoeur, Paul. *Interpretation Theory: Discourse and the Surplus of Meaning*. Fort Worth, TX: Texas Christian University Press, 1976.

Robertson, David. "The Comedy of Job: A Response." *Semeia* 7 (1977) 41–44.

Rogerson, John. *Old Testament Criticism in the Nineteenth Century: England and Germany*. London: SPCK, 1984.

Rosas, L. J. III. "Kierkegaard, Søren Aabye." In *Historical Handbook of Major Biblical Interpreters*, edited by Donald K. McKim, 330–36. Downers Grove, IL: InterVarsity, 1998.

Sandywell, Barry. "The Shock of the Old: Mikhail Bakhtin's Contributions to the Theory of Time and Alterity." In *Bakhtin and the Human Sciences*, edited by Michael Mayerfeld Bell and Michael Gardiner, 196–213. London: Sage, 1998.

Scalise, Charles J. "Canonical Hermeneutics: Childs and Barth." *SJT* 47.1 (1994) 61–88.

Schleifer, Ronald. "Irony, Identity and Repetition: On Kierkegaard's *The Concept of Irony*." *SubStance* 8.25 (1979) 44–55.

Scholder, Klaus. *The Churches and the Third Reich*. Vol. 1. London: SCM, 1987.

Schreiner, Susan E. "The Role of Perception in Gregory's *Moralia in Job*." *StPatr* 28 (1993) 87–95.

———. *Where Shall Wisdom be Found: Calvin's Exegesis of Job from Medieval and Modern Perspectives*. Chicago: University of Chicago Press, 1994.

Schulweis, Harold M. "Karl Barth's Job: Morality and Theodicy." *JQR* (1975) 156–67.

Seitz, Christopher R. *Figured Out: Typology and Providence in Christian Scripture*. Louisville: Westminster John Knox, 2001.

———. "Job: Full-Structure, Movement, and Interpretation." *Int* 43 (1989) 5–17.

———. *Word without End: The Old Testament as Abiding Theological Witness*. Grand Rapids: Eerdmans, 1997.

Shepherd, David. "The Authority of Meanings and the Meanings of Authority: Some Problems in the Theory of Reading." *Poetics Today* 7.1 (1986) 129–45.

———. "Bakhtin and the Reader." In *Bakhtin and Cultural Theory*, edited by K. Hirschkop and D. Shepherd, 91–108. Manchester: Manchester University Press, 1989.

———. "A Feeling for History? Bakhtin and 'the Problem of *Great Time*.'" *The Slavonic and East European Review* 84.1 (2006) 32–51.

Sherman, Robert J. "Reclaiming a Theological Reading of the Bible: Barth's Interpretation of Job as a Case Study." *IJST* 2.2 (2000) 175–88.

Simonetti, Manlio, and Marco Conti, and Thomas C. Oden, editors. *Job*. ACCS. Downers Grove, IL: InterVarsity, 2006.

Smeets, Arnold. "Une Lettre comme Don: Une Lecture Sémiotique de la Lettre de Grégoire dans les 'Moralia in Job.'" In *Lettres dans la Bible et Dans la Littérature*, 241–63. Paris: Cerf, 1999.

Steinmann, Andrew E. "The Structure and Message of the Book of Job." *VT* 46.1 (1996) 85–100.

Steinmetz, David C. "John Calvin as an Interpreter of the Bible." In *Calvin and the Bible*, edited by Donald K. McKim, 282–91. Cambridge: Cambridge University Press, 2006.

Stokes, Patrick. "Locke, Kierkegaard and the Phenomenology of Personal Identity." *International Journal of Philosophical Studies* 16.5 (2008) 645–72.

Straw, Carole E. Review of *"Remediarium Conversorum": A Synthesis in Latin of "Moralia in Job" by Gregory the Great*, by Peter of Waltham. *Speculum* 60 (1985) 1058.

Strawn, Brent A. "And These Three Are One: A Trinitarian Critique of Christological Approaches to the Old Testament." *PRSt* 31.2 (2004) 191–210.

Strolz, Walter. "Die Hiob-Interpretation bei Kant, Kierkegaard und Bloch." *Kairos* 23.1–2 (1981) 75–87.

Stump, Eleonore. "Biblical Commentary and Philosophy." In *The Cambridge Companion to Aquinas*, edited by Norman Kretzmann and Eleonore Stump, 252–68. Cambridge: Cambridge University Press, 1993.

———. "Faith and the Problem of Evil." In *Seeking Understanding: The Stob Lectures, 1986–1998*, 491–550. Grand Rapids: Eerdmans, 2001.

———. "The God of Abraham, Saadia and Aquinas." In *Referring to God*, 95–119. New York: St. Martin's, 2000.

Sykes, Stephen W. *Karl Barth: Studies of His Theological Method*. Oxford: Clarendon, 1979.

Syring, W.-D. *Hiob und sein Anwalt. Die Prosatexte des Hiobbuches und ihre Rolle Inseiner Redaktions- Und Rezeptionsgeschichte*. BZAW, Vol. 336. Berlin: de Gruyter, 2004.

Tanner, Michael. "Introduction." In *Beyond Good and Evil*, by Friedrich Nietzsche, 7–26. London: Penguin, 1990.

Taylor, Mark C. *Kierkegaard's Pseudonymous Authorship: A Study of Time and the Self*. Princeton: Princeton University Press, 1975.

———. "Text as Victim." In *Deconstruction and Theology*, edited by Thomas J. J. Altizer et al., 58–78. New York: Crossroad, 1982.

Taylor, Mark Lloyd. "Ordeal and Repetition in Kierkegaard's Treatment of Abraham and Job." In *Foundations of Kierkegaard's Vision of Community: Religion, Ethics, and Politics in Kierkegaard*, edited by George B. Connell and C. Stephen Evans, 33–53. Atlantic Highlands, NJ: Humanities, 1992.

Terrien, Samuel. *Job: Poet of Existence*. Indianapolis: Bobbs-Merrill, 1957.

The Bethel Confession: August Version. Cited 20 October 2008. Online: www.lutheranwiki.org/The_Bethel_Confession:_August_Version#The_Church_and_the_Jews.

Thulstrup, Niels. *Kierkegaard's Relation to Hegel*. Translated by George L. Stengren. Princeton: Princeton University Press, 1980.

Ticciati, Susannah. "Convergence and Divergence: Differing Jobs." *Journal of Scriptural Reasoning* 4.1 (2004): No Pages. Cited 21 January 2008. Online: http://etext.lib.virginia.edu/journals/ssr/issues/volume4/number1/ssr04-1-f01.html

———. "Does Job Fear God for Naught?" *Modern Theology* 21.3 (2005) 353–66.

———. *Job and the Disruption of Identity: Reading beyond Barth*. London: T. & T. Clark, 2005.

———. "Job, Debate, and the Shaping of Lives." *Journal of Scriptural Reasoning* 4.1 (2004) No Pages. Cited 21 January 2008. Online: http://etext.lib.virginia.edu/journals/ssr/issues/volume4/number1/ssr04-1-f01.html.

Timmermann, Jens. "Kant on Conscience, 'Indirect' Duty, and Moral Error." *International Philosophical Quarterly* 46.3 (2006) 294–309.

Bibliography

Uffenheimer, Benjamin, and Henning Graf Reventlow, editors. *Creative Biblical Exegesis: Christian and Jewish Hermeneutics through the Centuries*. JSOTsup, Vol. 59. Sheffield, UK: JSOT, 1988.
Vermes, Geza. "Isaac, the First Lamb of God." *Standpoint* 16 (2009) 62–67.
Vicchio, Stephen J. *Job in the Ancient World*. Eugene, OR: Wipf and Stock, 2006.
———. *Job in the Medieval World*. Eugene, OR: Wipf & Stock, 2006.
———. *Job in the Modern World*. Eugene, OR: Wipf & Stock, 2006.
Virno, Paolo. *A Grammar of the Multitude*. Translated by James Cascaito Isabella Bertoletti, Andrea Casson. Los Angeles: Semiotext(e), 2004.
Vischer, Wilhelm. "Das Alte Testament als Gottes Wort." *Zwischen den Zeiten* 5 (1927) 379–95.
———. "Das Alte Testament und die Geschichte." *Zwischen den Zeiten* 10 (1932) 22–42.
———. *Das Christuszeugnis Des Alten Testaments*. Vol. 1, Zurich: Evangelischer, 1946.
———. *Das Christuszeugnis Des Alten Testaments*. Vol. 2, Zurich: Evangelischer, 1946.
———. "Esther." *TEH Heft* 48 (1937) 1–29.
———. "Esther." *EQ* 11.2 (1939) 3–21.
———. "God's Truth and Man's Lie: A Study of the Message of the Book of Job." *Int* 15 (1961) 131–46.
———. "Der Gott Abrahams, Isaaks und Jakobs." *Zwischen den Zeiten* 9 (1931) 282–97.
———. "*Hiob*, Ein Zeuge Jesu Christi." *Bekenende Kirche* 8 (1934) 4–36.
———. "Isaak." *Zwischen den Zeiten* 9 (1931) 1–3.
———. "La Méthode de l'Exégèse Biblique." *RTP* 10.2 (1960) 109–23.
———. "The Witness of Job to Jesus Christ." *EQ* xlviii.1 (1934) 40–53.
———. "The Witness of Job to Jesus Christ." *EQ* xlviii.2 (1934) 138–50.
———. *The Witness of the Old Testament to Christ*. Translated by A. B. Crabtree. Vol. 1, London: Lutterworth, 1949.
von Rad, Gerhard. "Typological Interpretation of the Old Testament." *Int* 15 (1961) 174–92.
Wallace, Mark I. "Karl Barth's Hermeneutic: A Way Beyond the Impasse." *JR* 68.3 (1988) 396–410.
Walsh, Katherine, and Diana Wood, editors. *The Bible in the Medieval World: Essays in Memory of Beryl Smalley*. SCH, Subsidia, Vol. 4. Oxford: Blackwell, 1985.
Walsh, Sylvia. "Kierkegaard and Postmodernism." *International Journal for Philosophy of Religion* 29 (1991) 113–22.
Watson, Francis. "Barth's *Philippians* as Theological Exegesis." In *The Epistle to the Philippians*, by Karl Barth. 40th Anniversary Edition, xxvi–xl. Louisville: Westminster John Knox, 2002.
Webb, Geoff. "Bakhtin's Poetics and the Gospels: Genre-Memory and Its Possible Application to the Gospel of Mark." *Bulletin CSSR* 35.2 (2006) 38–42.
Webster, J. B., editor. *The Cambridge Companion to Karl Barth*. Cambridge Companions to Religion. Cambridge: Cambridge University Press, 2000.
———. *Word and Church: Essays in Christian Dogmatics*. Edinburgh: T. & T. Clark, 2001.
Weinandy, Thomas G., Daniel Keating, John Yocum, and Nicholas M. Healy, editors. *Aquinas on Scripture: An Introduction to His Biblical Commentaries*. London: T. & T. Clark, 2005.
Whedbee, William. "The Comedy of Job." *Semeia* 7 (1977) 1–39.

Bibliography

Whitman, Jon, editor. *Interpretation and Allegory: Antiquity to the Modern Period.* Brill's Studies in Intellectual History, Vol. 101. Leiden: Brill, 2000.
Wilken, Robert L. "Interpreting Job Allegorically: The Moralia of Gregory the Great." *ProEccl* 10.2 (2001) 213–26.
Williams, James G. "Comedy, Irony, Intercession: A Few Notes in Response." *Semeia* 7 (1977) 135–45.
———. "Job's Vision: The Dialectic of Person and Presence." *HAR* (1984) 259–72.
———. "'You Have Not Spoken Truth of Me': Mystery and Irony in Job." *ZAW* 83 (1971) 231–55.
Williams, Ronald J. "Current Trends in the Study of the Book of Job." In *Studies in the Book of Job*, edited by Walter Emanuel Aufrecht, 1–27. Waterloo, ON: Wilfred Laurier University Press, 1985.
Wimsatt Jr., W. K., and Monroe C. Beardsley. "The Intentional Fallacy." In *The Verbal Icon: Studies in the Meaning of Poetry*, 3–19. Lexington, KY: University of Kentucky Press, 1954.
Yaffe, Martin D. "Interpretive Essay." In *The Literal Exposition on Job*, by Thomas Aquinas, 1–65. Atlanta: Scholars, 1989.
Yarbrough, Robert W. "Wilhelm Vischer als Ausleger der Heiligen Schrift. Eine Untersuchung zum Chrstuszeugnis des Alten Testaments." *TJ* (2001) 31–49.
Yocum, John. "Aquinas' Literal Exposition on Job." In *Aquinas on Scripture: An Introduction to His Biblical Commentaries*, edited by Thomas G. Weinandy et al., 21–42. London: T. & T. Clark, 2005.
Zinn, Grover A. "Texts within Texts: The Song of Songs in the Exegesis of Gregory the Great and Hugh of St Victor." *StPatr* 25 (1993) 209–15.
Zuckerman, Bruce. *Job the Silent: A Study in Historical Counterpoint.* Oxford: Oxford University Press, 1991.

Name Index

Adams, Nicholas, 135, 165
Alonso-Schoekel, Luis, x
Aquinas, Thomas. *See* Thomas Aquinas

Bächli, Otto, 135–36
Bakhtin, Mikhail M., xvii–xviii, 1–21, 35–36, 163
Barr, James, 25–26
Barrett, Lee C., 69n8
Barth, Karl, ix–x, xv–xviii, 2, 4, 15–18, 22, 24, 31–37, 38–39, 42–44, 49–60, 63–65, 71, 74, 105–6, 117–18, 120, 127, 133–34, 135–62, 163–77
Bigelow, Pat, 85
Boer, Roland, 6
Bonhoeffer, Dietrich, 106–8
Brandt, Lori Unger, 67n1, 74
Brunner, Emil, 28–30
Bruns, Gerald L., 75n36
Budde, Karl, 119n47
Burgess, Andrew J., 89
Burnett, Richard E., 143n34

Calvin, John, 2, 25–26, 38, 41, 49, 51–59, 61, 120n50, 121n53, 135, 141, 160, 163, 172, 174
Caquot, André, 120n49
Chalemet, Christophe, 141n23
Childs, Brevard, 25
Clines, David J. A., 15n61, 128n77, 129, 155, 158n93, 174n24
Crites, Stephen, 99

Croxall, T. H., 69,
Cunningham, Mary Kathleen, 143n34, 150n59

Damgaard, Iben, 21, 69, 98
Davis, Leroy A., 143n34
Dawson, David, 23, 28–29
Delecroix, Vincent, 74n31, 91
Delitzsch, Friedrich, 126n74
Dhorme, Édouard, xn3, 116, 119n47, 128n77, 131, 159n97
Dorrien, Gary J., 141n23

Ebeling, Gerhard, 101–2n131
Evans, C. Stephen, 71n13, 86n75
Ellison, Allan, 106, 131–32

Felber, Stefan, 110
Frei, Hans W., 23, 25n93, 27n101, 28n104
Frye, Northrop, 27n101, 34

Gardiner, Michael, 3n6, 4
Gignilliat, Mark S., 142n25, 143n34, 145n39
Glatzer, Nahum Norbert, 52
Green, Barbara, 6
Green, Ronald Michael, 60
Greene-McCreight, Kathryn, 143n34, 145n39
Gregory I, Pope, xvii, 2, 16n63, 22, 38–46, 50, 56, 60, 66, 138, 163, 172
Greschat, Katharina, 40n10, 44n25

Name Index

Gunton, Colin, 142, 145, 157
Gutteridge, Richard, 107–8n9, 126n74

Habel, Norman C., xn3, 116n38
Hayashi, Tadayoshi, 74
Haynes, Stephen R., 107
Hendrix, Scott H., 75n36
Hendry, George S., 156–57
Higton, Mike, 151n61
Holm, Isak Winkel, 85n69, 88
Hölscher, Gustav, 144n37, 159n97

Jacobs, Louis, 147n48
Jauss, Hans Robert, 3–6
Jung, C. G., 146n44, 149n57

Kallas, Endel, 72n20, 73
Kant, Immanuel, xvii, 16–17, 39, 41, 59–66, 163
Keller, Roger R., 142n29, 143n31
Kessler, Stephan C., 40n6, 40n11
Kierkegaard, Søren Aabye, ix-xi, xv-xviii, 2, 7n25, 15n61, 16–17, 20–24, 33–37, 38–39, 41–44, 49–55, 59–60, 63–66, 67–102, 105, 117–18, 133, 144n37, 155n80, 160, 163–77

Lindsey, William D., 15
Loades, A. L., 60, 62n100
Lubac, Henri de, xviin4, 22, 24, 27–28, 33, 41n13, 154n75
Luther, Martin, 25–26, 51–52, 60, 66, 70, 75, 101n131, 163, 170

Markus, Robert Austin, 43n24
McCormack, Bruce, 143n34, 150
McGlasson, Paul, 143n34, 150n59
Migliore, Daniel L., 135
Mittleman, Alan, 62n103
Mooney, Edward R., 84
Morson, Gary Saul and Caryl Emerson, 13
Müller, Mogens, 70n11

Newsom, Carol A., 1–2, 15n61, 116n38

Nietzsche, Friedrich, xviii, 105, 112, 121–24
Noth, Martin, 144n38

Oettli, Samuel and Wilhelm Volck, 144n37

Parris, David Paul, 3
Percy, Walker, ix
Plato, 29, 85n73
Polk, Timothy H., 69n6, 69n8
Pons, Jolita, 20–21, 69n8
Poole, Roger, 71n13, 85

Rasmussen, Joel D. S., 67n1, 75n36
Reed, Walter L., 5
Rendtorff, Rolf, 25–26, 30n112, 110–11
Reventlow, Henning, 70n11
Rocoeur, Paul, 6–7, 19n68, 21
Rosas, L. J. III, 73

Sandywell, Barry, 8, 10–11
Schreiner, Susan E., 2, 42, 44n28, 47n48, 50, 55, 57, 126n74
Shulweis, Harold M., 135
Shepherd, David, 4–6, 13n56
Stokes, Patrick, 79

Tanner, Michael, 122n61, 123
Taylor, Mark Lloyd, 68n2
Thomas Aquinas, 16, 38, 44–51, 58, 120n50, 135, 163, 172
Ticciati, Susannah, 15n61, 136, 143, 160

Vermes, Geza, 34n123
Vicchio, Stephen J., 2n3, 16n62, 51n62, 55n77
Vischer, Wilhelm, xv-xviii, 2, 4, 16–19, 22, 24–37, 38–39, 42–44, 46n38, 49–53, 55–59, 63–65, 104–34, 137n9, 138–39, 144n37, 159n99, 169–78

Wallace, Mark I., 150n59

Yaffe, Martin D., 46–47
Yocum, John, 45

Scripture Index

Genesis

1	25
1:2	174
1:3	25–26
1:4	26
2–3	65
3:15	54
4	133

Numbers

13–14	144, 147n49

Deuteronomy

	57n83

1&2 Samuel

	59

Isaiah

53	54

Ezekiel

	133

Psalms

8	176
104:31	121n53

Job

1–2	19n67, 30, 144, 146
1:1	174–76
1:1, 5	175
1:3	113
1:9	44, 63, 169–70
1:10	113
1:20–21	69, 74–78, 102, 112, 115n37, 170
1:21	15n61, 148, 176, 177n28
1:22	40–41
1:23	113
2	112
2:9–10	176
2:10	148, 177n28
2–3	139
3	18–20, 113, 176
3–24	146
3–27	90
3–31	30, 147
3:1	114
3:3, 11–13	81n55
3:20	113
3:26	18–19
4	102, 146
4:6–11	53
4:7	53, 55
4:8	175
5:4	116
5:12–13	114
7	93, 115
7:4	144n37
7:11	49n55
7:17–18	94
8	174–77
8:2	174
8:5–7	174
8:6	176
8:8–9	122n62
8:8–10	175

Scripture Index

Job (cont.)

8:8–13	176
8:20	176
9	93
9–10	116n38
9:17	56
9:32	116
10:21	49
13:3	117
13:8	117
13:9–12	117
13:17–21	116
16	117–18
16:19	151
17	117–18
19	44–49, 118, 130
19:9	45
19:13	46n44
19:22	46n44
19:25	44, 58, 118, 151
19:27–29	131–132
21	119
21–37	128n77
23–27	128–29
23:3	49n55
23:13	64
24:18–24	128n77
25–26	128n77, 146
25:3–4	119n46
27	146
27:5–6	63
27:7–23	128n77
28	61, 120, 129–30, 146–47, 158–59
28:27–28	159
28:28	144n37
29	93, 102, 119n47, 154
29–31	90, 129, 146
29:2	119n47
29:8	81
29:13	81
30:1	81
31	98, 154
31:6	131
31:16–20	40
31:35	133
32–37	146
32:1	98
36	166
36:6	55
37	93, 174
38	121, 130
38:1	174
38:2	166
38–39	146
38–42	90
38:2	155
40–41	146
40:2	155
42	30, 46n44, 125, 153, 173
42:3	166–67
42:6	60, 166–67
42:7	53, 54, 56
42:7–8	152–53, 176

Wisdom of Solomon

2:23–24	114n33

Jubilees

18	34n123

Matthew

19:27	73

2 Corinthians

4:6	26

Philippians

2	139

1 Timothy

6:16	26

Hebrews

1:3	26
11:17–19	50n57

James

1:17	26

1 John

1:5	26

Revelation

	133

www.ingramcontent.com/pod-product-compliance
Lightning Source LLC
Chambersburg PA
CBHW070323230426
43663CB00011B/2200